New Frontiers in Work and Family Research

The purpose of this volume is to showcase alternative theoretical and methodological approaches to work and family research, and present methodological alternatives to the widely known shortcomings of current research on work and the family.

In the first part of the book, contributors consider various theoretical perspectives, including:

- positive organizational psychology
- system theory
- multi-level theoretical models
- dyadic study designs.

The chapters in Part Two consider a number of methodological issues including:

- key issues pertaining to sampling
- the role of diary studies
- case cross-over designs
- biomarkers
- cross-domain and within-domain relations.

Contributors also elaborate on the conceptual and logistical issues involved in incorporating novel measurement approaches.

The book will be essential reading for researchers and students in work and organizational psychology, and related disciplines.

Joseph G. Grzywacz is Kaiser Family Endowed Professor of Family Resilience at Oklahoma State University, USA. He is an interdisciplinary social scientist whose research focuses on the health-related implications of everyday work and family life for adults and children. His research emphasizes the role of work and family in creating and exaggerating health disparities, and programmatic and policy solutions for eliminating forced choices between work and family.

Evangelia Demerouti is a full-time professor at Eindhoven University of Technology, the Netherlands. Her research focuses on the processes enabling performance, including the effects of work characteristics, decision making, occupational well-being and work–life balance. Her articles have been published in journals including *Journal of Applied Psychology*, *Journal of Occupational Health Psychology* and *Journal of Vocational Behavior*.

Current Issues in Work and Organizational Psychology

Series Editor: Arnold B. Bakker

Current Issues in Work and Organizational Psychology is a series of edited books that reflect the state-of-the-art areas of current and emerging interest in the psychological study of employees, workplaces and organizations.

Each volume is tightly focused on a particular topic and consists of seven to ten chapters contributed by international experts. The editors of individual volumes are leading figures in their areas and provide an introductory overview.

Example topics include: digital media at work, work and the family, workaholism, modern job design, positive occupational health and individualized deals.

A Day in the Life of a Happy Worker
Edited by Arnold B. Bakker and Kevin Daniels

The Psychology of Digital Media at Work
Edited by Daantje Derks and Arnold B. Bakker

New Frontiers in Work and Family Research
Edited by Joseph G. Grzywacz and Evangelia Demerouti

New Frontiers in Work and Family Research

**Edited by
Joseph G. Grzywacz and
Evangelia Demerouti**

Routledge
Taylor & Francis Group

LONDON AND NEW YORK

First published 2013
by Psychology Press
27 Church Road, Hove, East Sussex BN3 2FA

Simultaneously published in the USA and Canada
by Psychology Press
711 Third Avenue, New York NY 10017

Psychology Press is an imprint of the Taylor & Francis Group, an informa business

British Library Cataloguing in Publication Data
A catalogue record for this book is available from the British Library

Library of Congress Cataloging in Publication Data
New frontiers in work and family research / edited by Joseph G. Grzywacz
and Evangelia Demerouti.
p. cm.
Includes bibliographical references and index.
1. Work and family--Research. 2. Work-life balance. I. Grzywacz, Joseph G.
II. Demerouti, Evangelia, 1970-
HD4904.25.N487 2013
306.3'6--dc23
2012035949

ISBN13: 978-1-84872-096-1 (hbk)
ISBN13: 978-1-84872-125-8 (pbk)
ISBN13: 978-0-203-58656-3 (ebk)

Typeset in Times
by Saxon Graphics Ltd, Derby

MIX
Paper from
responsible sources
FSC
www.fsc.org FSC® C004839

Printed and bound in Great Britain by
TJ International Ltd, Padstow, Cornwall

Contents

List of illustrations

List of tables and boxes

Tables

Boxes

Preface

The goal of this volume is lofty: we sought to enable a new generation of work and family research. Despite longstanding interest in the work–family interface, it is our belief that there has been relatively little advancement in reducing or eliminating challenges at the work–family interface. There is little doubt that scientific progress is being made. For example, the Work, Family and Health Network is currently conducting randomized trials of the effectiveness of supervisor supportiveness training and flexible schedule alternatives for reducing work–family conflicts. However, while the value of this research initiative is without question, the simple fact is that the burgeoning research literature offers few evidence-based solutions for creating "a well balanced" work and family life or mitigating the putatively negative consequences of a poorly fitted work and family arrangement. This means that research on this issue falls short in understanding the phenomenon and producing interventions that eliminate its unfavorable effects. Indeed, a recent special issue featured invited commentaries seeking to make work and family research more impactful (Kossek, Baltes and Matthews, 2011). Not surprisingly, organizations are frequently hesitant to help employees navigate their everyday lives: they are not persuaded that we (researchers and practitioners) can offer valid explanations and solutions.

This volume seeks to move work and family research forward theoretically and empirically. This goal is not motivated by the quest for something new for the sake of looking for something new. Rather, it is focused on developing new solutions to problems that remain unresolved. One ongoing problem is that work and family research remains theoretically underdeveloped. For example, researchers are told that theories used to understand conflicts between work and family are probably not useful for understanding the positive side of the work–family interface (Frone, 2003), yet theoretical tools for studying positive experiences like enrichment (Greenhaus and Powell, 2006) and facilitation (Grzywacz et al., 2007) remain elusive. Further, with the notable exception of the Job Demands and Resources Model (Bakker and Demerouti, 2008), theoretical tools for studying both positive and negative work and family experiences simultaneously remain underdeveloped. Theory is an analytical tool for understanding, explaining, and making predictions about a given subject matter (Wikipedia). We do not view theory as a goal in itself but as a means to improve people's lives (praxis). We need to invest in developing strong theories for work and family.

The impact of work and family research is also undermined by several methodological problems. The absence of clear conceptual definitions and consistent operationalization is a problem (Kossek *et al.*, 2011) that results from both conceptual underdevelopment and an almost monopolistic reliance on cross-sectional study designs that depend primarily on survey techniques and self-report measures. Impactful work and family research requires clarity of concepts, greater use of alternative study designs such as case-crossover designs, and alternative measurement strategies. Finally, the dominant segment of work and family research has relied on non-probabilistic samples, which create substantial problems drawing inferences and summarizing what is "known". Indeed, the recommendation to study effective policy and practice implementation (Kossek *et al.*, 2011) assumes that results obtained from non-probabilistic samples can reliably differentiate "effective" from "non-effective" solutions. Just as a medical specialist needs appropriate tools (instruments) and relevant evidence to diagnose and to cure disease, practitioners addressing work and family need appropriate instruments and rigorous evidence: it is these instruments and methods that we challenge in this volume.

Specifically, we commissioned chapters from an interdisciplinary team of experts and charged them to think "outside the box" in resolving one or more of the issues that keep work and family research from having greater impact. Experts and topics were selected to accomplish two primary aims: they were selected to delineate alternative or new theorizing about work and family, or to isolate methodological alternatives to overcome known shortcomings of work and family research. The commissioned authors were tasked with achieving these primary aims by writing chapters focused on one or more secondary aims:

1   advance work and family theorizing beyond basic notions of "stress" and "scarcity";
2   emphasize processes involved in work–family experiences, and the individual and contextual moderators shaping these processes;
3   critically analyze basic assumptions underlying key concepts in work and family research, and describing strategies for testing and refining those assumptions;
4   develop theoretical arguments that allow for and illustrate how to cross levels of analysis in work and family research;
5   illustrate the use and value of alternative study designs for understanding specific work and family issues;
6   elaborate conceptual and logistical issues involved in incorporating biomarkers into work and family research;
7   demonstrate the salience and need for rigorous sampling procedures in work and family research.

The first six chapters focus primarily on theoretical or conceptual issues, whereas the later five chapters focus primarily on methodological issues. The theoretical collection begins with an overview and application of Positive Organizational Scholarship (POS) to the study of work and family. **Spreitzer and colleagues** provide a concise overview of the POS perspective, including key tenets of POS and how the POS lens can be seen in existing work and family research. Most relevant to the aims of this volume, the chapter also provides a way of thinking conceptually about the interplay of positive and negative experiences at the work–family interface, and it provides several ideas from the POS lens for moving work and family research forward. Particularly compelling is positive deviance, or the idea of studying individuals who are thriving in their work and family situation, despite all of the challenges confronted in their daily lives. Such an approach would likely provide a more organic definition of what "work–family balance" is, and may be highly valuable in identifying useful strategies for creating better fitting work and family arrangements.

MacDermid and colleagues' chapter takes a fresh look at a longstanding theory; systems theory. MacDermid and colleagues provide a cogent recapitulation of systems theory and how it has been applied in existing work and family research. However, consistent with our charge to authors to "think outside the box", these researchers go on to isolate forgotten or overlooked aspects of the theory that raise questions about basic assumptions made in the work and family literature, and offer new and potentially useful avenues for future inquiry. The concepts of equifinality and feedback loops have been largely overlooked in work and family research, but they likely offer insights into how both macro-level forces such as social policy or organizational programs combine with micro-level decision making (within or between individuals) to create work and family solutions that work.

The next conceptual chapter takes a close look at several work and family concepts used in work and family research, particularly research focused on the work–family interface. **Demerouti and colleagues** review definitions and measurement strategies for work–family conflict and work–family enrichment. In the spirit of "thinking outside the box", these authors also pose five relevant venues for improving conceptualization of conflict and enrichment experiences, and improving understanding of these experiences through the use of alternative measurement strategies and data collection techniques. Perhaps most unique is the authors' suggestion that the "self" be construed as a domain distinct and separate from work and family. The authors' point out the salience of cultural beliefs in shaping work and family situations and experiences is also a vital area for inquiry.

Bakker and Demerouti introduce the spillover–crossover model (SCM) in the next chapter. The authors draw attention to a critical problem in the work and family literature: the general tendency to focus on individual-level work and family experiences (at the expense of others connected to the individual's work and family arrangement; e.g. spouse, children, coworkers) or the transmission of affect between individuals such as spouses (at the expense of considering the original source of the transmitted affect). The SCM provides a needed tool for answering basic social policy questions; for example, what potential consequences does growing underemployment in the wake of the "great recession" have for children's accumulation of human capital (e.g. educational success). Further, the SCM provides a framework for studying and understanding multilevel work and family issues, such as "does any type of employment contribute to family resilience?" and if not, "what types of jobs or which job attributes contribute to resilient families?"

Sonnentag and colleagues critically challenge the bucolic notion that "home" and "family" are inherently a haven for respite and recovery from the strains of work, and they argue that insufficient opportunity to recover is the fundamental source of conflicts between work and family. This conceptually rich chapter provides a trove of fresh ideas and fruitful areas of empirical inquiry and theorizing. Particularly compelling is the authors' thinking about complex boundary management strategies because in-depth understanding of these strategies offers potential insight into evidence-based practical solutions for helping individuals effectively meet their work and family responsibilities. Further, such an evidence base could inform organizational initiatives that assist workers at all levels within the organization in implementing, maintaining, and refining effective boundary management strategies.

In the last conceptually-focused chapter **Peeters and colleagues** took our request to think critically about the consequences of work–family experiences. The result is that they challenge the long-held assumption of domain-specific consequences of such experiences. For example, convention maintains the consequences of work–family conflict reside primarily in the "receiving" domain (i.e., "family" in the case of work-to-family conflict and "work" in the case of family-to-work conflict). Drawing on social exchange theory, Peeters and colleagues provide a compelling theoretical rationale for why work–family experiences should be expected to have meaningful consequences in multiple domains of life, not just the receiving domain. The authors also provide primary and secondary empirical support for revising the convention that work–family experiences have domain-specific consequences in the receiving domain. This type of thinking and the related theoretical explanation has substantial potential to inform more impactful work and family research, particularly for those researchers charged with estimating return on investment. If Peeters and colleagues' contention is true, the value of work-life initiatives would be seriously underestimated under the conventional view of domain-specific consequences.

Grzywacz and colleagues' chapter leads the more methodologically focused contributions to the volume. These authors provide a primer on sampling wherein they provide definitions of key ideas from sampling, and they illustrate the importance of rigorous and thoughtful attention to sampling issues. These illustrations range from the simple demonstration of how very different conclusions can be drawn from different random samples obtained from the same population, to complex data-driven simulations demonstrating the empirical consequence of over-representing women in studies of work–family experiences. Simulation results combined with a systematic review of sampling procedures used in work and family research suggests that inattention to sampling likely contributes to substantial inconsistency in study findings. The fundamental point of this chapter is that impactful work and family research requires greater purposeful attention to sampling to ensure that study samples and corresponding study results accurately reflect real populations of interest.

Butler and colleagues' chapter cogently articulates the necessity and value of greater use of experience sampling methods for advancing work and family research. After providing an overview of dominant approaches to experience sampling, the authors articulate clear problems in the work and family literature that can be overcome by greater use of experience sampling methods. Consistent with the volume's encouragement for authors to think critically, the chapter articulates a fundamental inferential error (of between-person analyses to make within-person inferences regarding work–family associations) that undermines the impact of work and family research. Also consistent with our charge to think "outside the box," the authors provide several concrete examples of how to apply experience sampling methods to important theoretical questions (e.g. understanding boundary transitions between work and family), as well as fruitful ideas for exploiting rapidly developing technological innovations for capturing detailed information on everyday aspects of life as it is lived.

Amstad and Semmer's chapter articulating a "chains of events" model complements and extends the chapter on experience sampling. Consistent with our request to "think outside the box", the authors encourage work and family researchers to focus on events to enable clearer understanding of the mechanisms involved in linking work and family, and they offer alternative study designs for operationalizing the study of event chains. For example, they describe case-crossover designs frequently used in epidemiological studies of "rare events" like myocardial infarction or injury on the job. This type of design could be applied to understand the family-related contributors to violence in the workplace, or the marital consequences of workplace displacement or relocation. They also demonstrate how to expand the case-crossover design into an event-chain framework, and they provide a concrete operational example using real data. The "chains of events" model offers substantial promise for informing impactful work and family research, particularly if discrete types of events can be generalized into classes of events that behave similarly. Such research would inform solutions that minimize exposure to threatening events, or that break the negative chains that follow event exposure.

Buxton and colleagues provide a primer on biomarkers and their use in work and family research. After a basic overview of what biomarkers are, the authors present a comprehensive review of biomarkers that can be applied to work and family research, how those biomarkers can be obtained (e.g. via saliva, urine, dried blood spots), and basic practical issues involved in incorporating biomarkers into studies of work and family. Greater use of biomarkers has substantial value for advancing new and impactful work and family research. Biomarkers are invaluable for falsifying core hypotheses in the work and family literature. Much of the literature maintains that specific experiences, notably work–family conflict, are stressors that trigger physiologic responses. Definitive evidence supporting this basic assumption is currently lacking, but is possible with current advances in biomarker methods. Likewise, biomarkers provide an alternative strategy for understanding health: a conceptually and practically important outcome of diverse work and family experiences.

The volume closes with a masterful chapter on observational methods in work and family research. **Repetti and colleagues** cogently argue the value of measures obtained through direct observation over self-report data by reviewing sources of measurement error that are avoided by direct observation. Most valuable to this volume is the detailed discussion of how to approach incorporating observational methods into work and family research: the authors answer basic questions about deciding what to observe, when to collect observations, as well as alternatives for how to record observations, and how to analyze the substantial amounts of data that direct observation can generate. Although a single chapter cannot provide a turnkey solution for novice work and family researchers to implement observational methods, the authors provide substantial insight into key issues to consider when designing an observational study and they provide useful experience-based recommendations.

Ultimately history will be the final judge in discerning whether the lofty goal of this volume is realized. In 20 to 30 years we will be able to conduct an author-citation search to determine whether chapters contained in this volume were the seeds of paradigm changing approaches to work and family research and evidence-based solutions that effectively help individuals create well-fitting work and family arrangements. In the meantime we rest in the fact that our aims were met. The chapters in this volume provide several new ways for conceptualizing and theorizing work and family, regardless of whether they were borrowed from other disciplines (e.g. Positive Organizational Scholarship) or they represent dusted off gems from well-established theory (e.g. systems theory) and conceptual frameworks (e.g. models of spillover and crossover). Likewise, the chapters provide methodological alternatives for overcoming established shortcomings in the work and family literature in order to better diagnose and intervene in the phenomenon. Although it is premature to conclude whether the ultimate goal of this volume is met, we are convinced that application of the theoretical and methodological tools described in this volume will enrich the work and family literature and result in scientific studies that satisfy the intellectual curiosity of researchers, and produce impactful results capable of resolving policy, organizational and individual concerns about work and family.

References

Bakker, A.B. and Demerouti, E. (2008). Towards a model of work engagement. *Career Development International* 13, 209–223.

Frone, M.R. (2003). Work–family balance. In J.C. Quick and L.E. Tetrick (eds), *Handbook of occupational health psychology* (143–162). Washington, DC: American Psychological Association.

Grzywacz, J.G., Carlson, D.S., Kacmar, K.M., and Wayne, J.H. (2007). Work–family facilitation: A multilevel perspective on the synergies between work and family. *Journal of Occupational and Organizational Psychology* 80, 559–574.

Greenhaus, J.H. and Powell, G.N. (2006). When work and family are allies: A theory of work–family enrichment. *Academy of Management Review* 31, 72–92.

Kossek, E.E., Baltes, B.B. and Matthews, R.A. (2011). How work–family research can finally have an impact in the workplace. *Industrial and Organizational Psychology: Perspectives on Science and Practice* 4, 352–369.

Acknowledgements

This research was supported by grants from the *Eunice Kennedy Schriver* National Institute for Child Health and Development (R01HD061010 & R01HD056360).

1 Using a positive organizational scholarship lens to enrich research on work–family relationships

Gretchen M. Spreitzer

The focus of this chapter is on applying insights from positive organizational scholarship (POS) to better understand work–family relationships. POS highlights positive deviance within organizational studies (Spreitzer and Sonenshein, 2004). It provides a focus on the generative (that is, life-building, capability-enhancing, capacity-creating) dynamics in organizations that contribute to human strengths and virtues, resilience and healing, vitality and thriving, and the cultivation of extraordinary states in individuals, groups and organizations (Dutton and Glynn, 2007). While in recent years, we have seen a more positive approach to understanding work–family relationships – reframing from a focus on work–family conflict to a focus on work–family enrichment or facilitation (Keeney and Ilies, 2011) – this chapter provides a more comprehensive approach to applying a positive lens to work–family relationships. My hope is that by applying a POS lens we can respond to Kossek, Baltes and Mathews' (2011) contention that "work–family researchers have not made a significant impact in improving the lives of employees relative to the amount of research that has been conducted".

I start this chapter with background on POS and how it offers new insights in organizational behavior generally. Then I examine the current literature on work–family relationships emphasizing developments that have a positive orientation. The remainder of the chapter identifies a number of ways in which a POS lens might offer new insights for understanding work–family relationships. I conclude the chapter with directions for future research and implications for practice.

Positive organizational scholarship

What is POS? A POS lens enriches organizational studies by expanding the range of topics and constructs seen as valuable within organizational behavior and organizational theory (Dutton and Sonenshein, 2009). The three words – positive, organizational, and scholarship – describes the core tenets of this perspective (Dutton, Glynn and Spreitzer, 2006):

- Positive: the term "positive" in POS research can be defined in four key ways (Spreitzer and Cameron, 2011): (1) as a positive lens – foregrounding strengths, capabilities, possibilities, backgrounds, weaknesses, problems, and threats, (2) as an affirmative bias – associated with resourcefulness, or with creating, unlocking, and multiplying latent resources in individuals and organizations, (3) as virtuous – defined as the best of the human condition and that which human beings consider to be inherently good, and (4) as positive deviance – successful performance that dramatically exceeds the norm in a positive direction.

- Organizational: where positive psychology focuses largely on individual states and traits (Seligman, 1999), POS focuses more specifically on individuals, groups, units, and collectives in context. POS is organizational in that it highlights the generative dynamics that unfold within and across organizations.
- Scholarship: By scholarship, we emphasize research that is theoretically-informed, backed by data and analyses, and provides insights on implications for organizational functioning, practice and teaching.

POS does not adopt one particular theory or framework, but, instead, draws from a full spectrum of organizational theories (Cameron, Dutton and Quinn, 2003). POS draws on the fields of organizational behavior, psychology, and sociology to better understand the generative dynamics in organizations that promote human strength, resiliency, healing, and restoration. POS assumes that understanding how to enable human excellence in organizations will unlock potential, reveal possibilities, and chart a more positive course of human and organizational functioning (Cameron & Sprietzer, 2011).

At its core, POS investigates the generative mechanisms through which organizations and their members flourish and prosper (Cameron and Spreitzer, 2011). Mechanisms explain the how and why (Hedstrom and Swedberg, 1998). They describe "a set of interacting parts—an assembly of elements producing an effect not inherent in any one of them. A mechanism is not so much about 'nuts and bolts' as about 'cogs and wheels'—the wheelwork or agency by which an effect is produced" (Hernes, 1998: 74). POS identifies the cognitive (e.g. meaning making, identity forming, and sense making), affective (e.g. broadens and builds theory of positive emotions; see Fredrickson, 1998), agentic (e.g. proactivity, initiative, voice, empowerment), and social structural (e.g. systems, structures, job designs) mechanisms that explain positive dynamics within organizations. In this way, POS is a field of inquiry within organizational studies that can help enrich organizational scholarship to see new possibilities. The POS community includes hundreds of scholars around the world working at the micro, meso, and macro levels of analysis.

The motivation for POS in the field

POS arose because key organizational phenomena were relatively invisible in organizational studies and, consequently, neither systematically studied nor valued (Cameron, Dutton and Quinn, 2003). POS helps us see new possibilities for organizational studies – it helps to move constructs and ideas that are often in the background to the foreground. POS is premised on the belief that enabling human excellence in organizations unlocks latent potential and reveals hidden possibilities in people and systems that can benefit both human and organizational welfare (Cameron and Spreitzer, 2011).

POS also arose from the need to broaden the set of outcome variables that dominated the organization literature which tended to focus on profitability, competitive advantage, problem solving, and economic efficiency (Davis and Marquis, 2005; Goshal, 2005). Outcomes such as job satisfaction, commitment, and justice also appeared frequently in the organizational studies literature (Smith, Kendall and Hulin, 1969), but alternative outcomes such as eudaemonia (Keyes, 2005) – especially at higher levels of positive intensity such as thriving (Spreitzer *et al.*, 2005) high quality connections (Dutton and Heaphy, 2003), or human sustainability (Pfeffer, 2010) have been relatively nascent. These more positively deviant (Spreitzer and Sonenshein, 2004) outcomes were largely outside the purview of mainline organizational science. The best of the human condition – what people care about deeply and profoundly – was less visible in organizational scholarship (Cameron and Spreitzer, 2011).

POS is more than just an exclusive focus on positive phenomena – it also examines the juxtaposition with negative phenomena

Research indicates that good things can come out of negative events or circumstances – compassion (Lilius *et al.*, 2011), resilience (Caza and Milton, 2011), healing (Powley, 2011), post-traumatic growth (Maitlis, 2011), and crisis response (James and Wooten, 2011). POS embraces, rather than ignores, the limits, set-backs, and problems that occur in organizations by looking at the good that comes out of them (Cameron and Spreitzer, 2011). Rather than viewing negative events as failures and threats, POS researchers often theorize them as catalysts or opportunities that can facilitate adaptation, resilience, and growth.

POS complements positive psychology

Positive psychology tends to focus on individual states and traits that enable human flourishing. POS goes beyond positive psychology by offering a number of new insights on theory and research relevant to the "O" in POS. The first is through increasing focus on organizational functions and practices. This is what Heath and Sitkin (2001) refer to as "Big O" in their commentary about making OB more organizational. POS offers theory and research on organization practices such as socialization (Ashforth, Meyers and Sluss, 2011), mentoring (Ragins, 2011), communications (Browning, Morris and Kee, 2011), career development (Hall and Las Heras, 2011), leadership development (DeRue and Workman, 2011), organizational development (Cooperrider and Godwin, 2011; Bartunek and Woodman, 2011), and diversity (Ramarajan and Thomas, 2011).

A second way that POS goes beyond positive psychology is by transcending constructs that have been originally studied at the individual level of analysis to a more organizational or collective level. For example, Goddard and Salloum (2011) build on the work of others (e.g. Bandura, 1977) to understand the social cognitive underpinnings of collective efficacy – a construct most often studied at an individual level of analysis. Similarly, Lilius *et al.* (2011) examine compassion through an organizational lens to better understand processes of compassion organizing and how compassionate practices can be institutionalized in a system.

A third way that POS goes beyond positive psychology involves the need to understand how organizational context affects phenomena that have been studied largely without focus on the role of context or embeddedness (Maitlis, 2011). This is what has been colloquially called "contextualized B" by Heath and Sitkin (2001) which discusses what is "organizational" about organizational behavior. As an example, while courage has been studied from a psychological perspective (especially the courage of the hero), Worline (2011) makes the case that everyday courage in a work context is a relevant and important area of investigation. Rather than studying the image of the "mythic hero", courage can be found in "every corner of the cubicle". Courage goes beyond the makeup of the individual and has implications for the organizational context and the how it enables or impedes performance at work.

In these ways, POS provides an enriching lens for organizational studies. It encourages organizational scholars to expand their horizons in theorizing about and investigating empirically macro and micro topics in organizational behavior. It expands the range of topics seen as valuable and legitimate in organizational science. When applied to work–family relationships, POS offers the potential to uncover new ways of thinking about antecedents and outcomes of work–family relationships and suggests new research questions about mechanisms for creating work–family balance, enrichment, and conflict.

How is a POS lens already (even implicitly) embedded within the literature on work–family relationships?

A broadening from conflict to enrichment/facilitation

Individuals perform different roles across their life domains (employee, husband, parent, and friend). The ways in which individuals manage the interface or transition between these roles has implications for their well-being as well as their work performance (Peng, Ilies and Dimotakis, 2011). Until recently, much of the work–family literature has assumed that the two domains are in conflict from simultaneous pressures and priorities (Kossek *et al.*, 2011). The literature often assumes that the finite nature of one's personal resources (time, energy, attention) creates potential for tension when allocating resources to meet competing demands of work and family, leading to experience of strain and conflict (Peng, Ilies and Dimotakis, 2011).

More recently, the literature has focused more attention on the potential for enrichment between work and family roles. An enrichment approach posits that one's participation in one role (i.e., work) can facilitate other roles (i.e., family) and vice versa (Greenhaus and Powell, 2006). A related concept to enrichment is work–family facilitation. Facilitation focuses more on systems level issues that contribute to how participation in one life domain benefits role-related performance and growth in another (Grzywacz *et al.*, 2007). Drawing on role expansion theory, these researchers suggest that experiences at home may make you a better employee and/or that being an employee may help you become a better parent or spouse. For example, a partner or children may offer a chance to practice new skills at home before translating them to the world of work – e.g. I may develop active listening skills at home that may help me be a better listener at work – (Kirchmeyer, 1992). Or a person's personal network ranging from friends to neighbors to community groups can provide a larger network that one can draw on for social capital when dealing with workplace issues.

The literatures on enrichment and facilitation help explain why work–family relationships may enable positive benefits. First, holding multiple roles can help obtain alternative resources (identity, health, financial security, and social support) that can outweigh the possible strain that comes from juggling multiple roles (Grzywacz *et al.*, 2007). Second, these effects may also come from positive spillover or the extent to which moods – such as joy or energy – and interpersonal and task-related skills – such as organization or budgeting – learned in one domain positively affect one's experience in another domain (Edwards and Rothbard, 2000; Ruderman *et al.*, 2002). And research suggests that strong engagement in both work and family can have a positive effect on health and well-being (Grzywacz, Butler and Almeida, 2008; Ruderman *et al.*, 2002). In this way, research on work–family enrichment and facilitation reflect one direction that implicitly draws on a POS lens (Keeney and Illies, 2011).

Support for more positive work–family relationships

The work–family literature also indicates a number of organizational and supervisory practices and policies that enable more generative and high quality work–family relationships (Kossek, Baltes and Mathews, 2011). In fact, there is a well-developed literature on another kind of POS – perceived organizational support (Eisenberger *et al.*, 1986) – that sometimes gets mixed up with Positive Organizational Scholarship. However, it does not tend to look specifically at work–family support (Kossek *et al.*, 2011). A recent review of research notes that it is clear that employers benefit from offering and supporting the use of work–family policies through more positive employee attitudes, better talent, and cost savings (Kossek and Michel, 2011). Three main types of support include:

1   *Employee control over work.* This might include "job conditions and the structure of work, such as work hours and job designs that give workers control over when, where, or how they do their job" (Kossek *et al.*, 2011: 7). Employee control or at least input into their work hours is important because it provides flexibility to address employees' needs outside of the workplace. Flexibility about where work is conducted can also contribute to more

positive work–family dynamics as employees can better juggle the needs of work and home life. It also provides more opportunities for recovery experiences during the evening/weekends necessary for restoration of energy that may have been depleted during the work day/week (Sonentag, *et al.* 2008).

2   *HR policies that support work–family balance.* Organizational practices that enable better balance are potent because they offer system level changes that have the possibility to be institutionalized over time for long term impact (Grzywacz *et al.*, 2007). These include organizational programs and practices such as flextime, telework, job sharing, paid time off, and family benefits like health care and assistance programs that assist employees with the joint management of a paid work role with non-work roles such as parenting, elder care, leisure, education, volunteering, and self care – e.g. exercise or medical needs – (Ryan and Kossek, 2008). These also include referral programs and formal benefits such as health and child and elder care and domestic partner inclusion. One particularly interesting research study on this topic was recently conducted by Perlow and Porter (2009). In their study of professional service employees, known to routinely work 60+ hour week, they found that consultants can provide the highest standards of service and still have planned, uninterrupted time off. The organization imposed a strict requirement for rotating evenings off from work. Employees reported not only better work–family relationship, but also indicated they had more open communication, increased learning and development, and delivered a better product to the client.

3   *Organizational culture/norms/expectations about work and family integration.* Employees often do not feel comfortable taking advantage of formalized work–family benefits. They may worry about cultural stigmatization and being evaluated less positively or seen as less committed when their managers do not see them working (Kossek, Baltes and Mathews, 2011). The best way to create a work–family supportive organizational culture is for managers and executives to be role models for employees in taking part in work–family policies and programs. When used successfully by managers and executives, employees will also feel comfortable participating in them. Recent research shows that interventions which increase bosses' consideration of work–family support also leads to higher productivity (Hammer *et al.*, 2011)

So clearly we already see some POS ideas leaking into the literature on work–family relationships. In the remainder of the chapter, we suggest additional ways that a POS lens may open up new insights into the work family literature.

Possible POS connections moving forward

In our introduction to POS, we identified several different ways that the term positive has been defined in POS research. By examining the work–family literature from several of these definitions, new insights can potentially be generated. These ideas can also stimulate future research.

Positive deviance

POS often seeks to identify examples of positive deviance by looking for exemplars that dramatically exceed the norm and identifying inspiring possibilities (Spreitzer and Sonenshein, 2004). Often, these exemplars show themselves in the rankings of Best Places to Work by *Fortune Magazine*. Who wouldn't want on-site fitness centers, health care, childcare, concierge services, and generous benefits programs that include eldercare and adoption support? While these are positively deviant examples, these kinds of work–family benefits are costly and not accessible to the average company, large or small. And not all employees seek the same kind of work–family integration (Kossek and Lautsch, 2008). Some workers may have higher work identities. Others have stronger family identities and still others are "dual-centric" (Kossek *et al.*, 2011). A positive deviance perspective would focus on identifying exemplars of these different types and how their organizations might support each simultaneously. We need greater understanding of how individuals can thrive (Spreitzer *et al.*, 2005) in their work–family relationships, regardless of their style of work–family integration.

Virtues

A second definition of positive has to do with virtues (or the best of the human condition). POS is based on the postulation that an inclination exists in all human systems toward achieving the highest aspirations of humankind (Dutton and Sonenshein, 2009). The study of virtues is the examination of excellence and goodness for its own sake – captured by the Latin *virtus* and the Greek *arête*. Whereas debate has occurred regarding what constitutes goodness and whether universal human virtues can be identified, all societies and cultures possess catalogues of traits that they deem virtuous, that represent what is morally good, and that define the highest aspirations of human beings (Peterson and Seligman, 2004).

Peterson and Seligman's (2004) typology of virtues and character strengths is a means to inventory the current state of research in this domain. They developed a classification for organizing 24 character strengths into six categories of virtues: courage, justice, humanity, wisdom, temperance, and transcendence (Park and Peterson, 2003). We suggest that specific virtues are specifically relevant to the work–family literature including compassion, hope, kindness and love, and justice. We offer suggestion on each below.

Compassion (Lilius *et al.*, 2011) for individuals non work-related life is one possibility. In a high performing business unit composed of 30 workers, the research findings demonstrated how showing compassion to a worker facing difficult times outside of work lifted up the whole office in terms of commitment and performance because they made a difference to the life of an employee (Lilius *et al.*, 2011). Compassion involves noticing, feeling, and acting to help a colleague in need. More compassion at work may contribute to stronger work–family enrichment. New ways of working like telework help employees such as disabled persons or those with young kids or seniors be able to be involved in a work organization. Work–family arrangements could provide new more compassionate ways of managing employees. It can provide new options that may enable labor force participation.

The virtue of hope may enable more work–family enrichment and facilitation. Hope may help open up generative pathways for positive work–family relationships to blossom. Hope is normally considered to involve two components; (1) agency, involving the expectancy of positive outcomes, and (2) pathways, involving the ability to see how those positive outcomes can be reached (Snyder, 2003). A sense of hope on the part of managers and employees may make a strong difference in the effective design and implementation of work–family policies and practices because individuals can see the possibilities for something better. For example, a parent trying to manage a dual career situation with small children at home may benefit from having stronger feelings of hope that a workable solution can be enacted. In this context, hope may nudge the worried parent to seek out the best quality childcare that can enrich the entire family's experience and not settle for a suboptimal solution that leaves the family stressed and struggling.

Another set of virtues has to do with humanity including kindness and love. The most relevant POS relational construct is high quality connections (Dutton and Heaphy, 2003). Connection quality may be defined in terms of the positivity of the emotional experience of interacting with another person at work and the feeling of potentiality for responsive action (Dutton, 2003; Dutton and Heaphy, 2003). Originating in relational theory, high quality connections focus on the human growth and development that can occur while in connection with – rather than separation from – others. High quality connections between bosses and employees provide the psychological safety necessary for employees to trust that they can take advantage of work–family policies and for bosses to trust that employees are working when they cannot be seen. And high quality connections between co-workers are crucial for them to provide social support and back up as necessary for people to fulfill family needs and obligations. When high quality connections are high, people assume professed needs are real and do not question when someone needs extra consideration in their workday or time off to take care of a need at home.

Justice is another virtue that is likely to be relevant for work–family relationships. One area this may be particularly relevant to is with regard to the meaning of "family". Many professional women do not have children, others are not married, and a substantial number of middle-aged workers have eldercare responsibilities. Still others devote themselves to other passions be it commitments to their communities, church, volunteer work, or athletics/fitness. The end result is that people can feel that family-friendly policies apply to only those with children and give preference to those in traditional family arrangements (Kossek *et al.*, 2011). Those who are single or without children may be expected to take more than their share of overtime or late night work assignments. In order to have just work–family policies, organizations need to be focused on a broadened conceptualization of family life. These practices may help to ameliorate societal injustice by serving as a way to help workers get access to positive life changing experiences that can help their families attain a better life.

Positive emotions

Positive emotions range from joy to happiness to energy to contentment. Fredrickson's broaden and build theory makes the case for how positive emotions lead people to become more creative, helpful, and open to information (Fredrickson, 1998, 2001; Isen, 1987, 2000). This can lead to the discovery of novel ideas (Fredrickson, 2001; Fredrickson and Branigan, 2005). A broad repertoire of thoughts and actions enables a person to come up with more ideas of things to do (Fredrickson and Branigan, 2005), be more inclusive with one's in-groups (Johnson and Fredrickson, 2005), and be more creative (Isen, 2000). How might individuals use positive emotions to contribute to better work–family relationships? We suggest that work–family capitalization to bringing more passion to work may be effective.

Illies, Keeney and Scott (2011) offer one specific practice – work–family interpersonal capitalization. Building on affective events theory (Weiss and Cropanzano, 1996), work–family interpersonal capitalization is defined as sharing positive events or experiences from work with a spouse or partner at home. Capitalization represents a social psychological mechanism that may explain the spillover across the work and family boundary. It is a process to enhance the possibility of work–family enrichment. They find that discussing positive work events and experiences with one's spouse or partner at home, increases not only job satisfaction but also relationships satisfaction, particularly when the partner is responsive (Illies, Keeney and Scott, 2011). A key advantage is that work–family capitalization does not involve the development of a new organizational policy or investment – it is a change in behavior. An interesting question is whether family-to-work capitalization (sharing good news from home to those at work) would have a similar positive effect.

Having more passion at work is another possible way to bring more positive emotions into one's work to possibly spill over into family relationships. Passion is defined as a strong inclination toward an activity that people like, find important, and in which they invest time and energy (Vallerand, 2008). When people play to their passions, they are more authentic and find that work requires less self-regulation (Perttula and Cardon, 2011). But in order for the positive emotions of passion at work to spill over into home life, the passion must be what Vallerand terms "harmonious". Harmonious passion originates from an autonomous internalization of the activity in identity and leads people to choose to engage in the activity that they love. It is expected to mainly lead to more adaptive outcomes like bringing positive emotions home from work. It can be contrasted with what Vallerand terms "obsessive" passion. This obsessive passion leads people to experience an uncontrollable urge to engage in the activity. It is found to predict less adaptive outcomes which could include more work–family conflict as the passion actively takes a person away from investments in their home life.

Managing human energy

POS research can also help us understand how to help people manage and restore their energy. Human energy can be seen as a resource (Hobfoll, 1989) that helps people regulate their behaviors and emotions in compliance with organizational or group norms and expectations. However, energy is limited and can be depleted over time due to work demands. These ideas on energy management and restoration may have important implications for work–family relationships in that, if individuals have more energy overall, they are better able to balance or enrich different roles in their lives. We discuss several energy-management threads as they may apply to work family relationships.

Research on recovery has found that employees can use their time *off* work – evenings (Sonnentag, Binnewies and Mojza, 2008) or weekends (Fritz and Sonnentag, 2005) – to recharge their energy and reduce their fatigue. For example, Fritz, Sonnentag, Spector and McInroe (2010) found that recovery experiences during the weekend were positively related to joviality – an experience similar to human energy – as well as to lower levels of fatigue at the end of the weekend. Further, research suggests that the kind of experiences during non-work time matter to the restoration of human energy as well. Specifically, experiences such as relaxation, mastery experiences, a sense of control, and psychological detachment from work have been found to be particularly beneficial for recovery (Fritz and Sonnentag, 2005, Fritz *et al.*, 2010; Sonnentag and Fritz, 2007). In addition, sleep is an important factor in replenishing human energy. Accordingly, results from day-level studies indicate that employees experiencing high-quality sleep at night reported higher levels of energy the next day (Scott and Judge, 2006; Sonnentag, Binnewies and Mojza, 2008).

But all of this research is focused on recovery activities *off of work time* which might intrude on work–family relationships. And with many individuals working a "second shift" (Hochschild and Machung, 1990) with chores and housework at home during non-work hours, time for recovery may be quite limited. Despite the significant progress recovery scholars have made in understanding what replenishes human energy during off-work time, research indicates that these beneficial effects of recovery activities fade over time. For example, vitality is sapped by the end of the workweek (Fritz *et al.*, 2010). The question becomes how to make energy at work more sustainable (Pfeffer, 2010) so that individuals still have energy at the end of the workday to engage in family relationships.

Recent research by Fritz, Lam and Spreitzer (2011) builds on the idea that energy is not finite (Marks, 1977) and suggests that individuals can engage in restoration activities at work. They found that breaks to detach from work such as surfing the web or shopping are not particularly restorative. What was found to be restorative were activities that imbue work with more meaning – e.g. reflect on how I make a difference at work; build relationships – e.g. show gratitude to someone at work; or create an opportunity to learn something new.

It may also be that individuals who are playing to their strengths and talents are likely to have more energy at the end of the workday that they can devote to work–family relationships. Recent research suggests that leveraging strengths builds important emotional, agentic and relational resources that can be drawn on during challenging times (Spreitzer, Stephens and Sweetman, 2009). A specific tool that has been found to identify core strengths, called the reflected best self feedback exercise (Roberts *et al.*, 2005), is particularly potent because it identifies strengths that cut across all aspects of one's life – work and family. By leveraging strengths, individuals build pathways to becoming extraordinary in ways that cut across different spheres of life. Another useful tool is the workstyle profile developed by Ellen Kossek and the Center for Creative Leadership that helps individuals to assess and leverage their own values and behaviors for integration and separation.

When individuals are doing work that makes them feel alive and generative, they are more likely to thrive (Spreitzer *et al.*, 2005), not just cope amidst change or challenges. And when individuals are thriving in one domain of life, they are also highly likely to be thriving in other aspects of life (Porath *et al.*, 2011). Thriving is generative in that it can be contagious across life domains – the energy from one life domain can flow into another. When a person has a great day at work with many accomplishments and positive interactions, that good energy can spill over at the end of the day. The extent to which domain-specific thriving can mediate or improve poor performance or experience in another domain is a promising area for work–family research.

Directions for future research

In the prior section, we outlined several ways, including positive deviance, virtues, positive emotions, and human energy, as possible POS avenues that may offer insights to the work–family literature. These serve merely as a starting point. In this final section of the paper, we offer a few specific directions for future research. One particularly fruitful area of research is using the positive deviance methodology (Pascale, J. Sternin and M. Sternin, 2010). In contrast to a best practice approach where organizations seek to learn from or borrow solutions to complex problems from other organizations, a positive deviance approach takes the perspective that solutions exist within your own organization. There are pockets of positive deviance within any system that are potent sources of learning and resources. The challenge is to find these pockets.

The quintessential example of positive deviance involves seeking solutions to reducing hunger and starvation in developing countries (Pascale, J. Sternin and M. Sternin, 2010). The normal approach was to bring in outside experts to evaluate the system and recommend solutions, often requiring large infusions of exogenous resources. Positive deviance scholars suggested a different approach that involved going to villages and seeking out those families with the best nourished children.

> The villagers discovered that there were well-nourished children among them, despite the poverty, and that those children's mothers broke locally accepted wisdom: they fed their children even when they had diarrhea; giving

them several small feedings each day rather than one or two big ones; adding sweet-potato greens to the children's rice even though they were considered to be low-class food. These ideas spread and still hold. In two years, malnutrition dropped 65 to 85 per cent in every village. Their program proved more effective than those of the outside experts.

(Pascale, R. Stenin and M. Stenin, 2010: x)

Work–family researchers might benefit from a positive deviance approach. This approach might identify some truly innovative unit practices, creative organization policies, or ingenious individual behaviors that offer new insights for work–family integration and facilitation.

Conclusion

There appears to be much potential for synergy between recent ideas radiating from a POS lens and the literature on work–family relationships. There has been some momentum already in applying a POS lens to work–family research. The ideas put forward in this chapter relating to positive deviance, virtues, positive emotions and energy management will intensify the momentum and contribute new insights back to the POS literature. Future research should also address how the literature on work–family relationships might provide new insights to POS. I invite you to join us on this journey by engaging in empirical research on these topics and more.

Acknowledgements

I thank Ellen Kossek and Dan Mulhern for interesting conversations on this topic that inspired ideas for this chapter.

References

Ashforth, B., Meyers, K. and Sluss, D. (2011). Socialization perspectives and positive organizational scholarship. In K.S. Cameron and G.M. Spreitzer (eds) *The Oxford handbook of positive organizational scholarship* (537–551). New York, NY: Oxford University Press.

Bandura, A. (1977). Self-efficacy: Toward a unifying theory of behavioral change. *Psychological Review* 84, 191–215.

Bartunek, J. and Woodman, R. (2011). The spirits of organization development or why OD lives despite its pronounced death. In K.S. Cameron and G.M. Spreitzer (eds) *The Oxford handbook of positive organizational scholarship* (727–736). New York, NY: Oxford University Press.

Browning, L., Morris, G. and Kee, K. (2011). The role of communication in positive organizational scholarship. In K.S. Cameron and G.M. Spreitzer (eds) *The Oxford handbook of positive organizational scholarship* (566–578). New York, NY: Oxford University Press.

Cameron, K.S. and Spreitzer, G.M. (2011). Introduction to the handbook. In K.S. Cameron and G.M. Spreitzer (eds) *The Oxford handbook of positive organizational scholarship* (1–14). New York, NY: Oxford University Press.

Cameron, K.S., Dutton, J.E. and Quinn, R.E. (2003). *Positive organizational scholarship: Foundations of a new discipline*. San Francisco, CA: Berrett-Koehler.

Caza, B.B. and Milton, L. (2011.). Resilience at work: Building capability in the face of adversity. In K.S. Cameron and G.M. Spreitzer (eds) *The Oxford handbook of positive organizational scholarship* (895–908). New York, NY: Oxford University Press.

Center for Positive Organizational Scholarship (2011). The essence of positive organizational scholarship: Unlocking the generative capabilities in human communities. Retrieved from http://www.bus.umich.edu/Positive/pdf/POS%20Essence.pdf

Cooperrider, D. and Godwin, L. (2011). Positive organizational development: Innovation-inspired change in an economy and ecology of strengths. In K.S. Cameron and G.M. Spreitzer (eds) *The Oxford handbook of positive organizational scholarship* (737–750). New York, NY: Oxford University Press.

Davis, G.F. and Marquis, C. (2005). Prospects for organization theory in the early twenty-first century: Institutional fields and mechanisms. *Organization Science* 16, 332–343.

DeRue, D.S. and Workman, K. (2011). Toward a positive and dynamic theory of leadership development. In K.S. Cameron and G.M. Spreitzer (eds) *The Oxford handbook of positive organizational scholarship* (784–797). New York, NY: Oxford University Press.

Dutton, J.E. (2003). *Energize your workplace: How to build and sustain high-quality connections at work*. San Francisco: Jossey-Bass.

Dutton, J.E. and Glynn, M. (2007). Positive organizational scholarship. In J. Baring and C.L. Cooper (eds) *The Sage handbook of Organizational Behavior: Micro approaches*, Vol. 1 (693–712). Thousand Oaks, CA: Sage.

Dutton, J.E. and Heaphy, E. (2003). The power of high quality connections. In K.S. Cameron, J.E. Dutton and R.E. Quinn (eds), *Positive organizational scholarships foundations of a new discipline* (263–278). San Francisco: Berrett-Koehler.

Dutton, J.E. and Sonenshein, S. (2009). Positive organizational scholarship. In S.J. Lopez (ed.) *Encyclopedia of positive psychology* (737–742). Oxford: Wiley-Blackwell.

Dutton, J. E., Glynn, M. and Spreitzer, G.M. (2006). Positive organizational scholarship. In J.H. Greenhaus and G.A. Callanan (eds) *Encyclopedia of career development*, Vol. 2 (641–644). Thousand Oaks, CA: Sage Publishers.

Edwards, J.R. and Rothbard, N.P. (2000). Mechanisms linking work and family: Clarifying the relationship between work and family constructs. *Academy of Management Review* 25, 178–199.

Eisenberger, R., Huntington, R., Hutchison, S. and Sowa, D. (1986). Perceived organizational support. *Journal of Applied Psychology* 71, 500–507.

Fredrickson, B.L. (1998). What good are positive emotions? *Review of General Psychology* 2, 300–319.

Fredrickson, B.L. (2001). The role of positive emotions in positive psychology: The broaden-and-build theory of positive emotions. *American Psychologist* 56, 218–226.

Fredrickson, B.L. and Branigan, C. (2005). Positive emotions broaden the scope of attention and thought-action repertoires. *Cognition and Emotion* 19, 313–332.

Fritz, C. and Sonnentag, S. (2005). Recovery, health and job performance: Effects of weekend experiences. *Journal of Occupational Health Psychology* 10, 187–199.

Fritz, C., Lam, C.F. and Spreitzer, G.M. (2011). It's the little things that matter: An examination of knowledge workers' energy management. *Academy of Management Perspectives* 25, 28–39.

Fritz, C., Sonnentag, S., Spector, P.E. and McInroe, J.A. (2010). The weekend matters: Relationships between stress recovery and affective experiences. *Journal of Organizational Behavior* 31, 1137–1162.

Ghoshal, S. (2005). Bad management theories are destroying good management practice. *Academy of Management Learning & Education* 4, 75–91.

Goddard, R.D. and Salloum, S.J. (2011). Collective efficacy beliefs, organizational excellence and leadership. In K.S. Cameron and G.M. Spreitzer (eds) *The Oxford handbook of positive organizational scholarship* (642–650). New York, NY: Oxford University Press.

Greenhaus, J.H. and Powell, G.N. (2006). When work and family are allies: A theory of work-family enrichment. *Academy of Management Review* 31, 72–92.

Grzywacz, J.G., Butler, A.B. and Almeida, D.M. (2008). Work, family and health: work-family balance as a protective factor against stresses of daily life. In A. Marcus-Newhall, D.F Halpern and S.J. Tan (eds) *The changing realities of work and family* (194–216). Oxford: Wiley-Blackwell.

Grzywacz, J.G., Carlson, D.S., Kacmar, K.M. and Wayne, J.H. (2007). A multi-level perspective on the synergies between work and family. *Journal of Occupational and Organizational Psychology* 80, 559–574.

Hall, D. and Las Heras, M. (2011). Personal growth through career work: A positive approach to careers. In Cameron, K.S. and Spreitzer, G.M. (eds) *The Oxford handbook of positive organizational scholarship* (507–518). New York, NY: Oxford University Press.

Hammer, L.B., Kossek, E.E., Anger, W.K., Bodner, R. and Zimmerman, K.L. (2011). Clarifying work-family intervention processes: The roles of work-family conflict and family-supportive supervisor behaviors. *Journal of Applied Psychology* 96, 134–150.

Heath, C. and Sitkin, S.B. (2001). Big-B versus big-O: What is *organizational* about organizational behavior? *Journal of Organizational Behavior* 22, 43–58.

Hedstrom, P. and Swedberg, R. (eds) (1998). *Social mechanisms: An analytical approach to social theory*. Cambridge: Cambridge University Press.

Hernes, G. (1998). Real virtuality. In P. Hedstrom and R. Swedberg (eds) *Social Mechanisms: An analytical approach to social theory* (74–101). Cambridge University Press.

Hobfoll, S.E. (1989). Conservation of resources: A new attempt at conceptualizing stress. *American Psychologist* 44, 513–524.

Hochschild, A. R. & Machung, A. (1990). *The second shift: working parents and the revolution at home*. California: Avon Books.

Isen, A.M. (1987). Positive affect, cognitive-processes and social behavior. In L. Berkowitz (ed.) *Advances in experimental social psychology* 20, 203–253. San Diego, CA: Academic Press.

Isen, A.M. (2000). Positive affect and decision making. In Lewis, M. and Haviland-Jones, J.M. (eds) *Handbook of emotions* (417–435). New York: Guilford Press.

Ilies, R., Keeney, J. and Scott, B.A. (2011). Work-family interpersonal capitalization: Sharing positive work events at home. *Organizational Behavior and Human Decision Processes* 114, 115–126.

James, E. and Wooten, L. (2011). Orientations of positive leadership in times of crisis. In K.S. Cameron and Spreitzer (eds) *The Oxford handbook of positive organizational scholarship* (882–8G.M. 94). New York, NY: Oxford University Press.

Johnson, K.J. and Fredrickson, B.L. (2005). "We all look the same to me": Positive emotions eliminate the own-race bias in face recognition. *Psychological Science* 16, 875–881.

Keeney, J. and Ilies, R. (2011). Positive work/family dynamics. In K.S. Cameron and G.M. Spreitzer (eds) *The Oxford handbook of positive organizational scholarship* (601–614). New York, NY: Oxford University Press.

Keyes, C.L.M. (2005). Mental illness and/or mental health? Investigating axioms of the complete state model of health. *Journal of Consulting and Clinical Psychology* 73, 539–548.

Kirchmeyer, C. (1992). Perceptions of nonwork-to-work spillover: Challenging the common view of conflict-ridden domain relationships. *Basic and Applied Social Psychology* 13, 231–249.

Kossek, E.E. and Lautsch, B.A. (2008). *CEO of me: Creating a life that works in the flexible job age*. Philadelphia: Wharton School Publishing.

Kossek, E.E. and Michel, J.S. (2011). Flexible work schedules. In S. Zedeck (ed.), *APA handbook of industrial and organizational psychology*, Vol. 1 (535–572). Washington, DC: American Psychological Association.

Kossek, E.E., Baltes, B. and Mathews, R. (2011). How work family research and finally have an impact in the workplace. *Industrial and organizational psychology: Perspectives on science and practice* 4, 3.

Kossek, E.E., Pichler, S., Bodner, T. and Hammer, L.B. (2011). Workplace social support and work-family conflict: A meta-analysis clarifying the influence of general and work-family specific supervisor and organizational support. *Personnel Psychology* 64, 289–313.

Lilius, J.M., Worline, M.C., Dutton, J.E., Kanov, J.M. and Maitlis, S. (2011). Understanding compassion capability. *Human Relations* 64, 873–899.

Lilius, J., Kanov, J., Dutton, J., Worline, M. and Maitlis, S. (2011). Compassion revealed: What we know about compassion at work. In K.S. Cameron and G.M. Spreitzer (eds) *Handbook of Positive Organizational Scholarship*. New York: Oxford University Press.

Maitlis, S. (2011). Post-traumatic growth: A missed opportunity for positive organizational scholarship. In K.S. Cameron and G.M. Spreitzer (eds) *The Oxford handbook of positive organizational scholarship* (909–923). New York, NY: Oxford University Press.

Marks, S.R. (1977). Multiple roles and role strain: Some notes on human energy, time and commitment. *American Sociological Review* 42, 921–936.

Park, N. and Peterson, C.M. (2003). Virtues and organizations. In K.S. Cameron, Dutton J.E. and R.E. Quinn (eds), *Positive organizational scholarship: Foundations of a new discipline* (33–47). San Francisco: Berrett Koehler.

Pascale, R., Stenin, J. and Sternin, M. (2010). The power of positive deviance: How unlikely innovators solve the world's toughest problems. Cambridge, MA: Harvard Business School Press.

Peng, A.C., Ilies, R. and Dimotakis, N. (2011). Work-family balance, role integration and employee well-being. In S. Kaiser, M. Ringlstetter, D.R. Eikhof and M.P. Cunha (eds). *Creating Balance? International perspectives on the work-life integration of professionals* (121–142). Berlin: Springer-Verlag.

Perlow, L.A. and Porter, J.L. (2009). Making time off predictable and required. *Harvard Business Review* 87, 102–109.

Perttula, K. and Cardon, M. (2011). Passion. In K.S. Cameron and G.M. Spreitzer (eds) *The Oxford handbook of positive organizational scholarship*, (190–200). Oxford, UK: Oxford University Press.

Peterson, C. and Seligman, M.E.P. (2004). *Character strengths and virtues. A handbook and classification.* Washington, DC: American Psychological Association.

Pfeffer, J. (2010). Building sustainable organizations: The human factor. *Academy of Management Perspectives* 24, 34–45.

Porath, C., Spreitzer, G., Gibson, C. and Garnett, F.G. (2011). Thriving at work: Toward its measurement, construct validation, and theoretical refinement. *Journal of Organizational Behavior*, Advance online publication, doi:10.1002/job756.

Powley, E.H. 2011. Organizational healing: A relational process to handle major depression. In K. Cameron and G. Spreitzer *Handbook of Positive Organizational Scholarship*. New York: Oxford University Press.

Ragins, B. (2011). Relational mentoring: A positive approach to mentoring at work. In K.S. Cameron and G.M. Spreitzer (eds) *The Oxford handbook of positive organizational scholarship* (519–536). New York, NY: Oxford University Press.

Ramarajan, L. and Thomas, D. (2011). A positive approach to studying diversity in organizations. In K.S. Cameron and G.M. Spreitzer (eds) *The Oxford handbook of positive organizational scholarship* (552–565). New York, NY: Oxford University Press.

Roberts, L.M., Spreitzer, G.M., Dutton, J., Quinn, R., Heaphy, E. and Barker, B. (2005). How to play to your strengths. *Harvard Business Review* 83, 75–80.

Ruderman, M.N., Ohlott, J.J., Panzer, K. and King, S.N. (2002). Benefits of multiple roles for managerial women. *Academy of Management Journal* 45, 369–386

Ryan, A.E. and Kossek, E.E. (2008). Work-life policy implementation: Breaking down or creating barriers to inclusiveness? *Human Resource Management* 47, 295–310.

Scott, B.A. and Judge, T.A. (2006). Insomnia, emotions, and job satisfaction: A multilevel study. *Journal of Management* 32, 622–645.

Seligman, M.E.P. (1999). The president's address. *American Psychologist* 54, 559–562.

Smith, P.C., Kendall, L.M. and Hulin, C.L. (1969). *The measurement of satisfaction in work and retirement: A strategy of the study of attitudes.* Chicago, IL: Rand McNally.

Sonnentag, S. and Fritz, C. (2007). The recovery experience questionnaire: Development and validation of a measure for assessing recuperation and unwinding from work. *Journal of Occupational Health Psychology* 12, 204–221.

Sonnentag, S., Binnewies, C. and Mojza, E.J. (2008). Did you have a nice evening? A day-level study on recovery experiences, sleep, and affect. *Journal of Applied Psychology* 3, 674–684.

Snyder, C.R. (2003). The *Psychology of hope: You can get there from here.* New York: Free Press.

Spreitzer, G.M. and Cameron, K.S. (2011). A path forward: Assessing progress and exploring core questions for the future of positive organizational scholarship. In K.S. Cameron and G.M. Spreitzer (eds), *The Oxford handbook of positive organizational scholarship* (1034–1048). New York, NY: Oxford University Press.

Spreitzer, G.M. and Sonenshein, S. (2004). Toward the construct definition of positive deviance. *American Behavioral Scientist* 47, 828–847.

Spreitzer, G., Stephens, J.P. and Sweetman, D. (2009). The reflected best self field experiment with adolescent leaders: Exploring the psychological resources associated with feedback source and valence. *Journal of Positive Psychology* 4, 331–348.

Spreitzer, G.M., Sutcliffe, K., Dutton, J., Sonenshein, S. and Grant, A.M. (2005). A socially embedded model of thriving at work. *Organization Science* 16, 537–549.

Vallerand, R.J. (2008). On the psychology of passion: In search of what makes people's live most worth living. *Canadian Psychology* 49,1–13.

Weiss, H. and Cropanzano, R. (1996). Affective events theory: A theoretical discussion of the structure, causes, and consequences of affective experiences at work. In B.M. Stan and L.L. Cummings (eds), *Research in Organizational Behavior. An annual series of analytical essays and critical reviews* 18, 1–74. Greenwich, CT: JAI Press.

Worline, M. (2011). Courage in organizations: An integrative review of the "Difficult Virtue". In K.S. Cameron and G.M. Spreitzer (eds), *The Oxford handbook of positive organizational scholarship* (304–315). New York, NY: Oxford University Press.

2 A systems perspective on work and family

Shelley MacDermid Wadsworth and Leah Hibel

The prospect of writing this chapter was at first daunting given its focus on a theory that, while having a long and distinguished history, is not highly visible in current studies of the relationships between work and family life (Perry-Jenkins and MacDermid Wadsworth, forthcoming). We wondered how systems theory, having been already in existence for so long, could contribute to the goal of this book to spawn a "new generation" of work–family research. It has been very instructive to revisit the books and articles that first introduced and then extended and refined systems theory. In the pages that follow, we aim to elevate readers:

- awareness of the magnitude of the paradigm shift that systems thinking represented in the study of families, employing organizations, and the interface between them;
- recognition of the degree to which systems theory has generated useful insights in these areas of study; and
- attention to aspects of systems theory yet to be fully applied to the study of the work–family interface.

General Systems Theory came into existence during a period of turbulence in both scientific and social culture. At the beginning of the twentieth century, scientists were using principles of physics to study organizations, especially the second law of thermodynamics, which specifies that "ordered systems ... tend toward ... destruction of existing order and ultimate decay" (von Bertalanffy, 1972: 409). Increasingly, these principles were proving insufficient to address "multi-variable" problems and unexpected outcomes (Drack, 2008). At the same time in the larger society, much of the first half of the century was spent preparing for, conducting, or recovering from large-scale wars that propelled significant societal change. The wars "sped up the line" for the development of new technologies that could take in and instantly adapt to new information, such as weapons systems that could track aircraft from ships (Whitchurch and Constantine, 1993). The wars and their resulting economic turmoil raised awareness of threats from far beyond the shores of the US, and compelled individual families to make changes at home as the employment of mothers skyrocketed from 8.6 per cent among mothers of children under 18 to 18.6 per cent and 39 per cent among mothers of children aged 0–5 and

6–17, respectively, in only a few short years (Blood, 1963). These scientific and social trends converged to produce fertile ground for the suggestion that social systems might operate to scientific principles other than those governing physics.

What is "systems theory"?

General Systems Theory (GST) is a transdisciplinary theoretical framework that overarches a variety of micro-level theories. The ultimate goal of GST is to explain the behavior of all multidimensional systems, defined as "set(s) of elements standing in interrelation among themselves and with the environment" (von Bertalanffy, 1972: 417) and found in almost any discipline in science. This theoretical perspective has been used to understand how complex and diverse systems, ranging from businesses and families to electrical networks and thermostats, act and react.

The GST framework represented a conscious shift away from previous mechanistic and vitalistic models that reduced explanations to a limited number of well defined interactions, or proposed a large number of factors with weak inter-relations. GST, however, stressed the importance of examining entire systems, rather than focusing only on the system's components. Properties specific to the system emerge only after viewing the system as a whole; these properties cannot be derived by examination of the individual parts of the systems in isolation. Further, GST highlighted interconnections within systems and the ability of systems to interact with the surrounding environment. Thus, according to the GST, systems are not closed like those governed by laws of thermodynamics, but open to interact with their environments and acquire new properties through these interactions.

GST concepts: application to family and organizational research

It took several decades for Bertalanffy's proposal of General Systems Theory to be taken up by family scholars, because his original work was published in German and because of interruptions by WWII. Marriage and family therapists were the first to apply GST to families. In particular, Bateson and colleagues believed that every element of the family was affected by one person's symptoms, and therefore, rather than treating patients separately from their families, as had been the traditional practice, healthy functioning required entire family involvement (Bavelas and Segal, 1982). General Systems Theory also is credited with inspiring the launch of modern organizational theory, an era preceded by a classical period focused on the anatomy of organizations, and a neo-classical period, launched by the Hawthorne studies, that acknowledged informal organizational structures (Diamond, 1967; Scott, 1961). As with family scholars, recognizing that organizations are not closed systems and focusing on flows of information or cybernetics led to several new trends in research (Katz and Kahn, 1966).

The GST perspective helped to explain why families sometimes seemed to go to great lengths to maintain their current patterns, even when pathological

(Doherty and Baptiste, 1993). Jackson applied the label "*homeostasis*" to describe the family phenomenon of maintaining the status quo (Jackson, 1957). Homeostasis is maintained by negative *feedback loops*, which discourage change by reverting new behaviors back into old behaviors. Changes may originate from an individual family member, but this *first-order change* is vulnerable to the predominant feedback loops exhibited by the family. For example, a family member may attempt to change a particular behavior (e.g. a mother returning to work) but if the predominant loops exhibited by the family are negative, family members may make the mother's re-entry into the workforce difficult or encourage the mother to stay at home. Feedback loops thus have the potential to facilitate or impede both functional and dysfunctional behaviors within a family system. Unlike first-order change, major higher level change (i.e., *second-order change*) has the ability to modify the entire family system. Second-order changes are therefore much more enduring than first-order changes because they generate new transactional patterns (D.S. Becvar and R.J. Becvar, 1988). Feedback loops are also recognizable in work organizations, and systems thinking encouraged organizational researchers to expand their focus beyond structures and central tendency to include these processes and variability over time. This shift increased the attention to the ways in which information flows throughout organizations, including how feedback loops operate; how components of organizations relate to one another; and how organizations learn and transform themselves (Buckley, 1968; Katz and Kahn, 1966; Scott, 1961; Skaržauskienė, 2010).

Systems theorists also noted the ability of various systems to result in the same end point, but via different processes (von Bertalanffy, 1968). This concept, termed *equifinality*, has been incorporated into family and organizational systems thinking. The concept of equifinality encourages attention to patterns of action such as communication, conflict, and cohesion (Bowen, 1974; Minuchin, 1988). Thus, a systems approach resulted in a shift away from "cause and effect" mechanistic thinking, to encouraging family and organizational scholars to understand processes and trajectories that can be used to explain widely divergent outcomes, or how similar outcomes can result from widely divergent situations.

As discussed previously, systems theorists highlight the importance of examining the system as a whole, rather than its components. Likewise, family systems theorists understand that families comprise not only smaller *sub-systems* (Cox and Paley, 1997), but also function and interact within other larger supra-systems. Thus, families are embedded within society's larger hierarchical structures (e.g. work, community, racial/ethnic, national) and also contain hierarchical structures within (e.g. parental, marital, sibling). For example, organizational subcultures have been shown to interact and influence family systems by limiting the resources available to families or conversely, provide opportunities that influence family structures or interactions (D. Segal and M. Segal, 2004). Similarly to the study of families, organizational researchers also now consider higher- and lower-order systems (supra- and sub-systems; Kast and Rosenzweig, 1972). According to Katz and Kahn (1966), systems thinking shifted the conceptualization of environmental influence, from a source of noise and error variance that muddied analyses, to an essential source of needed resources and insight into organizational functioning. Recognizing supra-system influences as a key dynamic opened up many new questions for analyses, such as expanding the focus on organizational performance beyond internal variables such as size or technology to environmental factors such as market competitiveness and attitudes toward stakeholders (Negandhi and Reimann, 1973).

The degree to which sub-systems interact and interfere depends upon the segmentation or integration of system *boundaries*. Boundaries refer to the borders that separate the time, space, individuals, affects and activities housed by sub-systems. Sub-systems that are particularly segmented exhibit low *permeability* (the degree to which elements from one domain enter into another domain) and lack *flexibility* (the extent to which temporal and spatial boundaries allow roles to be enacted in various settings and at various times). Conversely, sub-systems with integrated boundaries have boundaries that are highly permeable and flexible (Clark, 2000). A work–family example of an integrated boundary structure could be choosing work times based on family schedules (flexibility) and completing work related tasks while at home (permeability). Highly permeable boundaries, with repeated boundary violations, may result in *spillover* as when problems experienced at work are brought home.

Implications for research about families

The advent of systems perspectives called for changes in approaches to and interpretation of research about families (Broderick, 1970). Important conceptual, clinical, and empirical contributions "opened up" the internal dynamics of families to reveal Bowen's concepts of fusion, differentiation, and triangulation (Doherty and Baptiste, 1993); Kantor and Lehr's sub-systems, such as the mother–father or sibling sub-systems (White, 1978); and Hess and Handel's five "essential processes" of family interaction. Some researchers grouped constructs to form typologies, the best-known example of which is probably Olson's circumplex model of adaptability and cohesion (Whitchurch and Constantine, 1993).

Systems perspectives reshaped the understanding of family transitions such as divorce and developmental change in individuals. Fingerman and Bermann (2000), while also pointing out gaps in systems approaches to families, illustrated how systems approaches could enrich the understanding of the relationships between aging adults and their families. Considerable work was done to use systems perspectives to generate deeper understanding of the processes respon-sible for sustaining pathology within families, such as the relationship dynamics associated with persistent violence or substance use (Whitchurch and Constantine, 1993). Therapeutic approaches shifted from limiting contact with patients' families to conceptualizing individual symptoms as representing family problems (Bavelas and Segal, 1982).

With regard to families and their environments, perhaps the most notable influence of systems perspectives has been in connecting macro-level trends to dynamics within families. For example, in their recent decade review, Conger,

Conger and Martin (2010) present a Family Stress Model of romantic relationships that traces specific pathways by which economic downturns produce economic hardship; generating economic pressure that produces relationship hostility, conflict and withdrawal within couples; which in turn leads to reduced quality and stability. This model exemplifies many elements of systems theory, including specifying the connection between external environments and the proximal system, intra-system dynamics, and feedback loops that produce both first- and second-order change.

Implications for research about organizations

A specific example of organizational processes from organization science is that the understanding of the roles of organizational leaders changed. Rather than being seen as "operators" solving problems, they began to be seen as "pilots" navigating organizations across a complex landscape toward some strategically chosen position (Skaržauskiené, 2010). This expanded the study of leadership to include a wide variety of activities including aligning internal processes with external dynamics, understanding system forces that propel and resist change, and leading transformation.

Systems thinking began transforming approaches to organizational change and intervention. An example comes from LaMontagne and Keegel (2010), who concluded in a recent review of research on job stress interventions that interventions aimed only at individual workers tend to have few if any favorable impacts at the level of the organization, while interventions aimed at working conditions at the organizational level tend to have favorable impacts at *both* the individual – in the form of improved health – and organizational – in the form of reduced absenteeism – levels. The authors concluded (7), "Job stress can be prevented and controlled at the organizational level through the application of a systems or comprehensive approach. Despite the extensive evidence in support of systems approaches to job stress, prevalent practice … remains disproportionally focused on individual-level intervention."

A recent research example regarding work environments comes from Ashmos, Duchon and McDaniel (2000), who used a complex adaptive systems view to examine hospitals' responses to rapidly changing complex environments. Organizations that absorbed and engaged the complexity with aggressive change strategies outperformed those that responded with efforts to reduce the complexity of the change, with significantly higher returns on assets, revenue and income per hospital admission, margins, and utilization rates. Specifically, more successful organizations worked flexibly to maximize the flow of information among stakeholders and between the environment and the organization, fully acknowledged the multiple and conflicting goals prompted by environmental change; and created new organizational structures. In contrast, less successful organizations tended to adopt narrower and more rigid views of the environment, reduce complexity and the number of goals, formalize roles, and aim for stability and predictability.

How did systems theory enter research on the work–family interface?

Work–family researchers prior to 1960 focused their attention on the impact of parental work (or lack of it) on children. According to Bronfenbrenner and Crouter (1982) researchers' foci were both narrow, focusing primarily on implications for children without considering characteristics of parents' jobs or implications for parents themselves, and gendered, focusing on the negative aspects of employment by mothers, but *un*employment among fathers. In addition, there was little attention to interdependencies between mothers' and fathers' behavior.

Between 1960 and 1980, work–family research was one of many areas of science in which systems perspectives became popular. According to Bronfenbrenner and Crouter (1982), greater recognition of families as systems embedded in larger contexts widened researchers' lenses to include child care centers, schools, community programs for youth and social services, and relevant public policies at the state and national levels. Questions grew to incorporate not only parental work but also additional systems, such as those where children spent their time while parents were working.

The first very explicit application of a systems perspective to the work–family interface was Pleck's 1977 exposition of the work–family role system. In this groundbreaking work, he pointed out that while considerable research had focused on the ways in which characteristics of men's occupational roles, such as occupational status, shaped family life and the socialization of children, much less attention had been paid to the ways in which fathers' occupational roles constrained their involvement in family life. Pleck went further to suggest that external forces modulated the flow of influences between men's and women's occupational and family roles, and that these forces differed by sex. For example, both paid work in the economy and unpaid domestic work at home tend to be sex-segregated, with systematically different tasks for men and women. As a result, influences might be expected to flow more easily in one direction than the other for men and women, with stronger flows from family to work for women and stronger flows in the other direction for men. Westman *et al.* (2004) built on Pleck's work by exploring the dynamics of crossover, where influences from one spouse's work or family life flow to influence the other spouse. In one interesting study of Russian Army officers during a period of military downsizing, her team documented financial hardship leading to distress for both partners and undermining by officers' spouses, which produced marital dissatisfaction that fed back to promote greater distress for both partners.

Work–family researchers also debated the nature of energy, first articulating a scarcity view to recognize the role strain and conflict that arise when roles pose excessive demands (Goode, 1960; Kahn *et al.*, 1964), and later suggesting an expansionist view in which roles might create energy for one another (Marks, 1977). Subsequent efforts have documented the types of strain and enrichment that flow between work and home (Greenhaus and Beutell, 1985), and taxonomies of the specific mechanisms through which influences travel, such as spillover, compensation, and resource drain (e.g. Edwards and Rothbard, 2000).

Work–family research today

To examine how systems theory is currently influencing work–family research, we consulted the top 20 nominees in the most recent competition for the Rosabeth Moss Kanter award for Excellence in Work–family Research, each of which was published in 2009. These articles are selected by an international panel of over 30 scholars, who examine every article published in more than 70 journals to identify the "best of the best" in the work–family research domain. Several rounds of standardized quantitative reviews produced the leading candidates that are mentioned below. Although rarely mentioned explicitly, systems approaches are clearly embedded in these studies.

These studies exemplified several major themes in the rapidly-growing literature on work and family. One such theme is the connection between external job demands and children's experiences inside families. A second theme is the nature and management of boundaries between work and family. Finally, a growing number of studies are focusing on linking experiences within families to both proximal (e.g. local communities) and distal (e.g. cultural norms in the society) environmental influences.

Several Kanter studies focus on the connections between external demands in the form of parents' work conditions, and children's experiences. Using a national sample, Dockery, Li and Kendall, 2009 found that adolescents whose parents who worked nonstandard schedules *and* were in single parent families experienced less positive outcomes than adolescents whose parents worked standard schedules or had two parents. A shortcoming of this study, however, was a limited range of variables that prevented consideration of how children spent their time when parents were at work or the specific nature of parents' jobs. In a smaller but more richly descriptive study, DeMarco *et al.* (2009) examined how the working conditions of mothers in rural areas were related to the quality of child care received by their children, finding that most families relied on informal care and that hazardous working conditions or nonstandard shifts reduced the likelihood of using child care centers, where care is typically of higher quality than in informal settings. Both of these studies again illustrate the systems theory concept of links among systems, but the DeMarco *et al.* (2009) study in particular provides a detailed examination of variability *within* a group of interest, another important systems principle. Another study exemplifying this same theme was conducted by Roeters, Van Der Lippe and Kluwer (2009), who examined interdependencies among parents' work demands and their activities with their children. Consistent with Pleck's (1977) suggestion, and Westman *et al.*'s findings (2004), the strength of influences flowing between work and family were asymmetrical. Both the amount and type of mothers' activities with their children varied little as a function of mothers' or fathers' work demands, but fathers' involvement with children fell as a function of both their own and their partners' job demands, especially their involvement in routine daily activities. In addition to revealing connections between parents' work conditions and children's experiences, these findings suggest that mothers and fathers may differ in terms of the nature and management of the boundaries between their work and parenting lives.

Another way in which systems perspectives have been fruitfully used is to map the anatomy of boundaries between work and family. Border theory (Clark, 2000, 2002) and Boundary theory each use systems principles to consider the nature of boundaries; how they are created, reinforced, or weakened; and how they are crossed and managed. For example, Clark's exposition of Border theory (2002: 45) used the core general systems construct of cybernetics or information flow to consider workers' communication with family members about work demands, projects, and experiences, and with work associates about similar elements of family life. Contrary to hypotheses, communication with coworkers was not related to the permeability of the home border, suggesting that permeability may reflect not a smooth and synergistic integration of domains, but rather "defenselessness to invasion" of home by work. In addition, findings showed that balance appeared to be more strongly related to the quality of relationships among people than to the nature of boundaries, suggesting that there may be a type of energy or influence that was not fully captured by the conceptualization of boundary-crossing influences.

Similarly, Boundary Theory focuses on the ways in which people create, maintain, or change boundaries in order to simplify and classify the world around them (Ashforth, Kreiner and Fugate, 2000). In the most recent Kanter Award-winning article, Kreiner, Hollensbe and Sheep (2009) documented 12 specific tactics used by workers to manage boundaries between work and home, including behavioral tactics such as allowing selective permeability; temporal tactics such as finding respite; physical tactics such as managing space and artifacts; and communicative tactics such as setting expectations and confronting violators. These tactics help to illustrate how constructs from the theory, like the degree to which boundaries are thin, permeable, or integrating, are manipulated by workers and families to try to achieve a desired relationship between the domains.

Several Kanter-nominated articles used systems approaches to generate insights about internal family processes in response to external challenges or constraints. Unlike their early predecessors, these modern efforts took into account both marital partners and recognized the importance of gender without making unfounded assumptions about sex differences, such as assuming that only employment would be consequential for women and only unemployment for men. Sherman (2009) examined the impact of economic upheaval in a local community to see what kinds of family responses proved most adaptive. Shows and Gerstel (2009) examined how two groups of men – male physicians and emergency medical technicians – both working in medical professions but at different social classes practiced different types of masculinity. In both studies, fathers with more flexible views of fatherhood fared better, with greater personal happiness and higher-quality relationships at home. In the first study, families fared better when fathers could adjust their identities to their changed circumstances and the reality that they might no longer be able to be the primary breadwinner. In the second, the early prediction that working class men would feel threatened when they could not enact the primary breadwinner role proved incorrect. Instead, "physicians reinforce the gender order while the EMTs redo it" (Shows and Gerstel, 2009: 180). Both of these studies incorporated a focus on external environmental conditions crossing the boundary to influence internal family dynamics, as well as feedback loops within families that prove more or less adaptive in the face of those challenges.

Finally, an example of a study linking distal super- and sub-systems was conducted by Greenstein (2009), who tied the characteristics of nations to internal dynamics within families. Based on studies of individual women within couples, he was able to show that women who lived in countries where the culture was more supportive of gender equity were more likely to recognize and reject inequality in the division of labor in their homes. Women who lived in countries that were less supportive of gender equity were more likely to see unequal divisions of labor at home as fair and less likely to see them as related to justice. Furthermore, the relationship between individual ideology and perceived fairness was entirely explained by national context.

Few if any of the examples just described explicitly acknowledge the roots of their approach in General Systems Theory, but the lineage is clear nonetheless. Tracing the paths through which economic influences from the environment enter and reverberate within families, examining variations in the internal dynamics of families in response to work conditions, mapping the construction and management of boundaries between work and home, and tying together the functioning of very large and very small systems are all examples of areas of study that might never have emerged had it not become clear that systems are open to environmental influences.

Limitations of systems theory

Systems theory has been criticized, both in its general form and more specific applications such those to families and organizations. Some of the scholars who were originally most enthusiastic about General Systems Theory eventually expressed disillusionment, arguing that they had been swayed to the notion of the openness of systems and the idea of the growth of systems by the exuberance of the economy at the time. In the cold light of later economic stagnation and supply shortages, they rejected the notion of perpetual growth as unsustainable (Scott, 1970). They questioned whether it is really true that systems are open. While it may seem that a firm or a family are open and receive new energy from the outside, they may be part of some much larger system which in fact is closed and faces finite limits. As Thayer (1972: 481) commented, "The systems debate ... will turn on the question of whether the planet Earth can be conceptualized as a "closed" or "open" system."

Another concern is the degree to which systems perspectives meet the fundamental criterion of good theory for falsifiability. Theories that cannot be proven false cannot be tested, and some scholars wonder whether systems theory is a "philosophical perspective" rather than a true theory (Whitchurch and Constantine, 1993: 346). Still another concern focuses on the degree to which the theory really has led to explanatory innovations. Early expectations were that old mechanistic approaches where system components were "pulled apart" and studied separately would no longer be needed. But in fact, it has proven difficult to quantify "greater than the sum of its parts," and methods for collecting and in many instances data are still tied tightly to "parts" rather than the whole. At other times, parts are ignored in favor of the "whole." (Thayer, 1972; Yerby, 1995).

Particularly as it has been applied to families, it is not clear whether the fault for some limitations lays in the theory itself, or in the way it has been applied (Whitchurch and Constantine, 1993). For example, one criticism is that the theory has been applied too much to processes through which families maintain homeostasis and too little to the processes through which families change and adjust (Yerby, 1995). Another concern, raised in particular by feminists, is that applications of the theory to family life have imperfectly attended to power differentials and hierarchies within families, and have failed to attend to the power of social expectations and social structures in shaping the opportunities and constraints experienced by family members (Yerby, 1995). Knudson-Martin (1994), for example, criticizes Bowen's conceptualization of family systems for framing tendencies more characteristic of women than men – such as sensitivity to the views of others – as coming at the expense of individuality and appropriate differentiation. In this and other ways, systems perspectives are sometimes seen as disproportionately "privileging" the characteristics of men.

Complaints about lack of attention to gender have also been raised in the organizational realm. In the 1970s, Kanter (1977) complained that persistent structural inequities in the opportunities available to women were persistent and powerful influences on women's progress within organizations. Despite the fact that women were regularly advised or steered toward different activities than men, downstream differences in outcome were persistently attributed to the women themselves (Kanter, 1977). Decades later, Williams (2000: 1) observed that little progress had been made:

> Domesticity remains the entrenched, almost unquestioned, American norm and practice. The ideology of domesticity held that men "naturally" belong in the market because they are competitive and aggressive; women belong in the home because of their "natural" focus on relationships, children, and an ethic of care. In its original context, domesticity's descriptions of men and women served to justify and reproduce its breadwinner/housewife roles by establishing norms that identified successful gender performance with character traits suitable for those roles.

Finally, a critique that applies both to systems theory and to the work–family literature overall is that dimensions of social stratification other than gender, such as ethnicity and class, also have not yet received sufficient attention (Whitchurch and Constantine, 1993; Yerby, 1995). Research on minority or working-class families has made it clear that they can experience unique configurations of constraints and opportunities (Perry-Jenkins and MacDermid Wadsworth, forthcoming). For example, middle class families may be especially at risk for work–family conflict in the form of strain travelling home from work, but working-class families may face the challenge of finding sufficient hours of work to cover basis expenses, an entirely different form of conflict.

Challenges for the future

We believe that addressing three as-yet-unresolved challenges posed by systems theory will deepen our understanding of the relationships between work and family life. The first is to resolve the nature of energy. The second is to fully document all of the key mechanisms of the theory at the work–family interface. And the third is to connect the full range of system levels involved in the work–family interface.

Researchers have yet to fully articulate the nature of energy as it relates to work and family. The scarcity perspective that underlays many studies of the work–family interface is predicated on the notion of finite resources, consistent with closed systems, and tends to emphasize work–family conflict. In contrast, expansionist perspectives focus less on the degree to which resources are finite and more on resource transfer. In both cases, studies of work and family tend – for understandable but nonetheless problematic reasons – to exclude consideration of resource flows emanating from other systems, such as other roles in which workers might participate, or resources made available to workers by a spouse or others. Several different types of resources or energy are implicated in the relationship between work and family. Even time, which could be argued to be the most truly finite work–family resource, is perceived very differently across occasions.

Thompson and Bubolz (1986) proposed that several different types of energy exist within family systems. Among these were psychic or motivational energy that produces initiative or determination, and social-emotional energy directed at relationships with others. Work–family researchers have not yet completed mapping the different types of energy that are expended in the two domains and travel between them, identifying the degree to which, or the circumstances under which, each is more or less finite or identifying the implications for work–family relationships. For example, workers who perform demanding tasks are not similarly depleted every day – what opportunities reduce the likelihood that any day will be depleting, or reduce depletion for all workers? Based on her study of the work–family boundary, Clark (2002: 46) concluded: "If all across-the-border communication is viewed in terms of time and scheduling, both of which imply a fixed pie of 24 hours that must somehow be divided, then individuals are more likely to find conflict between work and family. On the other hand, if more communication is directed at sharing meaning, which is an infinite resource, then individuals may find increased synergy between work and family."

Systems theory contains two important constructs that have not yet been fully explored by work–family researchers, but which offer the opportunity to gain useful insights. The first is the notion of feedback loops. Although longitudinal research is revealing new insights about causal processes every day, feedback mechanisms are not yet fully understood. For example, once a worker has experienced work-to-family conflict, how does the existence of that experience color his or her perceptions of later events at work or at home – how does work–family conflict itself become a lens that filters robustness to other challenges, and with what implications?

A second principle of systems theory that has not been fully documented at the work–family interface is that of equifinality, or the notion that any particular outcome may be reached by multiple paths. This point was driven home to systems theorists by a biological study, when a sea urchin cut in half became two completely whole organisms instead of dying (Drack, 2008). The scientific drive for parsimony leads us to look for single best mechanisms, or those that are *most* useful, but in fact, the whole field of work and family was predicated in part on the notion that there should be multiple ways to pursue optimal functioning in both domains. The existence of equifinality was nicely illustrated in a Kanter-nominated article by Michel and colleagues (2009), who conducted meta-analyses to test the veracity of several theoretical pathways linking workplace experiences to life satisfaction. Although one model ultimately was selected as "best," several of the models tested fit the data well, reinforcing the notion of equifinality.

Another key element of systems theory that has yet to be fully explicated is the nature of boundaries both between and within systems. As technologies have increased the ability of workers to work anytime and anywhere, and the ability of employers to expect it, boundaries have become less structural and more negotiated. For example, prior to the era of cell phones, workers in some jobs experienced a structural boundary between work and family because there was simply no way for the worker to be reached during work hours (e.g. postal workers, many factory workers, outdoor workers). Today, those same workers experience a boundary that must be managed and negotiated. Thus, boundary regulation skills are becoming more consequential for workers' vulnerability to work-to-family conflict.

Another aspect of boundaries that is not yet fully understood is the variability in boundaries within systems. For example, do parents work harder to minimize the permeability of the boundary between their work and the parent–child than the marital subsystem? Do mothers and fathers differ systematically in the ways in which they manage boundaries between work and family, or do personal preferences for more or less permeable boundaries transcend gender or subsystem differences?

The final contribution of systems theory to future research on work and family is the opportunity to test models that more fully incorporate the full range of systems and subsystems implicated in this interface. As has been the case in many areas of science, our ability to test ideas has lagged behind the ideas themselves. Multilevel approaches have been a wonderful innovation, and they are increasingly being used to understand variation within individuals, dyads, or work groups over time, such as the studies by DeMarco *et al.* (2009) and Sherman (2009) mentioned earlier; or within layers of individuals, groups, and cultures, such as the work by Greenstein (2009). The "new frontier" is the interaction between biological substrates and multiple layers of the larger environment. Future research still has many opportunities to "stretch" multilevel models to connect "up" to the largest of all systems, such as cultures or countries, "down" to the most micro-levels of analysis such as electrical activity in the brain, and "across" to encompass a broader array of outcomes, including genetic expression, for example (Gottlieb, 2001).

Given that our methods do not yet permit inclusion of every possible system or subsystem in a single model, a dilemma is how to avoid conducting analyses that systems theorists would criticize for being "mechanistic," or treating systems as simply the sum of their parts. Studies that offer the most hope in this regard are those that pay careful attention to tracing the processes through which influences flow up and down through nested systems.

In conclusion, we began writing this chapter with the impression that systems theory had perhaps served its purpose and doubts that it could spur future theoretical innovations regarding relationships between work and family life. We end having recognized that the theoretical transformation launched by systems theory is still underway, with insights yet to be fully implemented. We look forward to future efforts to do so, with new and creative methodologies that will allow researchers to delve more broadly and more deeply into an understanding of these major domains of human life.

References

Ashforth, B.E., Kreiner, G.E. and Fugate, M. (2000). All in a day's work: Boundaries and micro role transitions. *Academy of Management Review* 25, 472–491.

Ashmos, D.P., Duchon, D. and McDaniel, R.R. (2000). Organizational responses to complexity: The effect on organizational performance. *Journal of Organizational Change Management* 13, 577–594.

Bailyn, L. (1978). Accommodation of work to family. In R. Rapoport and R. Rapoport, with J. Bumstead (eds) *Working couples* (159–174). New York: Harper Colophon.

Bavelas, J. and Segal, L. (1982). Family systems theory: Background and implications. *Journal of Communication* 32, 99–107.

Becvar, D.S. and Becvar, R.J. (1988). *Family therapy: A systemic integration.* Boston: Allyn and Bacon.

Blood, R.O. (1963). The husband-wife relationship. In F.I. Nye and L.W. Hoffman (eds) *The employed mother in America* (282–308). Chicago, IL: Rand McNally.

Bowen, M. (1974). Toward the differentiation of self in one's family of origin: Family Therapy in Clinical Practice. New York: Jason Aronson.

Broderick, C.B., Ed. (1970). Beyond the five conceptual frameworks: A decade of development in family theory. *A Decade of Family Research and Action* (3–24). Minneapolis, MN: National Council on Family Relations.

Bronfenbrenner, U. and Crouter, A.C. (1982). Work and family through time and space. In S.B. Kamerman and C.D. Hayes (eds) *Families that work: Children in a changing world* (39–83). Washington, DC: National Academy Press.

Buckley, W. (1968). Society as a complex adaptive system. In W. Buckley (ed.) *Modern systems research for the behavioral scientist* (490–513). Chicago: Aldine.

Clark, S.C. (2000). Work/family border theory: A new theory of work/family balance. *Human Relations* 53, 747–770.

—— (2002). Communicating across the work/home border. *Community, Work and Family* 5, 23–46.

Conger, R.D., Conger, K.J. and Martin, M.J. (2010) Socioeconomic status, family processes, and individual development. *Journal of Marriage and Family* 72, 685–704.

Cox, M.J. and Paley, B. (1997). Families as systems. *Annual Review of Psychology* 48: 243–267.

De Marco, A., Crouter, A.C., Vernon-Feagans, L. and The Family Life Project Key Investigators. (2009). The relationship of maternal work characteristics to childcare type and quality in rural communities. *Community, Work & Family* 12, 369–387.

Diamond, H. (1967). Implications of the behavioral sciences for management. *Public Personnel Review* 28, 26–30.

Dockery, A., Li, J. and Kendall, G. (2009). Parents' work patterns and adolescent mental health. *Social Science and Medicine* 68, 689–698.

Doherty, W.J. and Baptiste, D.A. (1993). Theories emerging from family therapy. In P.G. Boss, W.J. Doherty, R. LaRossa, W.R. Schumm and S.K. Seinmetz (eds) *Sourcebook of family theories and methods* (505–524). New York: Plenum.

Drack, M. (2008). Ludwig von Bertalanffy's early system approach. *International Society for System Sciences*. Madison, Wisconsin.

Edwards, J.R. and Rothbard, N.P. (2000). Mechanisms linking work and family: Clarifying the relationship between work and family constructs. *Academy of Management Review* 25, 178–199.

Fingerman, K.L. and Bermann, E. (2000). Applications of family systems theory to the study of adulthood. *International Journal of Aging and Human Development* 5, 5–29.

Goode, W.J. (1960). A theory of role strain. *American Sociological Review* 25, 483–496.

Gottlieb, G. (2001). The relevance of developmental-psychobiological metatheory to developmental neuropsychology. *Developmental Neuropsychology* 19, 1–9.

Greenhaus, J.H. and Beutell, N.J. (1985). Sources of conflict between work and family roles. *Academy of Management Review* 10, 76–88.

Greenstein, T.N. (2009). National context, family satisfaction, and fairness in the division of household labor. *Journal of Marriage and Family* 71, 1039–1051.

Jackson, D.D. (1957). The question of family homeostasis. *Psychiaric Quarterly supplement* 31, 79–90.

Kahn, R.L., Wolfe, D.M., Quinn, R.P. and Snoek, J.D. (1964). *Organizational stress: Studies in role conflict and ambiguity*. New York: John Wiley & Sons.

Kanter, R.M. (1977). *Men and women of the corporation*. New York: Basic.

Kast, F.E. and Rosenzweig J.E. (1972). General Systems Theory: Applications for organization and management. *Academy of Management Journal* 15, 447–465.

Katz, D. and Kahn, R.L. (1966). Common characteristics of open systems. In D. Katz and R.L. Kahn *The social psychology of organizations* (14–26). New York: Wiley.

Knudson-Martin, C. (1994). The female voice: Applications to Bowen's Family Systems theory. *Journal of Marital and Family Therapy* 20, 35–46.

Kreiner, G.E., Hollensbe, E.C. and Sheep, M.L. (2009). Balancing borders and bridges: Negotiating the work-home interface via boundary work tactics. *Academy of Management Journal* 52, 704–720.

LaMontagne, A.D. and Keegel, T.G. (2010). What organizational/employer level interventions are effective for preventing and treating occupational stress? Australia: Institute for Safety, Compensation and Recovery Research. Report 1210-022.1-R1. Downloaded from: http://www.iscrr.com.au/

Marks, S.R. (1977). Multiple roles and role strain: Some notes on human energy, time and commitment. *American Sociological Review* 42, 921–936.

Michel, J.S., Mitchelson, J.K., Kotrb, L.M., LeBreton, J.M. and Baltes, B.B. (2009). A comparative test of work-family conflict models and critical examination of work-family linkages. *Journal of Vocational Behavior* 74, 199–218.

Minuchin, P. (1988). Relationships within the family: A systems perspective on development. In R.A. Hinde and J. Stevenson-Hinde (eds) *Relationships within families: Mutual influences* (7–26). Oxford: Clarendon.

Negandhi, A.R. and Reimann, B.C. (1973). Correlates of decentralization: Closed and open systems perspectives. *Academy of Management Journal* 16, 570–582.

Perry-Jenkins, M. and MacDermid Wadsworth, S.M. (forthcoming). The state of theory in work and family research at the turn of the twenty-first century. In M.D. Fine and F.D. Fincham (eds) *Family Theories: A Content-based Approach..* Taylor & Francis/ Routledge: New York.

Pleck, J.H. (1977). The work-family role system. *Social Problems* 24, 417–427.

Roeters, A., Van Der Lippe, T. and Kluwer, E.S. (2009). Parental work demands and the frequency of child-related routine and interactive activities. *Journal of Marriage and Family* 71, 1193–1204.

Scott, W.G. (1961). Organization theory: An overview and an appraisal. *Academy of Management Journal* 4: 7–26.

Scott, W.G. (1970). Organization theory: A reassessment. Academy of Management Journal 17: 242–254.

Segal, D.R. and Segal, M.W. (2004). *America's Military Population. Population Bulletin* 59, 1–40.

Sherman, J. (2009). Bend to avoid breaking: Job loss, gender norms, and family stability in rural America. *Social Problems* 56, 599–620.

Shows, C. and Gerstel, N. (2009). Fathering, class, and gender: A comparison of physicians and emergency medical technicians. *Gender and Society* 23, 161–187.

Skaržauskienė, A. (2010). Managing complexity: Systems thinking as a catalyst of the organization performance. *Measuring Business Excellence* 14, 49–64.

Thayer, F. (1972). General system(s) theory: The promise that could not be kept. *Academy of Management Journal* 15, 481–493.

Thompson, J. and Bubolz, M.M. (1986, November). Energy in the family system: Meaning, usage, and assumptions. Presentation at the Theory Construction and Research Methodology Pre-Conference Workshop, annual meeting of the National Council on Family Relations, Dearborn, MI.

von Bertalanffy, L. (1968). General System Theory. Foundations, Development, Applications. New York: George Braziller.

von Bertalanffy, L. (1972). The history and status of General Systems Theory. *Academy of Management Journal* 15, 407–426.

Westman, M., Vinokur, A.D., Hamilton, V.L. and Roziner, H. (2004). Crossover of marital dissatisfaction during military downsizing among Russian Army officers and their spouses. *Journal of Applied Psychology* 89, 769–779.

Whitchurch, G.G. and Constantine, L.L. (1993). Systems theory. In P.G. Boss, W.J. Doherty, R. LaRossa, W.R. Schumm and S.K. Seinmetz (eds) *Sourcebook of family theories and methods* (325–352). New York: Plenum.

White, S.L. (1978). Family theory according to the Cambridge model. *Journal of Marriage and Family Counseling* 4, 91–110.

Williams, J. (2000). *Unbending gender: Why family and work conflict and what to do about it.* NY: Oxford University Press.

Yerby, J. (1995). Family Systems Theory reconsidered: Integrating social construction theory and dialectical process. *Communication Theory* 5, 339–365.

3 A closer look at key concepts of the work–nonwork interface

Evangelia Demerouti, Inés Martínez Corts and Marina Boz

In this chapter we adopt a critical view on whether there is a solid and consistent theoretical understanding of what the "work–nonwork interface" is. We challenge the theoretical meaning and practical value of different work–nonwork interface concepts by questioning whether current measures of conflict/enrichment are suitable to capture such constructs or whether more innovative measurement strategies are possible. Toward this end we overview existing key concepts and propose several venues for advancing research on the work–nonwork interface. Next, we propose the use of more neutral measures of work–nonwork experience and less reliance on survey items that imply causal attributions in relation to triggers of conflict and enrichment experiences. Further, we suggest within-person approaches (e.g. diary studies) to studying the work–nonwork interface can help uncover the nature of the experience, especially from an episodic perspective. Likewise, greater use of qualitative methods is also proposed to advance phenomenological understanding of the work–nonwork interface. Moreover, it is suggested that focusing solely on the interface between work and family does not capture the main roles that individuals are playing in the nonwork domain. Therefore, we suggest that the expansion of work–family literature to include also the relationship between work or family with the self is relevant. Moreover, we suggest that the detailed measurement/conceptualization of the family situation (at least as specific as the work situation) is also of paramount importance to further advance research into the work–nonwork interface. Finally, we propose that it is necessary to further improve the specification of the role of culture in the configuration of the experience of positive or negative work–nonwork interface relationships. With the suggestions that we offer, we aim to advance the conceptualization and measure of key concepts relevant for this domain.

Please note that we will refer to "work–family" or "family–work" constructs only when we describe studies that measured these specific types of work–nonwork roles while examining conflict or enrichment. As we understand that the scope of individual roles is broader than those of work and family only, we will refer to interrole or work–nonwork when we discuss constructs and processes that go beyond a specific study.

Conflict: construct definition and measurement

The conflict perspective has long been the dominant perspective used to study and understand the interface between work and nonwork roles. Although this perspective has been informed by multiple theoretical approaches such as boundary theory, compensation theory, ecological system theory, social identity theory, and spillover theory, the role strain has been the main theoretical background underpinning the development of the work–nonwork literature (Michel *et al.*, 2009). Role strain theory asserts that involvement in multiple roles will inevitably exhaust individual resources and lead to impaired functioning and strain (Goode, 1960).

Greenhaus and Beutell (1985: 77) defined work–family conflict as "a form of interrole conflict in which the role pressures from the work and family domains are mutually incompatible in some respect." Carlson, Kacmar and Williams (2000) operationalized the three types of work–family conflict originally identified by Greenhaus and Beutell, namely time-based, strain-based, and behavior-based conflict. Time-based conflict is characterized by a lack of time to accomplish the demands of multiple roles and occurs when time devoted to one domain (i.e., work) makes it difficult to successfully engage in the other (i.e., family) domain. Strain-based conflict occurs when the pressure experienced in one domain interferes with participation in the other domain. Behavior-based conflict happens when specific conducts required in one domain interfere with behavioral expectations in the other domain. Several studies have provided empirical evidence of the differential relationships of each of these dimensions of work–family conflict with putative antecedents and outcomes (i.e., Bruck and Allen, 2003; Lapierre *et al.*, 2008), thus demonstrating the relevance of investigating them separately.

Researchers have recognized the bi-directional nature of the work–nonwork conflict experiences by considering work interference with family and family interference with work (i.e., Grzywacz and Marks, 2000). Both forms of conflict are moderately correlated, but their antecedents (Michel *et al.*, 2009) and consequences (Mesmer-Magnus and Viswesvaran, 2005) are different. Work demands are primarily related to work-to-family conflict while family demands are related to family-to-work conflict (Byron, 2005). Work and family demands are associated with work–nonwork conflict because it implies processes that limit individuals' ability to cope with multiple roles (Voydanoff, 2005).

Although they are frequently used interchangeably, work–nonwork conflict and work–nonwork interference can be considered different concepts. Carlson and Grzywacz (2008) pointed out that work–nonwork conflict is related to experiences of mutually incompatible pressures, while work–nonwork interference is related to the behavioral responses to these incompatible experiences. Although differentiating between these two concepts can be theoretical useful, more research is needed to determine the associated empirical implications.

Work–nonwork conflict can also be differentiated from negative spillover. Spillover can be considered a linking mechanism between the work and family domains (Edwards and Rothbard, 2000), so that negative spillover occurs when the stress or strain from one domain surfaces in another domain. Evidence of this linking mechanism are the positive relationships between job stress and work–family interference and between family stress and family–work interference found by Byron (2005).

Consistent with several comprehensive reviews of the work–family literature, researchers have evidenced that experiencing work–family conflict has negative consequences to several individual outcomes, such as physical and mental health (Eby *et al.*, 2005; van Steenbergen and Ellemers, 2009), work and family satisfaction (Ford, Heinen and Langkamer, 2007), burnout and psychological strain (Allen, Herst, Bruck and Sutton, 2000).

Measurement

Work–family conflict is the best-developed topic in the work–nonwork literature in terms of both theoretical framework and measurement. Geurts *et al.* (2005) identified 19 existing instruments for measuring negative work–nonwork interaction. These measures can be classified in first-generation (i.e., Kopelman, Greenhaus and Connolly, 1983) and second-generation instruments (i.e., Geurts *et al.*, 2005; Netemeyer, Boles and McMurrian, 1996; Stephens Franks and Atziena, 1997), depending on whether they are based on previous scales or created directly from theory or specific frameworks. Mesmer-Magnus and Viswesvaran (2005) found that the most widely used measures of both work–family conflict and family–work conflict were Kopelman, Greenhaus and Connolly (1983) and Burley's (1989) scales. However, the most used measure to analyze the dimensions of work–nonwork conflict defined before is the Carlson, Kacmar and Williams (2000) scale. Although all of them try to capture the essence of work–nonwork conflict, results from studies using different measures cannot be comparable in some aspects. For example, most of these measures are validated on US samples, but others, like the SWING measure developed by Geurts *et al.*, was validated in Europe. Scales also use a different response format. For example, some use agree-disagree scales (e.g. Carlson, Kacmar and Williams, 2000; Kopelman, Greenhaus and Connolly, 1983) and others never–always scales (Geurts *et al.*, 2005). When using never–always response scales, the interval respondents are asked to recall must also be defined. For this, it is important to notice that even when people are asked to recall longer periods of time they are more likely to answer in accordance with their current mood because this is the most accessible information for them (Schwarz and Oyserman, 2001). Consistent with measurement threat Bellavia and Frone (2005) argued for the use of more discrete response anchors.

Regarding the validity of measures, most of the current measures have been validated using one source and method (i.e., self-reports from workers) to analyze the structure of the construct and its relationship with other variables. These measures use *family* or *home* as representatives of the nonwork domain, but individuals may engage in very diverse roles and activities not restricted to home or family when participating in their nonwork domain, which yet are not well reflected in existing scales. For instance, individuals may define their roles as primary and secondary, depending on the time spent in the roles, the specialization required to participate in them or the degree of involvement individuals have with each role (Pleck, 1977). It is important to note that, for example, for singles, maybe the family role is not the one in which they invest more time in, are more specialized in, or feel more involved with.

Enrichment: construct definition and measurement

Construct definition

Positive experiences derived from engaging in multiple roles within the work and nonwork domains have been named work–family synergy, work–family enhancement, positive spillover, work–family facilitation, and work–family enrichment. We prefer to use the scope of the enrichment concept (interrole or work–nonwork). In a convergent fashion, all the previous conceptualizations stem from the same positive perspective endorsed in role accumulation theory (Sieber, 1974), the expansion approach (Marks, 1977), the expansionist theory of gender, work, and family (Barnett and Hyde, 2001), and finally the enrichment argument (Rothbard, 2001). According to these theories, participating in several roles allows individuals to build personal, energy, and support resources, which can compensate for the increased demands that might arise in any life domain. The main differences among all previous conceptualizations of positive work and nonwork experiences are the quality of the effect of such experiences in the receiving domain and the level of analysis considered, i.e., whether it is the individual or the system that profits (Wayne *et al.*, 2007; Shein and Chen, 2010). In this sense, Wayne's recent review (2009) provides a comprehensive framework for differentiation between all the current positive work and nonwork interaction concepts in the literature, except for that of work–family synergy.

Work–family enhancement has been conceptualized in terms of acquisition of resources and beneficial experiences associated with occupying multiple roles (Tiedje *et al.*, 1990; Ruderman *et al.*, 2002). However, the concept of work–family enhancement does not specify particular gains or potential impacts derived from the interaction between work and nonwork domains. Positive work–family spillover has been defined as "the transfer of positively valenced affect, skills, behaviors, and values from the originating domain to the receiving domain, thus having beneficial effects on the receiving domain" (Hanson, Hammer and Colton, 2006: 251). In this sense, this concept differentiates from work–family enhancement for it specifies the gains involved (skills, values, etc.) and the bi-directional nature (work to nonwork vs. nonwork to work) of the positive work–nonwork interaction.

The subsequent conceptualizations of positive work and nonwork experiences are based on the notion that both directions of influence are distinct and require specific measures. Work–family facilitation has been defined as "the extent to which an individual's engagement in one life domain (i.e., work/family) provides gains (i.e., developmental, affective, capital, or efficiency) that contribute to enhanced functioning in another life domain (i.e., family/work)" (Wayne, Grzywacz, Carlson and Kacmar, 2007). Thus, a key distinction between positive spillover and facilitation is that work–family facilitation occurs when the individual successfully applies the gains acquired in one domain to the other domain, consequently enhancing its functioning on a system level (i.e., family members, co-workers). Lastly, work–family enrichment has been conceptualized as the extent to which experiences like enhanced affect and functioning in one role can improve the quality of life in the other role (Greenhaus and Powell, 2006: 73). A key distinction between work–family facilitation and work–family enrichment is that work–family facilitation focuses on the system level of analysis, whereas work–family enrichment focuses on the individual level improved functioning (Wayne's recent review (2009)).

Drawing on Greenhaus and Powell's (2006) conceptualization, Carlson, Kacmar, Wayne and Grzywacz (2006) extended the concept of work–family enrichment by differentiating amongst the following four dimensions: development, affect, capital, and efficiency. Development enrichment occurs when one domain stimulates the acquisition of skills, knowledge, behaviors, or ways of viewing things functional for the other domain, while affect enrichment occurs when involvement in one domain results in a positive emotional state or attitude that contributes to improve individuals' performance in the receiving domain. Capital enrichment refers to gains of psychosocial resources such as sense of security or self-fulfillment, while efficiency enrichment occurs when involvement in the family domain results in greater focus and time management skills in the work domain. The multidimensional conceptualization of the work–family enrichment experience has just recently started to receive further empirical support (Boz, Martínez-Corts and Munduate, 2009; Stoddard and Madsen, 2007).

Although the experience of work–family enrichment brings about a series of positive outcomes, it is not equal to the absence of work–family conflict, interference, or negative spillover. A recent review of empirical studies on the relationship between conflict and enrichment revealed a small non-significant negative relationship between both constructs. Such a result draws attention to the need for considering both types of experience in order to advance current knowledge on how individuals feel about the work–nonwork interface (Powell and Greenhaus, 2006a). In fact, previous studies that examined both conflict and enrichment have demonstrated that these experiences are indeed independent and that individuals may combine negative and positive experiences when performing work and family roles concurrently (e.g. Boz, Martínez-Corts and Munduate, 2009). Rather than considering the experience of conflict or enrichment separately, it makes sense to examine the profile of the negative as well as positive experiences initiated from both work and family (Demerouti and Geurts, 2004).

Measurement issues

So far, measurement of the various concepts representing the positive interaction between work and nonwork domains has been inconsistent, mainly due to the use and operationalization of these concepts interchangeably (Carlson *et al.*, 2006).

However, increasing attempts to empirically advance the literature resulted in the recent publication of two globally validated scales, for (1) measuring positive spillover (Hanson, Hammer and Colton, 2006), and (2) enrichment (Carlson *et al.*, 2006). As for work–family facilitation, no known study has developed a scale that captures the recent conceptualization proposed by Wayne *et al.* (2007), focused on the system level of analysis.

Having received more support for its validity than any other similar measure in the literature, the multi-dimensional scale of work–family enrichment (Carlson *et al.*, 2006) has been successfully used in several recent empirical investigations that added to the current knowledge on enrichment's specific dimensions (Bagraim and Mullins, 2009; Boz, Martínez-Corts and Munduate, 2009). Nevertheless, a few authors have highlighted difficulties in differentiating between the proposed dimensions of positive spillover and work–family enrichment (McNall, Nicklin and Masuda, 2009), suggesting that further investigation is still needed to disentangle the different conceptualizations of the positive work and nonwork interaction.

Challenging work–nonwork conceptualization

This short overview of the different concepts of positive and negative work–nonwork interface relationships shows that there is still no agreement about the way in which different roles influence each other, and neither do existing measurement instruments fully and sufficiently tap the total experience of interrole relationships. We suggest five relevant venues for improving conceptualization of conflict and enrichment experiences, and improving understanding of these experiences through the use of alternative measurement strategies and data collection techniques.

Towards a more accurate and neutral conceptualization of conflict/enrichment

Virtually all traditional survey measures of conflict and enrichment are "bidirectional" measures (e.g. Carlson, Kacmar and Williams, 2000; Carlson *et al.*, 2006; Netemeyer, Boles and McMurrian, 1996; van Steenbergen, Ellemers and Mooijaart, 2007; Geurts *et al.*, 2005). By this we mean that the items are phrased such that they capture in a simple and fast way not only that a causal attribution has taken place by the respondent but also that the result is obvious to the focal person. For example, consider the following items of conflict: "My job produces strain that makes it difficult to fulfill family duties" (Netemeyer, Boles and McMurrian, 1996); "I have to miss activities at home due to the amount of time I must spend on work responsibilities" (van Steenbergen, Ellemers and Mooijaart, 2007); "You do not fully enjoy the company of your spouse/family/ friends because you worry about your work" (Geurts *et al.*, 2005). A common assumption for all these items is that whether it is the "strain produced by work" (item 1), "amount of time spent on work" (item 2) or "worrying about work" (item 3), the causes attributions for experiencing conflict are found in work-related aspects. Moreover, the reason why one does not "fulfill family duties", "misses activities at home" or "does not enjoy the company of spouse/family/friends" is most apparently related to (a) long working hours and (b) hard (physically, intellectually and/or emotionally demanding) work.

There are several issues at stake here. First, it is critical to understand whether participants are able to have a clear idea of what are the work and nonwork domains and whether they are able to make the causal attributions to each domain. As Maertz and Boyar (2011) suggested, rather than assuming that individuals can make such attributions, it must be studied *how* they happen to do it, that is, how a given event triggers the conflict or enrichment experience. For instance, it is possible that the domain "blamed" would be where one *is not* when a trigger event occurs (Judge, Ilies and Scott, 2006), where one *is* when a trigger event occurs (Butler *et al.*, 2005), the domain to which the trigger event relates most closely (e.g. Stone, 1987), the domain that is least central and/or most permeable to the individual (e.g. Powell and Greenhaus, 2006b), or simply the domain that precedes and helps determine the choice of coping method (Greenhaus and Beutell, 1985).

Second, as hypothetical causes are included in the items, there is a serious danger that we find trivial or tautological relationships between causes of conflict or enrichment. Because of the particular wording of the items, it seems that explanations about conflict and enrichment are already given in the measurement of the work–family interface itself (Pichler, 2009). Findings that such as working hours or work pressure were the most significant predictors of work–life conflict (Eby *et al.*, 2005) are thus not surprising. In fact, as Pichler (2009) suggests, one does not need sophisticated statistical models to reveal these causes as they are already integrated in the measurement of work–family conflict as the dependent concept. A potential consequence of such scale construction strategy is that only causes named in the items can be recognized as such, while others not included in the items (like job insecurity or insufficient financial rewards) have a hard time to prove themselves as valid predictors.

In order to overcome these shortcomings, we suggest formulating the traditional items in a different way. First, future studies need to specify the forms of conflict and enrichment that can occur and develop items that capture these forms without forcing the participants to attribute specific causal implications implied in items. For instance, if we follow Carlson, Kacmar and Williams's (2000) operationalization, conflict can refer to time-based, strain-based, or behavior-based aspects. Instead of asking "I have to miss family activities due to the amount of time I must spend on work responsibilities" (time-based); "Due to all the pressures at work, sometimes when I come home I am too stressed to do the things I enjoy" (strain-based); "The problem-solving behaviors I use in my job are not effective in resolving problems at home" (behavior-based), we could ask about the frequency of the following experiences: "how often..." "do you have to miss family activities", "do you come home too stressed to do things you enjoy", "do you use ineffective problem-solving behaviors at home". These experiences could then be linked to different aspects of the work situation, e.g. working time requirements, work pressure, emotional and cognitive demands. . In this way, the causes for each specific dimension of work–family conflict may differ per individual and the findings regarding the prediction of this experience do not end up being circular. Moreover, family members can also provide independent and more objective information about the occurrence of interference.

Integration of diary designs and episodic approaches

Similar to the conceptualization of the work–nonwork interface, definitions of many constructs frequently leave open the question as to whether they describe a phenomenological experience (experiential state) or a hypothetical concept (Sonnentag, Dormann and Demerouti, 2010). To reflect an experiential state, ideally all items/statements of the work–nonwork interface should be *simultaneously* present. However, when individuals recall their experiences over an extended time period in the past (e.g. a couple of days), they could possibly score high on all items of, e.g. work–family enrichment, without ever having experienced them simultaneously. Hence, if one aims at investigating the full phenomenological experience of the work–nonwork interface, one has to focus on state work–nonwork interface as a rather momentary and transient experience that fluctuates within individuals within short periods of time (i.e., from day to day or from week to week). Moreover, a within-person design also allows for demonstrating the state nature of the conflict and enrichment experiences in case patterns of significant fluctuations across time are not found. Finally, Williams and Alliger (1994) identified three levels of analysis in measuring the quality of episodic experiences. These are immediate experience (reactions at that specific time), primary consolidation (end of day consolidation), and secondary consolidation (global assessment, focusing across many days). Measuring the immediate experience is superior to measuring primary or secondary consolidation because the last two rely on retrospective recollection and therefore tend to ignore specific aspects and sometimes include even contradictory dimensions of immediate experience (Maertz and Boyar, 2011).

Although the general approach of examining fluctuations of experiences and behaviors within persons (e.g. Bolger *et al.*, 1989) is not new, during the past years researchers in work–nonwork relationships have become increasingly interested in within-person processes (Butler *et al.*, 2005; Ilies *et al.*, 2007; Sanz-Vergel *et al.*, 2010; van Hooff *et al.*, 2006). Important, however, are the conceptual and theoretical prospects associated with such a within-person perspective. First, the within-person approach allows for a closer look at temporal patterns of work-related experiences and behaviors. As several of these diary studies have demonstrated, individuals do not experience that work and family conflict with or enrich each other every day. There are days (or weeks) when they experience more conflict or enrichment than on other days (or weeks). "Averaging" across these situations by assessing a general level of the work–nonwork interface (i.e., by asking individuals to retrospect over the previous months or even the year and providing summary accounts of their psychological states) ignores the dynamic and configurational part of this phenomenon (Sonnentag, Dormann and Demerouti, 2010).

Second this approach enables us to examine – in addition to general predictors such as stable demands and resources of the work and family environments – the more proximal predictors of the experience of conflict or enrichment. Thus, this approach promises answers to the question: When do persons feel interrole conflict or enrichment? Are there specific situational features that have to be present during a specific day in order to experience conflict or enrichment? For example, Butler *et al.* (2005) found that the relationship between daily demands and daily work–family conflict was stronger when daily control was high. Similarly, are there person-specific states that foster the experience of interrole conflict or enrichment during a specific day or week? For example, Sanz-Vergel *et al.* (2011) found that daily detachment from work is especially important for individuals with high home role salience as it increases evening cognitive liveliness and reduces work–home interference.

Third, as an experiential state, the conceptualization of interrole conflict or enrichment is probably more closely tied to real work-, family- or other life-related events and behavioral outcomes than judgments based on aggregations of previous experiences over time. Consequently, investigating state experience of interrole relations may yield much stronger evidence of its antecedents and consequences than investigating its trait-like counterpart. In addition, it may also provide evidence for different causal antecedents and consequences of conflict or enrichment because it might involve fewer human judgmental processes and errors than more trait-like conceptualizations and, by this, might better reflect true causal relations.

Thus, from a conceptual and theoretical point of view, the within-person approach offers a compelling alternative for developing a more accurate understanding of interrole conflict or enrichment. In addition, research following this within-person approach is also practically relevant. In many work settings there are specific times and periods when it is unavoidable that employees will experience conflict or enrichment between work and family, for example, when travelling for a business trip (conflict), or when the employer organizes a party for employees and their families (enrichment). Knowledge about the more proximal situational and person-related predictors of state interrole conflict or enrichment is crucial to create a setting that optimally supports enrichment and minimizes conflict during such critical times and periods.

Notwithstanding these advantages, when applying the within-person approach researchers are asked to respond to several challenges, including specifying whether the measurement instruments of the between-person approach can be used for diary research, developing short but also reliable and valid instruments that can be used for frequent measures, specifying the appropriate number of days/weeks that are necessary to ensure an adequate sampling of individuals' usual work and nonwork experiences. Finally, a further fundamental question is whether the theoretical models of the between-person approach can be applied to the within-person approach (see Sonnentag *et al.*, 2010 and Ohly *et al.*, 2010 for further challenges).

Use of qualitative studies

As recent reviews have demonstrated, the work–nonwork literature has been largely dominated by a positivist perspective, which has developed mainly through cross-sectional quantitative studies with employees from large organizations, in administrative job positions, in traditional white middle-class nuclear families, and mainly in the USA (Casper *et al.*, 2007; Chang, McDonald and Burton, 2010; Özbilgin *et al.*, 2011). Consequently, our current knowledge on conflict and enrichment both in terms of conceptual and measurement development is still limited and does not fully reflect the reality of minorities and individuals from different national contexts. Thus, in order to address these gaps we propose the use of qualitative methods. Qualitative studies are interpretive and contextualized as they originate from individuals' perceptions of their own experiences in their own voices, so they are "essential for uncovering deeper processes in individuals, teams, and organizations, and understanding how those processes unfold over time" (Bluhm *et al.*, 2011, p. 5). In this sense, we argue that qualitative methods are well-suited for broadening knowledge on the types of conflict and enrichment, and consequently on how these experiences unfold as individual processes. Additionally, we suggest that qualitative methods are especially suitable for investigating more specific samples and therefore are valuable for uncovering the conflict and enrichment experiences of minorities.

From a phenomenological standpoint, qualitative methods surface individuals' voices, spontaneous subjective meanings to phenomena that have been long examined through constructs defined by researchers (Maertz and Boyar, 2011). In this sense, qualitative research can contribute to expand theoretical development by presenting alternative views of phenomena and opening new venues for investigating potential antecedents and outcomes. For example, Hill *et al.* (2007) adopted an inductive approach to investigate work–family facilitation, and by doing so, expanded the five role resources previously identified by Greenhaus and Powell (2006) as a function of the direction of influence (work-to-family or family-to-work). Similarly, in the study conducted by Poppleton, Briner and Kiefer (2008), the use of a qualitative diary design allowed them to uncover the salient nature of the negative spillover compared to that of conflict for negative spillover episodes would last longer and were more emotionally intense. Furthermore, we previously highlighted the episodes approach, which suggests the study of conflict and enrichment as processes that unfold in the form of discrete episodes (Maertz and Boyar, 2011). From this perspective and adopting a phenomenological standpoint, we recommend the use of qualitative methods such as critical incident techniques or diary designs to the identification of key events that are encompassed in the conflict and enrichment processes (Poppleton, Briner and Kiefer, 2008; Shein and Chen, 2010).

Finally, qualitative research addresses more specific samples and therefore allows to deepen knowledge on targeted populations that have long been ignored in the work–nonwork interface literature, such as religious and ethnic minorities, and homosexual individuals and families (Özbilgin *et al.*, 2011). Although the use of non-probability sample techniques and the subsequent restrictions in terms of generalizability have been identified as critical drawbacks in qualitative research (Chang, McDonald and Burton, 2010), it still proves to be a valuable method for building theory that can be further validated in diverse and large samples embedded in different contexts (Kreiner, Hollensbe and Sheep, 2009).

The "self" domain

Does conflict and enrichment between work and family really capture what matters for individuals when they cross domain borders? Work on self-construal, self-determination theory and individualism–collectivism seems to suggest that people view themselves both as independent and autonomous individuals and as interdependent on others (e.g. Deci and Ryan, 1985; Markus and Kitayama, 1991). According to De Dreu and Nauta (2009), humans are born with the tendency to be concerned with their self-interests, and their primary motive underlying their behavior is to safeguard and improve their self-interests. Moreover, self-concern influences information processing since it stimulates individuals to consider personal characteristics and qualities (e.g. needs) as well as individual outcomes. Similarly, humans are characterized by their admonitions to be true to themselves (Sheldon *et al.*, 1997). According to this view, to be true to oneself within a role means to be able to behave in ways that feel personally expressive (Waterman, 1990), authentic (Ryan, 1993), or self-determined (Deci and Ryan, 1991). Individuals who constantly behave themselves in line with role-related pressures or demands lack integrity and self-direction (Block, 1961) and might suffer accordingly. In support of this assumption, Sheldon *et al.* (1997) demonstrated that satisfaction in each of several life roles (e.g. student, employee, friend), relative to the individual's own mean satisfaction, was attributable to the degree to which that role supported authenticity and autonomous functioning. Also, the work–family literature has indicated the importance of self in the interrole relationships. Specifically, Barnett, Gareis and Brennen (1999) emphasized with their fit model the need to consider the fit of the work (home) domain with the personal interests of the individual.

Identity theory could be used to justify that work or family aspects may impact personal interests in a positive or negative way. Identity is generally defined as a person's perception of him/herself as he/she relates to his/her environment (Hall, 1972). People can define themselves as members of groups (collective or group identity), as partners in close relationships (relational or role identities), and in terms of personal aspects or traits (personal or individual identities) (Brewer and Gardner, 1996). Identities are often activated by the occurrence of particular situations that activate relevant identities (Bargh, Chen and Burrows, 1996). When a supervisor assigns you a new task, your professional identity is activated, while when you play tennis with your friend, your personal identity is activated. In general, demands or pressures and their personal conception by the individual represent the triggers that activate a specific identity.

Based on identity theory, it can be suggested that focusing solely on work and family represents a rather limited view of interrole management. A more comprehensive view of humans would be to integrate personal identity or individuals' sense of self as another 'domain', operationalized as personal desires, activities, and interests in the work–nonwork interface, or simply me-time. Imagine, for instance, a successful manager of a multinational company who also has a happy marriage with two children. Although such a person might experience high work–nonwork enrichment, he/she might be unable to spend time on personal interests like hobbies or other preferred social activities. The typical work–family conflict measures would not uncover the existence of conflict but the person might feel a conflict between work or family domain and the self.

Kreiner, Hollensbe and Sheep (2006) introduced the term work–self balance, which is conceptualized as an optimal overlap between aspects of individual and organizational identities. Kreiner and colleagues set the basis for viewing individuals as active agents who are able not only to respond to identity pressures, but also to proactively initiate identity dynamics and to co-construct the interface of identity boundaries. For instance, individuals may use a foreign language at work, which they might want to improve further during personal time (e.g. following language courses). Alternatively, one's personal interest (e.g. in languages) might influence the work assignments one is choosing (e.g. international collaboration).

Recently, Demerouti (2012) introduced the concept of work–self and family–self facilitation in a study among working couples to examine the positive spillover and crossover resources and individual energy. While work–self facilitation was found to mediate the relationships between job resources and individual energy, family–self facilitation mediated the relationship between partner's home resources and individual energy. In this sense, work/family–self facilitation was able to uncover why resourceful environments stimulate positive experiences within individuals. It seems therefore promising for future research to focus on such expanded conceptualizations of interrole management and to examine possible predictors and outcomes in order to uncover not only family-friendly but also individual-friendly interventions.

The impact of culture on the configuration of interrole relations

The globalization of work processes, increases in the number of foreign and transnational companies, the internationalization of workers, and the development of operations in emerging countries all necessitate a broader view of work–nonwork experiences. Culture plays a very important role in understanding both direct and indirect impacts of certain demands and resources on the experiences of work–nonwork interrole relations, as well as their consequences on the individuals' health and the organizational outcomes (Aycan, 2008). Casper *et al.*, (2007) reported that 75 per cent of samples in work–nonwork studies were from the United States and were characterized by middle to upper class white men and women in traditional families. Thus, as Casper *et al.* have pointed out, we know little about work–nonwork issues of other national cultural contexts. National culture has been defined as "the collective programming of the mind that distinguishes the members of one group or category of people from another" (Hofstede, 2001: 9); "shared motives, values, beliefs, identities, and interpretations or meanings of significant events that result from common experiences of members of collectives that are transmitted over generations" (House and Javidan, 2004: 15); and "shared beliefs, attitudes, norms, roles, and behaviors" (Triandis, 1995: 4). National culture defines aspects such as social norms, social policies and programs that provide formal and informal support for the people who work and have families (Andreassi and Thompson, 2008), as well as gender equality.

From a methodological perspective, Casper *et al.* (2007) noticed that although most studies conducted in non-US contexts measured work–nonwork constructs with existing scales, the necessary adaptations to these scales were rarely reported. It should be noticed that adapting measures can alter their content and construct validity (Schriesheim *et al.*, 1993) due to differences in the meaning of words across cultures attributed to language and other differences (Powell, Francesco and Ling, 2009). Therefore, we strongly recommend reporting evidence of the adaptation procedure and the associated results when publishing a study conducted with measures that were developed in different cultural backgrounds.

From a theoretical perspective, so far, studies have considered the role of national culture in three main ways according to the typology developed by Powell, Francesco and Ling (2009): 1) Culture-as-nation studies, 2) Culture-as-reference studies, and 3) Culture-as-dimensions studies. Firstly, *culture-as-nation studies* compare individuals' experiences of the work–nonwork interface from different countries, but do not consider culture as a specific construct. These studies have failed to consider culture as a key element in determining the nature and strength of relationships embedded in the interface between individuals' work and nonwork domains (Powell, Francesco and Ling, 2009). For example, considering the different aspects of our life like work, family, friends, health and spirit or self (Byrne, 2005), in some traditional countries such as Spain, family is an important source of support, while in other less traditional cultures, for example the Netherlands, friends can also be a comparable relevant source of support.

Second, the *culture-as-reference studies* consider the role of culture – because they are developed in a non-US country – in the hypotheses and in explaining the results, but do not measure culture or make cross-cultural comparisons. These studies have failed to report valid conclusions about cultural differences because they do not measure cultural characteristics to confirm if and how these characteristics have influenced the results.

Finally, the *culture-as-dimensions studies* specify the influence of specific cultural dimensions like gender egalitarianism (i.e., Lyness and Kropf, 2005), individualism and collectivism (i.e., Yang *et al.*, 2000), level of economic development, and government work–family policies and supports (i.e., Hill *et al.*, 2004), to develop theories about work–nonwork relationships. These studies provide the most accurate explanations of cultural influences on the work–nonwork interface relationships, as they consider the cultural dimensions that can really make a difference for the phenomena studied and they do not associate culture with nations so that they can also identify subcultures within nations.

As we believe that future studies should consider the role of cultural dimensions and the transnational perspective when theorizing work–nonwork interface relationships, we suggest, further research to focus on the identification of discrete dimensions or domains of culture that shape work–nonwork experiences or give rise to differential patterns of effects. However, it is important to avoid the simple conflation of nation and culture to allow for the differentiation of subcultures in one nation. In relation to the transnational perspective we propose: a) To analyze the impact of the new demands that emerge as a consequence of the globalization of work processes on work–nonwork experiences, b) To consider the positive and negative aspects that diversity generates to incorporate new demands and resources which allow a better understanding of work–nonwork experiences, c) To value the consequences on work–nonwork experiences derived from the work of immigrants whose country of origin maintains an unequal power relationship with the country in which they are working, d) To carry out studies that permit the identification of the demands and resources of the people who work in developing countries and the cultural dimensions that influence work–nonwork experiences the most.

Conclusion

The goal of this chapter was to critically reflect on the theoretical meaning and practical value of different work–nonwork interface concepts by referring to the question whether current measures of conflict and enrichment are the most suitable to capture the essence of interrole relationships. Our suggestions concern three main categories. First, we suggest advancing the measurement of conflict and enrichment by using more objective measures as well as to better operationalize the nonwork domain to address the specific conditions that may impact on interrole relationships. Second, we suggest that the use of within-person designs (e.g. diary studies) may allow for examining specific episodes of conflict or enrichment as well as the use of more qualitative research to expand current knowledge on phenomenological issues in the work–nonwork experiences. Thus, more insight into the underlying mechanisms can be gained and questions related to new potential antecedents and consequences, prevalence and frequency of specific dimensions can be answered. Third, we propose the expansion of the traditional measures of conflict and enrichment in order to integrate the self as an active player of interrole relations and the role of culture in forming the configuration of the work–nonwork interface. Integrating these suggestions in future research may enhance our understanding of the phenomena and provide us the means to improve interrole relations such that all stakeholders (i.e., the individual, the family, the employer, the community) can have an advantage.

References

Allen, T.D., Herst, D.E.L., Bruck, C.S. and Sutton, M. (2000). Consequences associated with work-to-family conflict: A review and agenda for further research. *Journal of Occupational Health Psychology* 5, 278–308.

Andreassi, J.K. and Thompson, C.A. (2008). Work-family culture: current research and future directions. In K. Korabik, D.S. Lero and D.L. Whitehead *Handbook of work-family integration* (31–35). USA: Academic Press

Aycan, Z. (2008). Cross-cultural perspectives to work-family conflict. In K. Korabik & D. Lero (Eds.). *Handbook of Work-Family conflict* (pp. 359–371). London: Cambridge University Press.

Bagraim, J. and Mullins, J. (2009). *The effects of social support on work-family enrichment: A preliminary South African study.* Paper presented at the III International Conference of Work and Family of the International Centre for Work and Family at the IESE Business School, Barcelona.

Bargh, J. A., Chen, M. and Burrows, L. (1996). Automaticity of social behavior: Direct effects of trait construct and stereotype activation on action. *Journal of Personality and Social Psychology* 71, 230–244.

Barnett, R.C. and Hyde, J.S. (2001). Women, men, work, and family. *American Psychologist* 56, 781–796.

Barnett, R.C., Gareis, K.C. and Brennan, R.T. (1999). Fit as a mediator of the relationship between work hours and burnout. *Journal of Occupational Health Psychology* 4, 307–317.

Bellavia, G.M. and Frone, M.R. (2005). Work-family conflict. In J. Barling, E.K. Kelloway and M.R. Frone (eds) *Handbook of work stress* (113–147).Thousand Oaks, CA: SAGE Publications.

Block, J. (1961). Ego-identity, role variability, and adjustment. *Journal of Consulting and Clinical Psychology* 25, 392–397.

Bluhm, D.J., Harman, W., Lee, T.W. and Mitchel, T.R. (2011). Qualitative research in Management: A decade of progress. *Journal of Management Studies* 48, 1866–1891.

Bolger, N., DeLongis, A., Kessler, R.C. and Schilling, E.A. 1989. Effects of daily stress on negative mood. *Journal of Personality and Social Psychology* 5, 808–18.

Boz, M.A., Martínez-Corts, I. and Munduate, L. (2009, July). *Gender Differences in the Experience of Family-to-Work Conflict and Enrichment.* Paper presented at the III International Conference of Work and Family of the International Centre for Work and Family at the IESE Business School, Barcelona.

Brewer, M.B. and Gardner, W. (1996). Who is this "we"? Levels of collective identity and self representations. *Journal of Personality and Social Psychology* 71, 83–93.

Bruck, C.S. and Allen, T.D. (2003). The relationship between big five personality traits, negative affectivity, type A behavior, and work-family conflict. *Journal of Vocational Behavior* 63, 457–472.

Burley, K. (1989). *Work-family conflict and marital adjustment in dual career couples: A comparison of three time models.* PhD thesis, Claremont Graduate School, Claremont, CA.

Butler, A.B., Grzywacz, J.G., Bass, B.L., Linney, K.D. (2005). Extending the demands-control model: A daily diary study of job characteristics, work-family conflict and work-family facilitation. *Journal of Occupational & Organizational Psychology* 78, 155–169.

Byrne, U. (2005). Work-life balance: Why are we talking about it at all? *Business Information Review* 22, 53–59

Byron, K. (2005). A meta-analytic review of work-family conflict and its antecedents. *Journal of Vocational Behavior* 67, 169–198.

Carlson, D.S. and Grzywacz, J.G. (2008). Reflections and Future Directions on Measurement in Work Family Research. In: K. Korabik, D. Lero and D. Whitehead (eds) *Handbook of Work-family Integration: Reasearch, Theories and Best Practices.* UK: Elsevier.

Carlson, D.S., Kacmar, K.M. and Williams, L.J. (2000). Construction and initial validation of a multidimensional measure of work-family conflict. *Journal of Vocational Behavior* 56, 249–276.

Carlson, D.S., Kacmar, K.M., Wayne, J.H. and Grzywacz, J.G. (2006). Measuring the positive side of the work-family interface: Development and validation of a work-family enrichment scale. *Journal of Vocational Behavior* 68, 131–164.

Casper, W.J., Eby, L.T., Bordeaux, C., Lockwood, A. and Lambert, D. (2007). A review of research methods in IO/OB work-family research. *Journal of Applied Psychology* 92, 28–43.

Chang, A., McDonald, P. and Burton, P. (2010). Methodological choices in work-life balance research 1987 to 2006: A critical review. *The International Journal of Human Resource Management* 21, 2381–2413.

De Dreu, C.K.W. and Nauta, A. (2009). Self-interest and other-orientation in organizational behavior: Implications for job performance, prosocial behavior, and personal initiative. *Journal of Applied Psychology* 94, 913–926.

Deci, E.L. and Ryan, R.M. (1985). *Intrinsic motivation and self determination in human behavior.* New York: Plenum.

—— (1991). A motivational approach to self: Integration in personality. In R. Dienstbier (ed.) *Nebraska Symposium on Motivation: Developmental perspectives on motivation* (Vol. 38: 227–288). Lincoln: University of Nebraska Press.

Demerouti, E. (2012). The spillover and crossover of resources among partners: the role of work-self and family-self facilitation. *Journal of Occupational Health Psychology* 17(2), 184–195.

Demerouti, E. and Geurts, S.A.E. (2004). Towards a typology of work-home interaction. *Community, Work & Family* 7, 285–309.

Eby, L.T., Casper, W.J., Lockwood, A., Bordeaux, C. and Brinley, A. (2005). Work and family research in IO/OB: Content analysis and review of the literature (1980–2002). *Journal of Vocational Behavior* 66, 124–197.

Edwards, J.R. and Rothbard, N.P. (2000). Mechanisms linking work and family: Clarifying the relationship between work and family constructs. *Academy of Management Review* 25, 178-199

Ford, M.T., Heinen, B.A. and Langkamer, K.L. (2007). Work and family satisfaction and conflict: A meta-analiysis of cross-domain relations. *Journal of Applied Psychology* 92, 57-80.

Geurts, S.A.E., Taris, T.W., Kompier, M.A J., Dikkers, J.S.E., van Hooff, M.L.M. and Kinnunen, U.M. (2005). Work-home interaction from a work psychological perspective: Development and validation of a new questionnaire, the SWING. *Work & Stress* 19, 319–399.

Goode, W.J. (1960). A Theory of Role Strain. *American Sociological Review* 25, 483–496.

Greenhaus, J.H. and Beutell, N.J. (1985). Sources of conflict between work and family roles. *Academy of Management Review* 10, 76–88.

Greenhaus, J.H. and Powell, G.N. (2006). When work and family are allies: A theory of work-family enrichment. *Academy of Management Review* 31, 72–92.

Grzywacz, J.G. and Marks, N.F. (2000). Reconceptualizing the work-family interface: An ecological perspective on the correlates of positive and negative spillover between work and family. *Journal of Occupational Health Psychology* 5, 111–126.

Hall, D.T., (1972). A model of coping with role conflict: The role behavior of college educated women. *Administrative Science Quarterly* 17, 471–486.

Hanson, G.C., Hammer, L.B. and Colton, C.L. (2006). Development and validation of a multidimensional scale of perceived work-family positive spillover. *Journal of Occupational Health Psychology* 11, 249–265.

Hill, E.J., Allen, S., Jacob, J., Bair, A.F., Bikhazi, S.L., van Lageveld, A., Martinengo, G., Parker, T.T. and Walker, E. (2007). Work-family facilitation: Expanding theoretical understanding through qualitative exploration. *Advances in Developing Human Resources* 9, 507–526.

Hill, E.J., Yang, C., Hawkins, A.J. and Ferris, M. (2004). A cross-cultural test of the work-family interface in 48 countries. *Journal of Marriage and Family* 66, 1300–1316.

Hofstede, G. (2001). *Culture's consequences: Comparing values, behaviors, institutions, and organizations across nations.* 2nd ed. Thousand Oaks, CA: Sage.

House, R.J. and Javidan, M. (2004). Overview of GLOBE. In R.J. House, P.J. Hanges, M. Javidan, P.W. Dorfman and V. Gupta (eds) *Culture, leadership, and organizations: The GLOBE study of 62 societies* (9–28). Thousand Oaks, CA: Sage.

Ilies, R., Schwind, K., Wagner, D.T., Johnson, M., DeRue, D.S. and Ilgen, D.R. (2007). When can employees have a family life? The effects of daily workload and affect on work – family conflict and social activities at home. *Journal of Applied Psychology* 92, 1368–1379.

Judge, T.A., Ilies, R. and Scott, B.A. (2006). Work-family conflict and emotions: Effects at work and at home. *Personnel Psychology* 59, 779–814.

Kopelman, R.E., Greenhaus, J.H. and Connolly, T.F. (1983). A model of work, family, and interrole conflict: A construct validation study. *Organizational Behavior and Human Performance* 32, 198–213.

Kreiner, G.E., Hollensbe, E.C. and Sheep, M.L. (2006). Where is the "me" among the "we"? Identity work and the search for optimal balance. *Academy of Management Journal* 49, 1031–1057.

—— (2009). Balancing borders and bridges: Negotiating the work-home interface via boundary work tactics. *Academy of Management Journal* 54, 704–730.

Lapierre, L.M., Spector, P.E., Allen, T.D., Poelmans, S., Cooper, C.L., O'Driscoll, M-P., Sanchez, J.I., Brough, P. and Kinnunen, U. (2008). Family-supportive organization perceptions, multiple dimensions of work-family conflict, and employee satisfaction: A test of model across five samples. *Journal of Vocational Behavior* 73, 92–106.

Lyness, K.S. and Kropf, M.B. (2005). The relationships of national gender equality and organizational support with work-family balance: A study of European managers. *Human Relations* 58, 33–60.

Maertz, C.P. and Boyar, S.L. (2011). Work-family conflict, enrichment and balance under "levels" and "episodes" approaches. *Journal of Management* 37, 68–98.

Marks, S.R. (1977). Multiple roles and role strain: Some notes on human energy, time and commitment. *American Sociological Review* 42, 921–936.

McNall, L.A., Nicklin, J.M. and Masuda, A.D. (2009). A meta-analytic review of the consequences associated with work-family enrichment, *Journal of Business and Psychology* 25, 381–396.

Markus, H.R. and Kitayama, S. (1991). Culture and the self: Implications for cognition, emotion and motivation. *Psychological Review* 98, 224–253.

Mesmer-Magnus, J.R. and Viswesvaran, C., (2005). Convergence between measures of work-to-family and family-to-work conflict: A meta-analytic examination. *Journal of Vocational Behavior* 67, 215–232

Michel, J.S., Mitchelson, J.K., Kotrba, L.M., LeBreton, J.M. and Baltes, B.B. (2009) A comparative test of work-family conflict models and critical examination of work-family linkages. *Journal of Vocational Behavior* 74, 199–218.

Netemeyer, R.G., Boles, J.S. and McMurrian, R. (1996). Development and validation of work-family conflict and family-work conflict scales. *Journal of Applied Psychology* 81, 400–410.

Ohly, S., Sonnentag, S., Niessen, C. and Zapf, D. (2010). Diary studies in organizational research: An introduction and some practical recommendations. *Journal of Personnel Psychology* 9, 79–93.

Özbilgin, M.F., Beauregard, A., Tatli, A. and Bell, M.P. (2011). Work-life, diversity and intersectionality: A critical review. *International Journal of Management Reviews* 13, 177–198.

Pichler, F. (2009) Determinants of work-life balance: Shortcomings in the contemporary measurement of WLB in large-scale surveys. *Social Indicators Research* 92, 449–469.

Pleck, J.H. (1977). The work-family role system. *Social Problems* 24, 417–427.

Poppleton, S., Briner, R.B. and Kiefer, T. (2008). The roes of context and everyday experience in understanding work-non-work relationships: A qualitative diary study of white- and blue- collar workers. *Journal of Occupational Health Psychology* 81, 481–502.

Powell, G.N. and Greenhaus, J.H. (2006a). Is the opposite of positive negative? Untangling the complex relationship between work-family enrichment and conflict. *Career Development International* 11, 650–659.

—— (2006b). Managing incidents of work-family conflict: A decision-making perspective. *Human Relations* 59, 1179–1212.

Powell, G.N., Francesco, A.M. and Ling, Y. (2009). Toward culture-sensitive theories of work-family interface. *Journal of Organizational Behavior* 30, 597–616.

Rothbard, N.P. (2001). Enriching or depleting? The dynamics of engagement in work and family roles. *Administrative Science Quarterly* 46, 655–668.

Ruderman, M.N., Ohlott, P.J., Panzer, K. and King, S.N. (2002). Benefits of multiple roles for managerial women. *Academy of Management Journal* 45, 369–386.

Ryan, R.M. (1993). Agency and organization: Intrinsic motivation, autonomy and the self in psychological development. In J. Jacobs (ed.) *Nebraska Symposium on Motivation: Developmental perspectives on motivation* (Vol. 40: 1–56). Lincoln: University of Nebraska Press.

Sanz-Vergel, A.I., Demerouti, E., Moreno-Jiménez, B. and Mayo, M., (2010). Searching for Work-family Balance and Energy: A Day-Level Study on Recovery Inhibiting and Enhancing Conditions. *Journal of Vocational Behavior* 76, 118–130.

—— (2011). Work-Home Interaction and Psychological Strain: The Moderating Role of Sleep Quality. *Applied Psychology: An International Review* 60, 210–230.

Schriesheim, C.A., Powers, K.J., Scandura, T.A., Gardiner, C.C. and Lankau, M.J. (1993). Improving construct measurement in management research: Comments and a quantitative approach for assessing the theoretical content adequacy of paper-and-pencil survey-type instruments. *Journal of Management* 19, 385–417.

Schwarz, N. and Oyserman, D. (2001). Asking questions about behavior: Cognition, communication, and questionnaire construction. *American Journal of Evaluation*, 22 127–160.

Shein, J. and Chen, C.P. (2010). *Work-family Enrichment. A Research of Positive Transfer.* Rotterdam, NL: Sense Publishers.

Sheldon, K.M., Ryan, R.M., Rawsthorne, L. and Ilardi, B. (1997). Trait self and true self: Cross-role variation in the Big Five traits and its relations with authenticity and subjective well-being. *Journal of Personality and Social Psychology* 73, 1380–1393.

Sieber, S.D. (1974). Toward a theory of role accumulation. *American Sociological Review* 39, 567–578.

Sonnentag, S., Dormann, C. and Demerouti, E. (2010). Not all days are created equal: The concept of state work engagement. In A.B. Bakker and M.P. Leiter (eds) *Work engagement: A handbook of essential theory and research* (25–38). Hove, UK: Psychology press.

Stephens, M.A.P., Franks, M.M. and Atziena, A.A. (1997). Where two roles intersect: Spillover between parent care and employment. *Psychology and Aging* 12, 30–37.

Stoddard, M. and Madsen, S.R. (2007). Toward and understanding of the link between work-family enrichment and individual health. *Journal of Behavioral and Applied Management* 9, 2–15.

Stone, A. (1987). Event content in a daily survey is differentially associated with concurrent mood. *Journal of Personality and Social Psychology* 52, 56–58.

Tiedje, L.B., Wortman, C.B., Downey, G., Emmons, C., Biernat, M. and Lang, E. (1990). Women with multiple roles: Role-compatibility perceptions, satisfaction, and mental health. *Journal of Marriage and Family* 52, 63–72.

Triandis, H.C. (1995). *Individualism and collectivism.* Boulder, CO: Westview.

Van Hooff, M.L.M., Geurtz, S.A.E., Kompier, M.A J. and & Taris, T.W. (2006). Work-home interference: How does it manifest itself from day to day? *Work and Stress* 20, 145–162.

van Steenbergen, E.F. and Ellemers, N. (2009). Is managing the work-family interface worthwhile? Benefits for employee health and performance. *Journal of Organizational Behavior* 30, 617–642.

van Steenbergen, E.F., Ellemers, N. and Mooijaart, A. (2007). How work and family can facilitate each other: Distinct types of work-family facilitation and outcomes for women and men. *Journal of Occupational Health Psychology* 12, 279–300.

Voydanoff, P. (2005). Toward a conceptualization of perceived work-family fit and balance: A demands and resources approach. Journal of Marriage and Family 67, 822–836.

Waterman, A.S. (1990). Personal expressiveness: Philosophical and psychological foundations. *Journal of Mind and Behavior* 11, 47–74.

Wayne, J.H., Grzywacz, J.G., Carlson S. and Kacmar, K.M. (2007). Work-family facilitation: A theoretical explanation and model of primary antecedents and consequences. *Human Resource Management Review* 17, 63–76.

Wayne, J.H. (2009). Reducing conceptual confusion: Clarifying the positive side of work and family. In D.R. Crane and J. Hill (Eds.), Handbook of families and work: Interdisciplinary perspectives (pp. 105–140). Lanham, MD: University Press of America.

Williams, K.J. & Alliger, G.M. (1994). Role stressors, mood spillover, and perceptions of work-family conflicto in employed parents. *Academy of Management Journal* 37, 837–868.

Yang, N., Chen, C.C., Choi, J. and Zou, Y. (2000). Sources of work-family conflict: A Sino-US comparison of the effects of work and family demands. *Academy of Management Journal* 43, 113–123.

4 The spillover–crossover model

Arnold B. Bakker and Evangelia Demerouti

Many studies have shown that job demands (e.g. a high workload and emotionally demanding customers) have a negative impact on employee well-being (Quick and Tetrick, 2003), whereas job resources (e.g. social support, performance feedback, task identity) have a positive impact, particularly on employee engagement (Bakker, 2011; Bakker and Demerouti, 2008). However, less attention has been paid to possible consequences of the work environment for those with whom employees frequently interact – their intimate partners. In this chapter, we introduce a model that integrates two lines of research, the Spillover–crossover model.

To illustrate the gap in the work–family research that this chapter aims to fill, we will provide an example. Imagine an employee who has a poor relationship with her supervisor. This employee will experience some sort of negative strain (like disappointment, negative emotions, mental preoccupation), which will not only be present during working time but most probably also during nonwork time. The employee should be a good actor in order to be able to hide these negative experiences and thus tensed interactions with the partner can arise. Such conflicts and arguments at home can also enhance the experience of negative emotions of the partner as well as disturb his recovery at home. The example illustrates how employees' experiences at work (e.g. a poor relationship with the supervisor) may spill over to the home domain (in the form of negative strain), which then influence their behaviors at home (e.g. conflicts with the partner), and cross over to their partner's well-being (i.e., negative emotions and lack of recovery).

The central aim of this chapter is to integrate two lines of research: spillover and crossover. Spillover researchers have generally neglected the possibility to examine the impact of employees' experiences at work on the well-being of the partner at home. Similarly, crossover researchers have generally ignored the work-related *causes* of the experiences that cross over from the employee to the partner at home. By integrating both literatures, we may get a better insight in the processes that link the work and family domains.

First spillover, then crossover

Researchers have identified two different ways in which demands or strain are carried over (Bolger *et al.*, 1989). *Spillover* is a within-person, across-domains transmission of strain from one area of life to another. Previous research has primarily focused on how reactions experienced in the work domain are transferred to and interfere with the non-work domain for the same individual (Eby *et al.*, 2005). For example, an employee may experience a time-based conflict between work and private life when work overload results in overwork at the expense of leisure time. Similarly, a worker may experience a strain-based work–family conflict when confronted with something unfair during the day at work, about which he or she continues worrying during the evening at home. Indeed, many studies have now found evidence for such spillover effects (for meta-analyses, see Allen *et al.*, 2000; Amstad *et al.*, 2011; Ford, Heinen and Langkamer, 2007).

In contrast, *crossover* involves transmission across individuals, whereby demands and their consequent strain cross over between closely related persons (Westman, 2001). Thus, in crossover, job strain experienced by an individual may lead to strain being experienced by the individual's partner at home. For example, a person who feels chronically fatigued and has become cynical about the meaning of work may transfer such feelings and attitudes to the partner during conversations at home. Indeed, research suggests that frequent exposure to a burned-out partner may increase one's levels of burnout (Demerouti, Bakker and Schaufeli, 2005; Westman, Etzion and Danon, 2001). Whereas spillover is an intra-individual transmission of stressors or strain, crossover is a dyadic, inter-individual transmission of stressors or strain. Crossover research is based upon the propositions of role conflict theory, recognizing the fluid boundaries between work and family life. Crossover of work-related experiences actually implies spillover to happen first. However, the crossover approach adds another level of analysis to previous approaches by adding the inter-individual level, specifically the dyad, as an additional focus of study (Westman, 2001).

Spillover

Conflict theory claims that the work and family environment are incompatible because they have distinct norms and requirements (Zedeck and Mosier, 1990). Specifically, work–family conflict is defined as "a form of interrole conflict in which the role pressures from the work and family domains are mutually incompatible in some respect. That is, participation in the work (family) role is made more difficult by virtue of participation in the family (work) role." (Greenhaus and Beutell, 1985, 77). Although the latter authors explicitly stated that work–family conflict is inherently non-directional (84), most scholars distinguish between two types of interrole conflict: (1) *work–family conflict* (WFC), referring to a situation in which role pressures at work hamper functioning at home; and (2) *family–work conflict* (FWC), referring to role pressures at home interfering with functioning at work. Since the Spillover–crossover model mainly focuses on the impact of work on family, we will restrict ourselves here to discussing research on WFC.

In addition to dispositional variables such as Type A and negative affectivity (Carlson, 1999), work characteristics have been consistently related to WFC (see Byron, 2005; Frone, 2003). Job demands found to be predictors of WFC are work pressure (e.g. Dollard, H. Winefield and A. Winefield, 2001; Grzywacz and Marks, 2000; Wallace, 1997), an unfavorable working time schedule (Demerouti, E., Geurts, S.A.E. and Kompier, M.A.J. 2004; Geurts, Rutte and Peeters, 1999), work-role overload (Butler *et al.*, 2005; Demerouti, Bakker and Butlers, 2004), and emotional demands, such as having frequent interactions with demanding patients or customers (Bakker and Geurts, 2004).

The role scarcity hypothesis (Edwards and Rothbard, 2000) has been used to explain negative spillover. Accordingly, people possess limited and fixed amounts of resources (e.g. time and energy). Managing multiple roles (e.g. of employee, spouse, and parent) is problematic as they draw on the same, scarce resources. High job demands require employees to devote more resources (e.g. time, emotions) to work, leaving them with fewer resources to devote to their family (Frone, Yardley and Markel, 1997). Previous research has demonstrated that especially time- and strain- based conflict (i.e., fulfilment of demands in one domain is difficult owing to the time devoted to and strain produced in the other domain, respectively) are associated with various negative work-, family-, and stress- related outcome variables (see, Allen *et al.*, 2000; Amstad *et al.*, 2011). Thus, employees who are confronted with work overload and high emotional demands have more problems in combining their work and family. In other words, job demands can spill over to the home domain and interfere with family life.

Fortunately, interrole management may not only result in the experience of conflict but also in the experience of positive spillover between life domains. Generally, positive spillover or work–family enrichment has been defined as the extent to which experiences in one role improve the quality of life in another role (Greenhaus and Powell, 2006). Work–family enrichment is generally positively related to job resources, like autonomy and social support (Demerouti, Geurts and Kompier, 2004), and positively related to outcomes like job performance (Demerouti, Bakker and Voydanoff, 2010).

According to Marks' (1977) *expansion hypothesis*, participation in multiple roles may provide a greater number of opportunities and resources to the individual, which can be used to promote growth and better functioning in both life domains. This is consistent with the notion that identification with and engagement in a role can be enriching to other roles and identities (Rothbard, 2001). According to Greenhaus and Powell (2006), interrole enrichment can occur in one of two pathways. The first is an instrumental pathway and occurs when resources such as skills and opportunities for self-growth gained from one role directly improve functioning in another role. The second pathway is affective and occurs when a resource in one domain produces positive affect such as positive emotions and energy within that domain, which, in turn, improves individual functioning in another domain (Wayne *et al.*, 2007).

Crossover

Once experiences built up at work have spilled over to the family domain, they may influence the partner. Crossover is the term used to describe the interpersonal process that occurs when job stress or psychological strain experienced by one person affects the level of strain of another person in the same social environment (Bolger *et al.*, 1989). Some researchers have focused on the crossover of job stressors from the individual to the spouse, others have examined the process whereby job stressors of the individual affect the *strain* of the spouse, and yet others have studied how psychological strain of one partner affects the strain of the other (see Westman, 2001). Note that most previous crossover studies have focused on the transference of strain – that is why we will use strain crossover as a starting point. However, we will see later in this chapter that positive experiences can also cross over between partners.

Westman (2006) suggested several possible mechanisms to explain the crossover process. First, direct crossover can take place between two spouses/ partners through empathic processes. That is, since spouses/partners spend considerable time together they become aware of and are affected by each others' affective states. Second, spouses/partners may share some common stressors (e.g. financial pressures, life events) that can lead to increased levels of common strains (e.g. negative affect). Third, crossover may be an indirect process in which the transmission of strain is mediated by the communication and interaction of spouses/partners (e.g. coping strategies, social undermining, and lack of social support).

Most studies have investigated and found evidence for the crossover of psychological strains, such as anxiety (Westman, Etzion and Horovitz, 2004), burnout (e.g. Bakker and Schaufeli, 2000), distress (Barnett *et al.*, 1995), depression (Howe, Levy and Caplan, 2004), and marital dissatisfaction (Westman *et al.*, 2004). A few studies investigated crossover of health complaints and perceived health between partners (Bakker, 2009; Gorgievski-Duijvesteijn, Giesen and Bakker, 2000; Westman *et al.*, 2008). There are, however, also studies that have detected direct crossover of *positive* experiences, like work engagement (Bakker, Demerouti and Schaufeli, 2005; Bakker and Demerouti, 2009), life satisfaction (Demerouti, Bakker and Schaufeli, 2005), and vigor (Westman, Etzion and Chen, 2009). Some studies focused on unidirectional crossover from husbands to wives, whereas others looked for bi-directional crossover, from husbands to wives and from wives to husbands (Westman and Bakker, 2008).

Hatfield, Cacioppo and Rapson (1994) have argued that there are several circumstances under which people should be especially likely to catch others' emotions. Emotional contagion or direct crossover is particularly likely, for example, if individuals pay close attention to others, and if they construe themselves as interrelated to others rather than as independent and unique. Furthermore, a number of studies have shown that there exist stable individual differences in people's susceptibility to emotional stimuli (Doherty *et al.*, 1995; Stiff *et al.*, 1988), and that these individual differences are good predictors of the extent to which people catch positive and negative emotions from others.

Westman and Vinokur (1998) have argued that empathy can be a moderator of the crossover process. Literally, the root meaning of the word empathy is "feeling into". Starcevic and Piontek (1997) define empathy as interpersonal communication that is predominantly emotional in nature. It involves the ability to be affected by the other's affective state, as well as to be able to read in oneself what that affect has been. Similarly, Lazarus (1991) defined empathy as "sharing another's feelings by placing oneself psychologically in that person's circumstances" (287). The core relational theme for empathy would have to involve a sharing of another person's emotional state, distressed or otherwise. Accordingly, an individual's strain produces an empathic reaction in the partner that increases the partner's strain, by way of what may be called *empathic identification*. Social learning theorists (e.g. Bandura, 2001; Stotland, 1969) support this view, and have explained the transmission of emotions as a conscious processing of information. They suggested that individuals imagine how they would feel in the position of another – empathic identification – and thus come to experience and share the other's feelings.

The spillover–crossover model

The Spillover–crossover model (SCM) combines the spillover and crossover literatures, and proposes that work-related experiences first spill over to the home domain, and then cross over to the partner through social interaction. As can be seen in Figure 4.1, we assume that the spillover process can start in both partners' work environment. Using the Job Demands–Resources model (Bakker and Demerouti, 2008; Demerouti and Bakker, 2011; Demerouti *et al.*, 2001), we first propose that although every job may be characterized by different working conditions, these conditions can still be categorized as either job demands or job resources. Job demands are the aspects of work that cost effort, like workload and mental demands. Confrontation with job demands is therefore straining; repeated confrontation may even lead to a state of exhaustion or burnout (Demerouti *et al.*, 2001). In contrast, job resources are those aspects of work that help to deal with the job demands, and have motivational potential. Job resources such as social support from colleagues, performance feedback, and task significance have been shown to satisfy basic human needs (van den Broeck *et al.*, 2008), and have positive effects on work engagement and job performance (Demerouti and Bakker, 2011).

The SCM typically departs from the work domain. Job demands are hypothesized to evoke strain which can spill over into the home domain, and lead to work–family conflict. For instance, employees who are confronted with high emotional demands may feel fatigued after a day at work, and may continue to ruminate about work when at home. According to the SCM, this state of work–family conflict will have a negative impact on the interaction with the partner at home and indirectly on the partner's well-being (see Figure 4.1). In contrast, job resources are hypothesized to foster engagement, which leads to work–family enrichment when these resources are high. Employees who enjoy their work because they have, for instance, ample opportunities for professional development and interesting interactions with others (clients, colleagues), may feel self-efficacious after a day at work, and may go home in a positive mood. According to the SCM, this state of work–family enrichment will have a positive impact on partner's well-being through positive interactions.

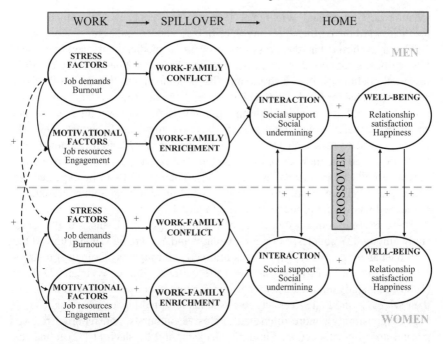

Figure 4.1 The spillover–crossover model

The SCM suggests that the impact on partner's well-being occurs either through direct crossover of negative and positive experiences or through indirect crossover (see Figure 4.1). The indirect crossover uncovers the mechanism through which the inter-individual transmission occurs. Evidence for indirect crossover, i.e., a transmission mediated by interpersonal exchange, can explain why crossover among partners happens. Up to now, particularly social undermining and social support have been examined as behavioral transmitters of crossover in the SCM. These behavioral transmitters influence one's partner well-being directly or through impacting the family level demands and resources. For instance, Bakker, Demerouti and Dollard (2008) found that work–family conflict increased the partner's home demands because the employee undermined the partner. We will now zoom in on the specific process through which experiences built up at work cross over to the partner.

Exchange between partners

Westman (2001) has used the stress and coping literature to argue that crossover may be the result of an indirect process of social undermining. Social undermining consists of behaviors directed toward the target person that express negative affect, convey negative evaluation or criticism, or hinder the attainment of instrumental goals (Vinokur and Van Ryn, 1993). The construct of social undermining comes close to what has been called "hostile marital interactions"

(Matthews, Conger and Wickrama, 1996) – the frequency with which one is hostile toward the partner (gets angry, criticizes, shouts, and argues).

The hypothesis that the crossover process is mediated by negative social interactions is supported by empirical findings from two lines of research. First, research documents that distress and its accompanying frustration leads to aggressive behavior (Berkowitz, 1989). Second, the literature on family processes shows that stressed couples exhibit high levels of negative interactions and conflicts (Schaefer, Coyne and Lazarus, 1981; Westman and Vinokur, 1998). The increased distress (associated with the experience of WFC) and its accompanying frustration lead an individual to initiate or exacerbate a negative interaction sequence with the partner (Westman, 2005). Therefore, it can be expected that strain-based WFC is positively related to social undermining and, consequently, to reduced well-being of the partner (see Figure 4.1).

There is some indirect evidence for the latter process. Using a multi-source study among 337 couples, Matthews, Conger and Wickrama (1996) showed that both husbands' and wives' WFC was indirectly (through psychological distress) related to hostile interactions between the partners. Burke, Weir and DuWors (1980), in a study among 85 senior administrators in correctional institutions and their wives, found that wives whose husbands reported higher job demands (e.g. high responsibility), more often had explosive outbursts, and reported reduced marital and life satisfaction. Similarly, Jackson and Maslach (1982) found that police officers with high levels of stress were more likely to display anger and be less involved in family life, whilst their wives showed a corresponding increase in distress. In short, WFC seems to foster social undermining behaviors, and reduces involvement in family life. This means that the partner is confronted with increased emotional demands and may experience lower levels of relationship satisfaction.

Until now, we have particularly focused on negative spillover and crossover, but we will see later in this chapter that positive spillover and crossover is probably equally likely. As can be seen in Figure 4.1, the SCM proposes that stress factors like job demands and burnout spill over to the home domain, and have an indirect negative impact on the social support offered to the partner. This process holds for both partners, and the social support offered by men is positively related to the social support offered by women – in other words, support is reciprocated. This means that, in the long run, work–family conflict also reduces the social support one *receives* – work–family conflict undermines the quality of the relationship. This proposition is based on equity theory (Adams, 1965). Accordingly, people evaluate their relationships with others in terms of investments and outcomes. A central proposition is that people have a deeply rooted tendency to pursue reciprocity in interpersonal relationships and that they feel distressed if they perceive these relationships as inequitable (F. Walster, G. Walster and Berscheid, 1978). Buunk and Schaufeli (1999) have argued that reciprocity is a universal and evolutionary rooted psychological principle that increased the likelihood of our ancestors' survival in the evolutionary past.

We further argue that social support offered to the partner has a positive effect on own and the partner's well-being. Lyubomirsky, Tkach and Sheldon (2004) showed that simply asking people to commit random acts of kindness can significantly increase happiness levels for several weeks. In their study, Lyubomirsky and colleagues randomly assigned students to a no-treatment control group or to an experimental group, in which students were asked to commit five random acts of kindness a week for six weeks. As predicted, students who engaged in random acts of kindness were significantly happier than controls. Consistent with these findings, experimental work suggests a causal relationship between giving (support) and happiness. For example, when Field *et al.* (1998) asked a volunteer group of retired senior citizens to give infants a massage three times a week for three weeks, these seniors experienced less anxiety and depression. The seniors also showed improved health and a reduction in stress-related hormones.

Many studies have shown how received social support has a positive impact on well-being. One reason for this is that social support is a key resource, in that it is functional in achieving one's goals. Thus, instrumental support from one's partner can help to get something done in time, and may therefore alleviate the impact of time pressure on strain (van der Doef and Maes, 1999). In addition, the stress-buffering hypothesis states that social support protects individuals from the pathological consequences of stressful experiences (Cohen and Wills, 1985).

Finally, the SCM proposes that well-being crosses over directly between partners. We have already discussed studies showing a positive relationship between the strain of partners (see, for an overview Bakker, Westman and van Emmerik, 2009). Since crossover is particularly likely if individuals pay close attention to others, and if they construe themselves as interrelated to others rather than as independent and unique, direct crossover between intimate partners is highly likely. Indeed, since partners are likely to discuss their feelings and be attuned to each other, it is rather likely that their states cross over. Demerouti, Bakker and Schaufeli (2005) found that women's job demands were positively related to their own exhaustion via work–family conflict; women's exhaustion consequently predicted their partner's level of exhaustion. Additionally, they found that men's job demands were negatively related to their own life satisfaction via work–family conflict; men's life satisfaction consequently predicted their partner's level of life satisfaction. This study also indicated that partners influence each other with their happiness.

Evidence for the SCM

A series of studies has provided evidence for the SCM – although it should be noted that most studies focused exclusively on negative spillover and crossover. In a study among Dutch couples of dual-earner parents, Bakker, Demerouti and Dollard (2008) hypothesized and found that for both genders job demands fostered their own work–family conflict (WFC), which, in turn, contributed to their partner's home demands and exhaustion. In addition, as predicted, social undermining mediated the relationship between individuals' WFC and their partner's home demands. Thus, as employees' work overload and emotional demands increased, their work started to interfere with family life, resulting in negative behaviors toward the partner. This behavior increased the partner's home demands (overload of household tasks and emotional demands at home), resulting in high levels of partner exhaustion.

This study was replicated and expanded using the data of 99 couples of dual-earner parents in Japan. Shimazu, Bakker and Demerouti (2009) showed that men's job demands (i.e., overload and emotional demands) were positively related to own and partner's reports of WFC. Consequently, men's WFC was negatively related to the quality of the social interaction (i.e., decreased social support from and increased social undermining by men), which, in turn, led to women's ill-health (i.e., depressive symptoms and physical complaints). We found similar findings for the model starting with women's job demands; gender did not affect the strength of the relationships in the model. Taken together, these two studies clearly indicate that high job demands initiate a process of work–family conflict and poor relationship quality, which may eventually affect the intimate partner's well-being in an unfavorable way.

Using workaholism as the trigger in the SCM, Bakker, Demerouti and Burke (2009) hypothesized that workaholism would result in reduced support provided to the partner, through work–family conflict. In addition, it was predicted that individuals who receive considerable support from their partners are more satisfied with their relationship, and that relationship satisfaction would cross over between the partners. The results of structural equation modeling analyses using the matched responses of both partners supported these hypotheses. Again, gender did not affect the strength of the relationships in the proposed model. These findings indicate that employees who feel compelled to work excessively hard are more likely to bring their work home, which results in lower efforts to help the partner. This reduced social support has a negative impact on partner's relationship satisfaction.

Shimazu *et al.* (2011) tried to replicate parts of these findings using a large sample of Japanese dual-earner couples. The results of logistic regression analyses showed that "workaholics" (i.e., employees scoring high on both working excessively and working compulsively) were more likely to experience work-to-family conflict (i.e., WFC) and psychological distress compared to "relaxed workers" (i.e., low on both working excessively and working compulsively) for both genders. In addition, husbands of workaholic women were more likely to experience family-to-work conflict (i.e., FWC) whereas wives of workaholic men were not.

Finally, Bakker, Petrou and Tsaousis (in press) conducted a study among 267 Greek teachers and their partners to test the SCM and to integrate equity theory in the model by formulating hypotheses about exchange in interpersonal relationships. Structural equation modeling analyses supported the spillover hypothesis that teachers who lose their work engagement as a result of an inequitable relationship with their students invest less in the relationship with their partner. In addition, the results supported the crossover hypothesis that teachers' relationship investments, in turn, show a negative relationship with inequity in the intimate relationship as perceived by the partner; and inequity in the intimate relationship contributed to partner depression. These findings shed more light on the exchange between partners, and offer additional support for the central claim of the SCM that experiences built up at work can spill over to the home domain, and consequently have an impact on one's partner.

Positive spillover and crossover

Although the focus in most work–family studies has primarily been on negative spillover, research has clearly indicated that positive spillover is also possible (Greenhaus and Powell, 2006; Wayne *et al.*, 2007). Whereas work–family conflict refers to incompatibility between work and family roles, work–family enrichment is defined as "the extent to which participation at work (or home) is made easier by virtue of the experiences, skills, and opportunities gained or developed at home (or work)" (Frone, 2003: 145). This means that participation in the family role is facilitated by what has happened at work. There are only two tests of the combined, positive spillover and crossover process. Bakker, Shimazu, Demerouti, Shimada and Kawakami (2012) conducted a longitudinal study among Japanese couples to investigate how two types of heavy work investment, workaholism and work engagement, influence one's partner's family satisfaction through a process of negative or positive spillover. The results of structural equation modeling showed that whereas workaholism has a negative impact on family satisfaction through work family conflict; work engagement has a positive influence on family satisfaction through work–family enrichment. Moreover, the findings indicated that partners influenced each other's life satisfaction, also over a longer time period. Life satisfaction was thus the result of own workaholism and engagement, but also the workaholism and engagement of the partner.

Demerouti (in press) tested the positive spillover–crossover model in a study among Dutch dual-earner couples. Job resources of one partner were predicted to spill over to their individual energy, i.e., reduced fatigue and increased motivation. Consequently, individual energy was predicted to influence the partner's family resources (i.e., autonomy, social support and developmental possibilities at home), which eventually were hypothesized to influence the partner's level of individual energy. Rather than focusing on work–family enrichment as a measure of positive spillover, this study examined work-self enrichment and family-self enrichment as the mechanisms through which the favorable effects of job and home resources, respectively, impact on individual energy. Work-self and family-self enrichment represent the degree to which individual's engagement in one life domain (i.e., work/family) contributes to enhanced functioning during time spent on personal interests. Results confirmed that job resources influence one's own individual energy through work-self enrichment. Consequently, the levels of individual energy positively influence one's partner's perception of home resources, which eventually influence partner's individual energy through experienced family-self enrichment. Work-self and family-self enrichment were useful in explaining why job and family resources may enhance the levels of energy that individuals invest in different life domains.

A few other studies have detected crossover of positive experiences between intimate partners, without necessarily examining the spillover process that precedes it (Bakker, Demerouti and Schaufeli, 2005; Demerouti, Bakker and Schaufeli, 2005; Prince, Manolis and Minetor, 2007). For example, Bakker, Demerouti and Schaufeli (2005) tested the hypothesis that burnout and work engagement may cross over from husbands to wives and vice versa among couples working in a variety of occupations. Their findings provided evidence for the crossover of burnout (exhaustion and cynicism) and work engagement (vigor and dedication) among partners. The bi-directional crossover relationships were significant and about equally strong for both partners, after controlling for important characteristics of the work and home environment.

In a similar vein, Bakker and Demerouti (2008) investigated the crossover of engagement from working wives to their husbands. The results of moderated SCM analyses showed that work engagement crossed over from wives to husbands. Furthermore, they found that empathy (particularly perspective taking) moderated the crossover effect. Men who were perspective takers were more strongly influenced by their partners' work engagement than their counterparts who were not perspective takers. Finally, in an international context, Westman, Etzion and Chen (2009) studied 275 business travelers and their working spouses and found crossover of vigor from business travelers to their working spouses.

Practical implications

The negative consequences of an imbalance between work and family mainly concerned outcomes within the individual (Allen *et al.*, 2000; Frone, 2003; Kossek and Ozeki, 1998). The SCM suggests that work–family conflict is only one part of the multiple challenges that employed parents experience in balancing work and family demands. The conflict of work with family is also linked to the quality of social interactions at home, and these linkages are alike for both men and women. To date, strategies implemented by employers have sought to mitigate the impact of family on work behavior with an eye toward improving employee productivity while on the job, and have paid less attention to how working conditions can be improved in order to mitigate the negative influence and promote a positive influence of work on family. Most employers use family responsive policies such as maternity and parental leaves, child care programs, alternative work schedules, and employee assistance and relocation programs (Zedeck and Mosier, 1990) which are appropriate for dealing with family demands and consequently for reducing the negative influence of family life on work. Undoubtedly, such practices can help employees balance both life domains. However, the SCM suggests that organizations should simultaneously pay attention to work related characteristics – i.e., the job demands and job resources – that influence work to family interference and enrichment.

Future research

As we have seen in the reviewed studies, work–family/self conflict and, less often, enrichment play the role of mediator/transmitter in spillover processes. Montgomery *et al.* (2006) have argued that the definition of work–family conflict implies mediation, as there will be no conflict when there are no demands at work. Similarly, there will not be any enrichment from work to home when there are no resources to facilitate functioning in the other domain. In essence, variables such as work–life conflict or enrichment cannot exist without reference to the relevant life domains. The challenge for future research is to examine whether there are alternative ways to capture spillover (or interrole conflict and enrichment) in a more direct, objective way.

Essential for the crossover effect is that the individual's energy is influencing the energy of other system members (cf. Wayne *et al.*, 2007). We have suggested social undermining and social support as the ways or behavioral transmitters through which crossover in the family occurs. However, we are aware that other possible ways might exist that can be relevant for specific cultural and family contexts. Future research is therefore necessary to expand our view, and shed more light on the possible transmitters of crossover.

It is clear from the literature review that the majority of the studies has focused on negative spillover–crossover processes. Although there are some studies on positive spillover–crossover there is definitely a need for more research on such positive processes. Such research can uncover whether other transmitters than provided social support might be involved in the positive processes. Moreover, future studies can examine whether there are differences between positive and negative spillover–crossover processes. One difference between the crossover of positive vs. negative experiences from one partner to the other is that in the study of Demerouti (2012) individual energy was directly and positively related to partner's home resources, while negative experiences crossed over to the partner through increased social undermining (Bakker, Demerouti and Dollard, 2008; Shimazu, Bakker and Demerouti, 2009), and diminished social support (Bakker, Westman and van Emmerick, 2009; Shimazu *et al.*, 2009).

Finally, currently the SCM has been applied to examine the processes through which work is influencing family life. However, it is conceivable that the model can also be applied to examine the impact of family life on work. To this end and similar to the study of Demerouti, Bakker and Voydanoff (2010), family demands and resources would be supposed to spill over to the work domain through family-work conflict and enrichment which consequently would impact colleague's strain. Bakker and colleagues (Bakker and Xanthopoulou, 2009; Bakker, Demerouti and Schaufeli, 2005) have found evidence for the crossover of positive and negative strain among colleagues.

Conclusion

Whereas previous research has shown that job demands and job resources may influence employee well-being through work–family conflict and enrichment, the SCM goes one step further and shows how experiences built up at work can influence the partner at home. The SCM integrates two lines of research and shows how negative, but also positive experiences at work can have an impact on one's partner's well-being. Whereas job demands and burnout seem to undermine social support provided to the partner, job resources and engagement seem to facilitate social support and have a positive impact on partner's well-being. We hope that this chapter inspires researchers to test the model in other countries than The Netherlands, Japan, and Greece.

References

Adams, J.S. (1965). Inequity in social exchange. *Advances in Experimental Social Psychology* 62, 335–343.

Allen, T.D., Herst, D.E.L., Bruck, C.S. and Sutton, M. (2000). Consequences associated with work-to-family conflict: A review and agenda for future research. *Journal of Occupational Health Psychology* 5, 278–308.

Amstad, F.T., Meier, L.L., Fasel, U., Elfering, A. and Semmer, N.K. (2011). A meta-analysis of work-family conflict and various outcomes with a special emphasis on cross-domain versus matching-domain relations. *Journal of Occupational Health Psychology* 16, 151–169.

Bakker, A.B. (2009). The crossover of burnout and its relation to partner health. *Stress & Health* 25, 343–353.

—— (2011). An evidence-based model of work engagement. *Current Directions in Psychological Science* 20, 265–269.

Bakker, A.B. and Demerouti, E. (2008). Towards a model of work engagement. *Career Development International* 13, 209–223.

—— (2009). The crossover of work engagement between working couples: A closer look at the role of empathy. *Journal of Managerial Psychology* 24, 220–236.

Bakker, A.B. and Geurts, S. (2004). Toward a dual-process model of work-home interference. *Work & Occupations* 31, 345–366.

Bakker, A.B. and Schaufeli, W.B. (2000). Burnout contagion processes among teachers. *Journal of Applied Social Psychology* 30, 2289–2308.

Bakker, A.B. and Xanthopoulou, D. (2009). The crossover of daily work engagement: Test of an actor-partner interdependence model. *Journal of Applied Psychology* 94, 1562–1571.

Bakker, A.B., Demerouti, E. and Burke, R. (2009). Workaholism and relationship quality: A spillover-crossover perspective. *Journal of Occupational Health Psychology* 14, 23–33.

Bakker, A.B., Demerouti, E. and Dollard, M. (2008). How job demands influence partners' experience of exhaustion: Integrating work-family conflict and crossover theory. *Journal of Applied Psychology* 93, 901–911.

Bakker, A.B., Demerouti, E. and Schaufeli, W.B. (2005). Crossover of burnout and work engagement among working couples. *Human Relations* 58, 661–689.

Bakker, A.B., Westman, M. and van Emmerik, I.J.H. (2009). Advancements in crossover theory. *Journal of Managerial Psychology* 24, 206–219.

—— (2006). The socially induced burnout model. In Columbus (ed.) *Leading edge research in cognitive psychology*. New York: Nova Science.

Bakker, A.B., Petrou, P. and Tsaousis, I. (2012). Inequity in work and intimate relationships: A Spillover-crossover model. *Anxiety, Stress, and Coping*, *25*, 491–506.

Bakker, A.B., Shimazu, A., Demerouti, E., Shimada, K. and Kawakami, N. (in press). Work engagement versus workaholism: A test of the Spillover-crossover model. *Journal of Managerial Psychology*.

Bandura, A. (2001). Social cognitive theory: An agentic perspective. *Annual Review of Psychology* 52, 1–26.

Barnett, R.C., Raudenbush, S.W., Brennan, R.T., Pleck, J.H. and Marshall, N.L. (1995). Changes in job and marital experience and change in psychological distress: A longitudinal study of dual-earner couples. *Journal of Personality and Social Psychology* 69, 839–850.

Berkowitz, L. (1989). The frustration-aggression hypothesis: Examination and reformulation. *Psychological Bulletin* 106, 59–73.

Bolger, N., DeLongis, A., Kessler, R. and Wethington, E. (1989). The contagion of stress across multiple roles. *Journal of Marriage and the Family* 51, 175–183.

Burke, R.J., Weir, T. and DuWors, R.E. (1980). Work demands on administrators and spouse well-being. *Human Relations* 33, 253–278.

Butler, A.B., Grzywacz, J.G., Bass, B.L. and Linney, K.D. (2005). Extending the demands-control model: A daily diary study of job characteristics, work-family conflict and work-family facilitation. *Journal of Occupational and Organizational Psychology* 78, 155–169.

Buunk, B.P. and Schaufeli, W.B. (1999). Reciprocity in interpersonal relationships: An evolutionary perspective on its importance for health and well-being. *European Review of Social Psychology* 10, 259–291.

Byron, K. (2005). A meta-analytic review of work-family conflict and its antecedents. *Journal of Vocational Behavior* 67, 169–198.

Carlson, D.S. (1999). Personality and role variables as predictors of three forms of work-family conflict. *Journal of Vocational Behavior* 55, 236–253.

Cohen, S. and Wills, T.A. (1985). Stress, social support, and the buffering hypothesis. *Psychological Bulletin* 98, 310–357.

Demerouti, E. (2012). The spillover and crossover of resources among partners: The role of work-self and family-self facilitation. *Journal of Occupational Health Psychology*, *17*, 184–195.

Demerouti, E. and Bakker, A.B. (2011). The Job Demands-Resources model: Challenges for future research. *South African Journal of Industrial Psychology* 37, 1–9.

Demerouti, E., Bakker, A.B. and Bulters, A. (2004). The loss spiral of work pressure, work-home interference and exhaustion: Reciprocal relationships in a three-wave study. *Journal of Vocational Behavior* 64, 131–149.

Demerouti, E., Bakker, A.B. and Schaufeli, W.B. (2005). Spillover and crossover of exhaustion and life satisfaction among dual-earner parents. *Journal of Vocational Behavior* 67, 266–289.

Demerouti, E., Bakker, A.B. and Voydanoff, P. (2010). Does home life interfere with or facilitate performance? *European Journal of Work and Organizational Psychology*, 19, 128–149.

Demerouti, E., Geurts, S.A.E. and Kompier, M.A.J. (2004). Positive and negative work-home interaction: Prevalence and correlates. *Equal Opportunities International* 23, 6–35.

Demerouti E., Bakker, A.B., Nachreiner, F. and Schaufeli, W.B. (2001). The Job Demands-Resources model of burnout. *Journal of Applied Psychology* 86, 499–512.

Demerouti, E., Geurts, S.A.E., Bakker, A.B. and Euwema, M. (2004). The impact of shiftwork on work-home interference, job attitudes and health. *Ergonomics* 47, 987–1002.

Doherty, R.W., Orimoto, L., Singelis, T.M., Hatfield, E. and Hebb, J. (1995). Emotional contagion: Gender and occupational differences. *Psychology of Women Quarterly* 19, 355–371.

Dollard, M.F., Winefield, H.R. and Winefield, A.H. (2001). *Occupational strain and efficacy in human service workers*. Dordrecht, The Netherlands: Kluwer.

Eby, L.T., Casper, W.J., Lockwood, A., Bordeaux, C. and Brinley, A. (2005). Work and family research in IO/OB: Content analysis and review of the literature (1980–2002). *Journal of Vocational Behavior* 66, 124–197.

Edwards, J.R. and Rothbard N. (2000). Mechanisms linking work and family: Clarifying the relationship between work and family constructs. *Academy of Management Review* 25, 178–200.

Field, T.M., Hernandez-Reif, M., Quintino, O., Schanberg, S. and Kuhn, C. (1998). Elder retired volunteers benefit from giving massage therapy to infants. *Journal of Applied Gerontology* 17, 229–239.

Ford, M.T., Heinen B.A. and Langkamer K.L.J. (2007). Work and family satisfaction and conflict: a meta-analysis of cross-domain relations. *Journal of Applied Psychology* 92, 57–80.

Frone, M.R. (2003). Work-family balance. In J.C. Quick and L.E. Tetrick (eds) *Handbook of occupational health psychology* (143–162). Washington, DC: American Psychological Association.

Frone, M.R., Yardley, J.K. and Markel, K.S. (1997). Developing and testing an integrative model of the work-family interface. *Journal of Vocational Behavior* 50, 145–167.

Geurts, S.A.E., Rutte, C. and Peeters, M. (1999). Antecedents and consequences of work-home interference among medical residents. *Social Science & Medicine* 48, 1135–1148.

Gorgievski-Duijvesteijn, M.J., Giessen, C. and Bakker, A.B. (2000). Financial problems and health complaints among farm couples: Results of a ten-year follow-up study. *Journal of Occupational Health Psychology* 5, 359–373.

Greenhaus, J.H. and Beutell, N.J. (1985). Sources of conflict between work and family roles. *Academy of Management Review* 10, 76–88.

Greenhaus, J.H. and Powell, G.N. (2006). When work and family are allies: A theory of work family enrichment. *Academy of Management Review* 31, 72–92.

Grzywacz, J.G. and Marks, N.F. (2000). Reconceptualizing the work-family interface: An ecological perspective on the correlates of positive and negative spillover between work and family. *Journal of Occupational Health Psychology* 5, 111–126.

Hatfield, E., Cacioppo, J.T. and Rapson, R.L. (1994). *Emotional contagion*. New York: Cambridge University Press.

Howe, G., Levy, M. and Caplan, R. (2004). Job loss and depressive symptoms in couples: Common stressors, stress transmission, or relationship disruption? *Journal of Family Psychology* 18, 639–650.

Jackson, S.E. and Maslach, C. (1982). After-effects of job-related stress: Families as victims. *Journal of Occupational Behavior* 3, 63–77.

Kossek, E.E. and Ozeki, C. (1998). Work-family conflict, policies, and the job-life satisfaction relationship: A review and directions for organizational behavior-human resources research. *Journal of Applied Psychology* 83, 139–149.

Lazarus, R.S. (1991). *Emotion and adaptation.* New York: Oxford.

Lyubomirsky, S., Tkach, C. and Sheldon, K. M. (2004). *Pursuing sustained happiness through random acts of kindness and counting one's blessings: Tests of two six-week interventions.* Unpublished data, Department of Psychology, University of California, Riverside.

Marks, S.R. (1977). Multiple roles and role strain: Some notes on human energy, time and commitment. *American Sociological Review* 42, 921–936.

Matthews, L.S., Conger, R.D. and Wickrama, K.A.S. (1996). Work-family conflict and marital quality: Mediating processes. *Social Psychology Quarterly* 59, 62–79.

Montgomery, A.J., Panagopoulou, E., de Wildt, M. and Meenks, E. (2006). Work-family interference, emotional labor and burnout. *Journal of Managerial Psychology* 21, 36–51.

Prince, M., Manolis, C. and Minetor, R. (2007). Life satisfaction crossover among couples. In R.J. Estes (ed.) *Advancing Quality of life in a Turbulent World*, (191–208). Dordrecht, Nederland: Springer.

Quick, J.C. and Tetrick, L.E. (2003). *Handbook of occupational health psychology.* Washington, DC: American Psychological Association.

Rothbard, N. (2001). Enriching or depleting? The dynamics of engagement in work and family roles. *Administrative Science Quarterly* 46, 655–684.

Schaefer, C., Coyne, J.C. and Lazarus, R.S. (1981). The health-related functions of social support. *Journal of Behavioral Medicine* 4, 381–406.

Shimazu, A., Bakker, A.B. and Demerouti, E. (2009). How job demands influence partners' well-being: A test of the Spillover-crossover model in Japan. *Journal of Occupational Health* 51, 239–248.

Shimazu, A., Demerouti, E., Bakker, A.B., Shimada, K. and Kawakami, N. (2011). Workaholism and well-being among Japanese dual-earner couples: A spillover-crossover perspective. *Social Science and Medicine* 73, 399–409.

Starcevic, V. and Piontek, C.M. (1997). Empathic understanding revisited: Conceptualization, controversies, and limitations. *American Journal of Psychotherapy* 51, 317–328.

Stiff, J.B., Dillard, J.P., Somera, L., Kim, H. and Sleight, C. (1988). Empathy, communication, and prosocial behavior. *Communication Monographs* 55, 198–213.

Stotland, E. (1969). Exploratory investigations of empathy. In L. Berkowitz (ed.) *Advances in experimental social psychology* (vol. 4, 271–314). New York: Academic Press.

van den Broeck, A., Vansteenkiste, M., De Witte, H. and Lens, W. (2008). Explaining the relationships between job characteristics, burnout, and engagement: The role of basic psychological need satisfaction. *Work & Stress* 22, 277–294.

van der Doef, M. and Maes, S. (1999). The job demand-control(-support) model and psychological well-being: A review of 20 years of empirical research. *Work & Stress* 13, 87–114.

Vinokur, A.D. and Van Ryn, M. (1993). Social support and undermining in close relationships: Their independent effects on the mental health of unemployed persons. *Journal of Personality and Social Psychology* 65, 350–359.

Wallace, J.E. (1997). It's about time: A study of hours worked and work spillover among law firm lawyers. *Journal of Vocational Behavior* 50, 227–248.

Walster, F., Walster, G.W. and Berscheid, E. (1978). *Equity: Theory and research*. Boston, MA: Allyn & Bacon.

Wayne J.H., Grzywacz J.G., Carlson, D.S. and Kacmar, K.M. (2007). Work-family facilitation: A theoretical explanation and model of primary antecedents and consequences. *Human Resource Management Review* 17, 63–76.

Westman, M. (2001). Stress and strain crossover. *Human Relations* 54, 557–591.

Westman, M. (2005). Cross-cultural differences in crossover research. In S.A.Y. Poelmans (Ed.), *Work and family: An international research perspective. Series in applied psychology* (241–260). Mahwah, NJ: Lawrence Erlbaum Associates Publishers.

Westman, M. (2006). Models of work-family interactions: Stress and strain crossover. In R.K. Suri (ed.) *International encyclopedia of organizational behavior* (498–522). New Delhi: Pentagon Press.

Westman, M. and Bakker, A.B. (2008). Crossover of burnout among health care professionals. In J. Halbesleben (ed.) *Handbook of stress and burnout in health care*. Hauppauge NY: Nova Science Publishers.

Westman, M., Etzion, D. and Chen, S. (2009). Crossover of positive experiences from business travelers to their spouses. *Journal of Managerial Psychology* 24, 269–284.

Westman, M., Etzion, D. and Danon, E. (2001). Job insecurity and crossover of burnout in married couples. *Journal of Organizational Behavior* 22, 467–481.

Westman, M., Etzion, D. and Horovitz, S. (2004). The toll of unemployment does not stop with the unemployed. *Human Relations* 57, 823–844.

Westman, M., Keinan, G., Roziner, R. and Benyamini, Y. (2008). The crossover of perceived health between couples: A theoretical model. *Journal of Occupational Health Psychology* 13(2), 168–180.

Westman, M. and Vinokur, A. (1998). Unraveling the relationship of distress levels within couples: Common stressors, emphatic reactions, or crossover via social interactions? *Human Relations* 51, 137–156.

Westman, M., Vinokur, A., Hamilton, L. and Roziner, I. (2004). Crossover of marital dissatisfaction during military downsizing among Russian army officers and their spouses. *Journal of Applied Psychology* 89, 769–779.

Zedeck, S. and Mosier, K.L. (1990). Work in the family and employing organization. *American Psychologist* 45, 240–25.

5   Not always a sweet home

Family and job responsibilities constrain recovery processes

Sabine Sonnentag and Ines Braun

Employment is a major source of stress for many adults. A recent study conducted on behalf of the American Psychological Association found that 70 per cent of surveyed Americans perceived work to be a "significant" or "very significant" cause of stress (American Psychological Association, 2010). When work is perceived to be stressful it results in strain reactions at the physiological, affective, cognitive, and behavioral level. To reduce these strain reactions and to protect health and well-being in the long run, some relief and recovery from the stressful experiences is needed.

The home and the family are domains where recovery is believed to be "natural". The above-mentioned study, however, demonstrated that family responsibilities often are also perceived to be stressful with 58 per cent of the respondents finding family responsibilities to be a (very) significant cause of stress. Moreover, many employees experience a conflict between work and family. More than two decades of research on the work–family interface suggests substantial potential for conflicts between work and family. In their seminal paper, Greenhaus and Beutell (1985) differentiated between strain-based conflict, time-based conflict, and behavior-based conflict. Strain-based conflict implies that strain (e.g. irritability, fatigue) originating from work impairs one's ability to comply with family demands. Time-based conflict means that the time devoted to work makes it impossible to meet the time demands associated with the family role. Behavior-based conflict refers to the incompatibility of role expectations at work and at home (being a self-reliant, dominant manager versus a warm, vulnerable spouse or parent).

We propose that particularly the experience of strain-based conflict is closely linked to a lack of recovery processes. Strain-based conflict between work and family occurs when people are exposed to stressful work situations in which job stressors increase their strain levels, including symptoms of fatigue and also states of high negative affect. Moreover, these strains originating from work impact negatively on one's family life when one does not have the opportunity to reduce the strain level before facing family demands. Imagine that employees had sufficient time and a suitable environment nearby so they could take a relaxed walk in the park, sleep, and do other enjoyable things before they arrive at home, strain-based conflict would be substantially reduced. They would come home in a refreshed state so that they could face family demands with new energy and the preceding strains being present at the end of the working day would have vanished. Of course, the walk-and-sleep-in-the-park scenario is unrealistic for most people, but it illustrates that daily routines that do not offer sufficient opportunities for recovery impact on people's strain-based work–family conflict. Similarly, also behavior-based conflict might be enhanced by a lack of recovery, particularly when not mentally disengaging from one's job while being at home. Taken together, our chapter starts with the premise that the tension many employees experience between work and family is augmented when recovery and recovery opportunities are lacking.

For time-based conflict, however, the pattern might be more complex: when time-based conflict between work and family is high, employees may be reluctant (and not able) to spend time on recovery activities. When spending time on (individual) recovery processes, time-based conflict between work and family might further increase. Moreover, the preoccupation with the work role while being at home – described as one aspect of time-based conflict (Greenhaus and Beutell, 1985) – might increase when not gaining mental distance from work while being at home. Overall, work–family conflict and recovery are closely intertwined phenomena.

However, it is not realistic to see the home mainly as a place of recovery and recuperation. Many employees continue to be occupied with job-related tasks when being at home (Schieman, Milkie and Glavin, 2009). Work and family stress have been found to co-occur (Grzywacz, Almeida and McDonald, 2002). Thus, the view of home and family as a place of rest and recuperation might be more of a wish than a reality for many employees. In our view, these constraints on recovery have not received sufficient attention in the recovery literature.

In this chapter we discuss recovery processes in light of constraints originating from the home domain and from job responsibilities that blur the boundary between work and home life. The first section of this chapter describes findings from recovery research. In the second section, we present housework and care activities as an important constraint on recovery, and in the third section we turn to job-related work at home as a constraint on recovery. In this section we pay particular attention to technology use at home. We suggest that complex boundary management, including the creation of mental boundaries, might help to take advantage of recovery opportunities when being at home. In the final section, we briefly summarize the findings from the literature and suggest directions for future research.

Recovery as an important mechanism for protecting well-being, health, and job performance

Recovery Concept

Generally, recovery can be defined as a process of regaining something that has been lost and of returning to a former state. Recovery at the work–family interface is often conceptualized as recovery from (paid) work. Working is an effortful activity that draws on employees' physical, cognitive and/or emotional resources. Often, working leads to an increase in strain symptoms such as state negative affect or fatigue. Such an increase in strain symptoms is particularly likely when working under stressful conditions. To reduce strain symptoms and to protect health and performance capabilities in the long run, it is important that employees recover from work, particularly from the stressful experiences encountered on the job. Recovery can be described as a process opposite to the strain process (Craig and Cooper, 1992; Meijman and Mulder, 1998). Recovery can occur in a broad range of settings, ranging from micro breaks during work (Fritz, Lam and Spreitzer, 2011) to vacations (Westman and Eden, 1997) and sabbaticals (Davidson *et al.*, 2010). Formal work breaks, leisure time in the evening, and weekends provide rather regular recovery opportunities for many employees. Other terms often used synonymously with recovery include unwinding, restoration, and recuperation.

Feeling recovered as a predictor of engagement and performance on the job

Empirical research supported the basic idea that recovery is related to positive job-related outcomes. Studies have found that employees who feel recovered when they return to work after a leisure period are more engaged at work and feel that they perform better. Based on a daily-survey study, Sonnentag (2003) reported that employees show higher work engagement and more proactive behavior at work on days when they felt that they recovered well during the preceding leisure time – as compared to days when they did not feel well recovered. Binnewies, Sonnentag and Mojza (2009) extended these findings and demonstrated that not only proactive behavior, but also in-role performance and organizational citizenship behavior (OCB) was higher when employees felt well recovered. Interestingly, the benefits of recovery were most prominent for employees who had high job control. Probably, when having a high level of control, employees can adjust their work behavior to their momentary energetic state, whereas when job control is low, employees have less discretion in influencing how they work.

Kühnel, Sonnentag and Bledow (2012) also reported an association between morning recovery level and engagement during the workday. Bakker, van Emmerik, Geurts and Demerouti (2008) found that the benefits of recovery were most prominent when job demands on the specific day were high. These authors suggested that "recovery turns job demands into challenges," implying that feeling recovered is most valuable when demands are high.

The beneficial effects of recovery do become obvious also after the weekend. For instance, Binnewies, Sonnentag and Mojza (2010) reported that when employees felt recovered after the weekend, they showed higher levels of task job performance, proactive behavior, and OCB during the week. Interestingly, when feeling recovered they also felt that they needed less effort to accomplish their tasks.

A recent study demonstrated that also the feeling of being recovered after a work break matters. Sanz-Vergel *et al.* (2011) reported that when employees felt recovered after a break at work they experienced higher levels of work–family facilitation (i.e., felt more in the mood to engage in activities with other family members or friends), and enjoyed a higher level of vigor at home.

Overall, these studies show that returning to work in a state of being recovered is associated with work engagement and various facets of job performance. Until now, most of the studies on recovery have tried to demonstrate the positive effect of recovery on work-related outcomes. However, the study by Sanz-Vergel *et al.* (2011) illustrates that feeling recovered (e.g. after a break) is also important for family-related outcomes. A study by Sonnentag and Niessen (2008) points into a similar direction: when employees felt recovered during a series of preceding evenings, they experienced a higher level of vigor at the end of the working day. Thus, it seems they were able to uphold a certain energy level during the day at work. Returning home from work with a high energy level helps employees to address family demands with more strength and persistence and might also contribute to more enjoyment at home. Later in this chapter, we discuss this issue in more detail.

Recovery at home

An employee's recovery level and overall state when returning to work after a period of leisure time or after a break seem to depend largely on how this employee has spent his or her non-work time and how he or she has experienced it (Sonnentag and Geurts, 2009). Here we will summarize research on activities that contribute to recovery. In addition, we will discuss specific experiences (e.g. mentally switching off) that were found to help in the recovery process.

Recovery activities

Studies that focused on recovery activities examined what employees are doing during the time when they are off the job. Studies have repeatedly shown that engaging in sport and exercise activities results in an elevated level of positive mood (Rook and Zijlstra, 2006; Sonnentag, 2001; Sonnentag and Bayer, 2005). For example, the more time people spent on sport and exercise activities during after-work hours, the more positive were their affective states later in the evening (Sonnentag, 2001; Sonnentag and Bayer, 2005). These findings from these studies are in line with other research that has demonstrated the affective benefits of sport and exercise activities (Reed and Ones, 2006).

With research to other types of activities the findings were less clear-cut. For instance, social activities (e.g. meeting with friends) were associated with more positive affective states in some of the studies (e.g. Sonnentag, 2001), but not in all (Sonnentag and Natter, 2004). Also so-called low-effort activities were found to be beneficial in some studies (e.g. Sonnentag, 2001), but not in others (Sonnentag and Bayer, 2005). It might be that the activity categories used in most of the studies are too broad to find a clear pattern. This is most evident with respect to the low-effort category that included activities such as watching TV, reading a book, taking a bath; also deliberate relaxation activities would be included in this category. It is obvious, that the recovery effects of such a divers set of activities differ. Moreover, it can be assumed that people differ with respect to specific activities that they like. Such interaction effects between individual preferences and time spent on activities have not been tested in these studies. Finally, it seems that work demands also play a role when it comes to the recovery effects of specific activities. For instance, in a sample of flight attendants who have high social-interaction demands on the job, social activities during leisure time were negatively related to favorable affective state (Sonnentag and Natter, 2004). Thus, a recovery activity can only unfold its positive potential if it does not put an additional demand on the functional system that has been challenged also during work (Meijman and Mulder, 1998).

Recovery experiences

In addition to analyzing the time spent on recovery activities, researchers have examined the experience quality associated with these recovery activities. The basic idea is that activities unfold their recovery potential by enabling specific experiences. For instance, going for a walk in nature might be recovering because this activity enables relaxation. Sonnentag and Fritz (2007) have argued that it might differ from person to person whether an activity is recovering or not, depending on the associated recovery experience. For example, watching a TV show might be recovering for one person because this person mentally detaches from work while watching the show, whereas it might not have any recovery potential for another person because this person keeps thinking about his or her work while watching the show.

Sonnentag and Fritz (2007) suggested to look at four specific recovery experiences: psychological detachment from work during non-work time, relaxation, mastery experiences, and control. Psychological detachment from work implies to mentally disengage from work. When someone detaches from work, he or she does not only refrain from job-related activities, but also does not think about job-related issues. Relaxation refers to an experience associated with a low (sympathetic) activation level, both with respect to the mental and the physical state. Mastery experiences refer to off-job processes associated with facing new challenges and learning. For instance, engaging in sport activities or learning a new language typically provides mastery experiences. Thus, recovering from one's job does not necessarily imply to be passive. Recovery can also be achieved by active pursuits that are complementary to the demands on the job. Finally, control implies to have some degree of self-determination in deciding how to spend one's time.

Empirical studies conducted in various countries showed that these four recovery experiences are positively related to positive indicators of well-being (e.g. life satisfaction) and negatively related to strain symptoms such as exhaustion and psychosomatic complaints (Sanz-Vergel *et al.*, 2010; Siltaloppi, Kinnunen and Feldt, 2009; Sonnentag and Fritz, 2007). Interestingly, a similar pattern of findings emerged in a study that examined recovery of students during a weekend (Ragsdale, Beehr, Grebner and Han, 2011).

In most of these studies, psychological detachment from work during non-work time turned out as the strongest predictor of well-being. In line with this finding, a range of additional studies specifically focused on the recovery benefits of psychological detachment. Some of these studies looked at between-person differences (i.e., compared persons who generally have a high level of detachment with persons who have a low level of detachment), while others looked at within-person relationships (i.e., examined high-detachment days with low-detachment days).

Similar to the findings from studies that looked at all four recovery experiences (e.g. Siltaloppi, Kinnuman and Feldt, 2009; Sonnentag and Fritz, 2007), between-person studies that concentrated on psychological detachment from work as a core recovery experience reported that lack of detachment was associated with poor well-being. For instance, Sonnentag, Kuttler and Fritz (2010) found that pastors who were more able to detach from their work during their spare free time had lower levels of emotional exhaustion and of need for recovery. Interestingly, psychological detachment mediated the relation between job stressors on the one hand and emotional exhaustion and need for recovery on the other hand. A longitudinal study by Sonnentag, Binnewies and Mojza (2010) found that lack of detachment predicted an increase in emotional exhaustion one year later, also when controlling for the initial level of emotional exhaustion, job stressors, and a broad range of background variables. Moreover, this study showed that psychological detachment from work during non-work time attenuated the relationship between high job demands and psychosomatic complaints and between high job demands and low work engagement. High job demands were only associated with an increase in psychosomatic complaints and a decrease in work engagement when employees did not detach from work during non-work time. Similarly, von Thiele Schwarz (2011) examined employed women's inability to withdraw from work during non-work time (a concept very similar to poor psychological detachment) and found that a high inability to withdraw from work predicted fatigue six months later. Although it is not possible to establish strong inferences about causality in correlational studies (even when they have a longitudinal design), research evidence tends to suggest that poor psychological detachment from work during non-work time contributes to poor well-being. Thus, employees who find ways to detach from their job during their non-work time seem to be better off in the long run.

Studies on worrying and rumination provide additional evidence that involuntarily thinking about work during non-work time may constitute a health risk (Brosschot, Pieper and Thayer, 2005). For instance Cropley and Millward-Purvis (2006) reported that rumination was related to poor sleep quality. Rydstedt *et al.* (2009) found that rumination predicted elevated evening cortisol levels. A follow-up study with the same sample 3.5 years later showed that the combination of role ambiguity and rumination predicted morning cortisol levels (Rydstedt, Cropley and Devereux, 2011).

In addition to analyzing associations with well-being indicators, Fritz *et al.* (2010) examined the association between psychological detachment and job performance. Using data from multiple sources this study demonstrated a curvilinear relation between psychological detachment and job performance with the highest level of job performance at intermediate levels of psychological detachment. It seems that job performance suffers both when psychological detachment is very low (because continuous thinking about one's work might deplete one's resources) and when psychological detachment is very high (because gaining too much distance from one's work during leisure time might decrease work motivation).

Overall, these between-person studies demonstrate that mentally disengaging from work during non-work time is associated with positive affective states and well-being; however, with respect to job performance the picture seems to be more complex. More studies are needed that explore the associations between psychological detachment and performance-related outcomes.

Research on psychological detachment from work did not only look at between-person differences but also at within-person processes. Here, the core question is if employees feel better on days when they succeed in detaching from work, compared to days when they continue to think or ruminate about their work during non-work time. A first diary study that addressed this question found that employees felt less fatigued and were in a better mood at bedtime when they had detached from work during the activities they pursued during leisure time (Sonnentag and Bayer, 2005). Another diary study examined whether psychological detachment from work mattered also for the next day (Sonnentag, Binnewies and Mojza, 2008). Results showed that employees felt less fatigued and reported lower levels of negative affect in the morning after they had detached from work during their preceding evenings.

Sanz-Vergel *et al.* (2011) showed that day-specific psychological detachment from work during evening hours predicted a low level of work–home interference. Interestingly, these authors identified an interaction effect with home role salience. The negative association between psychological detachment and work–home interference was particularly strong when home role salience was high, that is when attaching a high personal value to one's family and/or personal life. Sanz-Vergel and her co-workers also found an interaction effect between psychological detachment and home role salience on evening cognitive liveliness: Psychological detachment was positively related to cognitive liveliness in the evening for persons with a high home role salience, but not for persons with a low home role salience. Thus, it seems that employees with a high home role salience benefit most from gaining mental distance from work. This finding, however, does not imply that detachment does not matter for employees for whom work is important. A study using weekly surveys found that psychological detachment from work during weekday evenings predicted positive affect at Friday afternoon, particularly for employees with a high level of work engagement (Sonnentag, Mojza, Binnewies and Scholl, 2008). These studies suggest that psychological detachment during non-work time is particularly beneficial for employees who are highly engaged when being at work and for whom work is important.

Demerouti *et al*. (2012) examined the interplay between enjoyment at work (as an important facet of the flow experience) and psychological detachment from work when being at home. In line with what one would expect, enjoyment at work was positively related to vigor at night. Moreover, the positive association between enjoyment at work and vigor at home was most pronounced when psychological detachment during after-work hours was high. Thus, it seems that when one gets some mental distance from work during evening hours, one still feels energetic at home after an enjoyable day at work. However, when one stays mentally connected to one's work (i.e., does not detach) the energetic benefit of an enjoyable day at work wanes. Probably, continued mental connection to one's job depletes energy resources, even after an enjoyable day at work. Accordingly, in this study enjoyment at work was negatively related to exhaustion at night, but only on days with high levels of detachment from work during after-work hours.

Importantly, continued (negative) thinking about work during after-work hours seems to be also reflected in physiological processes. A study about work worries showed that both in men and in women work worries were associated with elevated cortisol levels in the evening of the same day (Slatcher *et al.*, 2010). Interestingly, whereas for men only their own work worries were associated with elevated cortisol levels, for women both their own work worries and their partners' work worries predicted elevated cortisol levels. Thus worrying about work and not detaching from one's job might not only affect the person him- or herself, but also his spouse – and maybe also the whole family.

It has to be noted that psychological detachment from work is not the only off-job experience that might matter at the day level. A recent diary study, for instance, showed that pleasure experienced during evening hours predicted high levels of vigor and low levels of fatigue at bedtime (van Hooff *et al.*, 2011). Moreover, mastery experiences during the evening predicted activated positive affect in the next morning and relaxation during the evening predicted low-activated positive affect in the next morning (Sonnentag, Binnewies and Mojza, 2008).

Overall, these studies show that the way employees spend their leisure time and how they experience this time is essential for short-term and long-term affective states and well-being. Not detaching from work during free time and particularly worrying about work undermine the recovery potential of leisure time.

Recovery during work breaks

Recovery does not only take place off the job but also during breaks when at work. Recovery can occur during short microbreaks when being at or near the workplace (Fritz, Lam and Spreitzer, 2011) and during more formal breaks, for example lunch breaks. In a pioneering study, Trougakos and his co-workers (2008) examined break activities of a group of cheerleader instructors and how break activities were related to subsequent affect and "affective delivery" – a proxy for work performance in this kind of job. Analyses of experience sampling data showed that spending time on typical respite activities such as napping, relaxing, and socializing was associated with subsequent high positive affect, low negative affect, and a high level of affective delivery after the break whereas spending time on chores such as working with customers, doing errands, practicing material, and preparing for upcoming sessions was associated with high levels of negative affect.

In a more recent study with administrative university employees, Trougakos, Hideg and Cheung (2011) studied lunch break activities in their relation to co-worker reports of fatigue at the end of the working day. Relaxing break activities were negatively related to fatigue at the end of the working day. Having engaged in work-related break activities was associated in increased fatigue levels. Interestingly, also social activities were related to fatigue. These authors tested control over break activities as a moderator and found that the positive relations between work-related activities and fatigue as well as between social activities and fatigue occurred only when control over break activities was low. This finding suggests that it might not be the break activity per se which is increasing fatigue but the fact of having to engage in this activity without one's own choice over it.

Also another recent study demonstrate that deliberately relaxing during breaks is particularly important for recovery (Krajewski, Wieland and Sauerland, 2010). However, it seems to be important that the break fits well into the work process. For instance, Demerouti *et al.* (2012) reported that enjoyment at work was positively related to vigor at work (and negatively to exhaustion at work) when recovery during breaks was low – as opposed to high. This finding may indicate that when breaks interrupt an enjoyable work process they are de-energizing. An alternative interpretation of this finding might be that recovery during break was experienced to be high after exhausting work periods, whereas after less exhausting work periods, recovery was experienced as low. Following this line of reasoning, one might argue that the effects of recovery during break reflect also pre-break strain levels.

Constraints on recovery

Overall, research on recovery has shown that spending time on recovery activities and particularly psychologically detaching from work when being at home plays an important role for employee health and well-being – and to some extent also for job performance. However, it would be overly naïve to assume that employees can devote all their at-home-hours to recovery.

It is self-evident that part of the non-work time has to be spent on activities such as sleeping (which in itself is crucial for recovery), eating, or personal hygiene. But in addition, also the time that does remain is no pure recovery time. Many employees face household duties and have to care for children and elderly when being at home. Moreover, often, employees continue with job-related activities during after-work hours. The amount of time devoted to job-related activities while being at home has been facilitated by the increased availability of technical connectivity with one's job in recent years. In this section of our chapter we address household and care activities as well as job-related activities as major constraints on recovery when being at home.

Household and care activities as a constraint on recovery

When being at home, many employees do not have all the off-job time at their full discretion. Having to complete household tasks and care for children and elder family members limit the time employees have available for recovery. Moreover, these household and care activities often require effort investment and therefore might further deplete energetic and affective resources.

The studies on recovery activities reported above also investigated time spent on household and childcare activities. Contrary to what one might expect, spending time on household and childcare activities were not related to subsequent negative affective states (e.g. Rook and Zijlstra, 2006; Sonnentag, 2001; Sonnentag and Natter, 2004). One explanation for this finding is that "household and childcare activities" is a very broad category comprising a range of both enjoyable and less enjoyable activities. Moreover, it might be that different people have very different preferences about what they like in terms of household or childcare activities. For instance, someone might find cooking pleasurable, while others might unwind when striking. Thus, asking about overall time spent in household and childcare activities might be an approach too rough to find substantial associations with affect and well-being.

Moreover, it might be that just looking at subjective indicators of well-being or affective states at bedtime only tells half of the truth. Day-level studies using cortisol data showed that the more time employees spent on household activities the higher were their evening cortisol levels (Klumb, Hoppmann and Staats, 2006; Saxbe, Repetti and Graesch, 2011). Thus, it seems that doing household activities slows down physiological recovery, maybe because housework often is physically demanding.

In addition, when it comes to household activities gender differences seem to play an important role. Overall, studies find substantial differences in time allocation patterns between women and men, particularly when comparing married women to married men with women spending more hours on housework and childcare activities (Sayer, 2007; Saxbe, Repetti and Graesch, 2011). With respect to recovery processes, the differences in time allocation patterns between men and women might imply that women have more difficulties to recover after work or during free days than men do (Lundberg and Frankenhaeuser, 1999).

In addition, there is some evidence that not only the amount of time oneself devotes to household activities, but also one's partner's engagement in household activities might matter. Using observational data of off-job activities, Saxbe, Repetti and Graesch (2011) reported that women's cortisol level decreased when their husbands spent more time on housework (in addition to the main effect women's time spent on housework had on their cortisol levels). No such pattern was found for men (but see Klumb, Hoppmann and Staats, 2006). Thus, it seems that it is not only the mere amount of time a person spends on specific activities that impedes versus fosters recovery. Also distribution of work within the family – and associated perceptions of justice and equality – might play a role.

Job-related work at home as a constraint on recovery

In many jobs, employees do not only work when they are at their (formal) workplace (e.g. the office), but also when they are at home. They finish tasks, prepare for the upcoming workday, or try to catch up with reading assignments. Moreover, by using job-related information technology when being at home, they can immediately respond to incoming emails and phone calls. Thus, in many jobs employees try to be available for their customers, supervisors, and co-workers long after the formal end of their working day, reflecting a 24/7 work culture. Without doubt, the option to continue working at home and the availability of information technology that helps to stay connected with one's workplace has clear advantages. Permanent availability at home might give employees a sense of control over things that happen while they are not physically present at work. For instance, if there is something really critical happening at work, they can be sure to get a call or an e-mail, otherwise when they do not get contacted they know that everything is all right, so they can mentally detach from work (without mobile technology some employees might ruminate a lot during leisure time and psychological detachment might not occur). Another advantage might be an increase in employees' flexibility with respect to working time and location. However, having job-related information technology available during after-work hours might have its drawbacks such as an increase in workload and longer workdays (Towers *et al.*, 2006).

Empirical studies suggest that blurring the boundaries between work and home might have some negative consequences. Diary studies found that spending time on job-related tasks when being at home is associated with an increase in more negative and a decrease in positive affective states (Sonnentag, 2001; Sonnentag and Zijlstra, 2006). Moreover, survey data from more than 2,000 men and women suggest that bringing work home and having job contacts at home predicts work-to-family conflict and perceived stress (Voydanoff, 2005). The author of this study identified "work–family multitasking" (i.e., working at the same time on job and home tasks) as the key underlying process that contributes to work-to-family conflict and perceived stress. Another large-scale survey study suggests that it is not necessarily the fact of completing work-related tasks at home that is related to work–family conflict (Eng *et al.*, 2010). This study found that working extra hours at home was related to a high level of work family conflict. However, the number of days working from home (instead of going to the office) was not related to work–family conflict.

Being contacted by colleagues and other job-related contacts during after-work hours seems to impact men and women differentially. A study by Glavin, Schieman and Reid (2011) found that guilt and distress increased in women as the frequencies of job-related contacts during after-work hours increased, also when controlling for work–family-conflict and a broad range of other variables. For men, however, there was no association between job-related contacts during after-work hours on the one hand and guilt or distress on the other hand. Nevertheless, it might be that being in contact with co-workers, supervisors, or customers might be stressful for other family members (Boswell and Olson-Buchanan, 2007).

With respect to technology use at home, Towers *et al.*, (2006) surveyed employees of a Canadian government department who used technologies such as blackberries, mobile phones, or laptop computers when working outside the office. Forty percent of the respondents agreed with a statement such as "I am never off duty: – I can be reached at any time, always expected to be accessible" (605). Boswell and Olson-Buchanan (2007) surveyed nonacademic university employees and found that using job-related communication technologies during after-work hours was positively related to the experience of work–family conflict. More recently, Fenner and Renn (2010) and Fender (2011) reported a similar finding. Interestingly, Fenner and Renn identified the time management strategy of setting goals and priorities to attenuate the association between using job-related technology at home and work–family-conflict. Thus, setting clear goals and priorities might help to reduce work–family conflict, also when using job-related technology at home. In a recent study, Park, Fritz and Jex (2011) reported that employees who used technology for work-related purposes at home reported a lower degree of psychological detachment from work during non-work time. Thus, overall it seems that the availability of job-related information technology at home may hinder recovery and psychological detachment from work.

Given the widespread use of job-related information technologies at home and its advantages in terms of flexibility, it would neither be realistic nor desirable to ban job-related technologies from the home domain and to advice employees to refrain from taking phone calls or checking email when being at home. Rather, it is important to find out how employees can use job-related information technologies when needed and at the same time protect their recovery time from too many intrusions.

Complex boundary management as a facilitator of recovery

Boundary theory

By drawing on boundary theory (Ashforth, Kreiner and Fugate, 2000; Nippert-Eng, 1996), we argue that it is important to set physical, temporal, and mental boundaries around the use of job-related information technologies when having them available at home (Olson-Buchanan and Boswell, 2006). According to role theory (Katz and Kahn, 1978), people fulfill several roles in their everyday lives, for instance the role of being an employee and the role of being a parent or a spouse. People differ in the degree to which they separate versus integrate these roles (Matthews and Barnes-Farrell, 2010; Rothbard, Philips and Dumas, 2005). For instance, traditional work arrangements where one commutes physically from home to work (as opposed to telecommuting) and does not complete job-related tasks at home refers to a high degree of segmentation, whereas completing job-related duties at home or working in a family business refers to a high degree of integration.

People tend to create boundaries around roles in order to simplify and structure their environment (Ashforth, Kreiner and Fugate, 2000). When moving from one role to another (for instance from the employee role to the parent role), people have to cross boundaries. In the case of highly separated roles, these role transitions are relatively effortful and boundary crossing occurs via "rites of transition" (Ashforth, Kreiner and Fugate, 2000: 478), whereas in case of highly integrated roles, the transition process is much less elaborate and effortful; often, it seems to occur automatically.

Ashforth, Kreiner and Fugate (2000) described boundary-crossing activities as micro-role transitions. When roles are highly segmented, a typical micro-role transition would be the daily commute from work to home. When roles are highly integrated, having a cup of coffee at one's desk might indicate the transition from the home-role to the work-role.

Boundary management when completing job-related tasks at home

What insights does boundary theory offer with respect to doing job-related work and using job-related information technology at home? First, job-related work and the use of job-related information technology at home refer to highly integrated roles of work and home. Second, the transition between the two roles can occur without much effort. This can be a positive feature because it allows for moving quickly between the roles. However, when it is so easy to transit from one role to the other, it may make the mental disengagement from work when being at home very difficult. Third, the more traditional transition rites between work and home (e.g. commuting from work to home) are not feasible when wishing to separate the roles in a highly integrated context.

Given the relevance of recovery – and particularly of mental disengagement from work when being at home – it is important that employees are able to temporally detach from work during after-work hours, also when they complete job-related tasks at home or when they have job-related information technology available at home. Because in such a situation, work and home roles tend to be highly integrated and because the traditional boundaries between work and home do not exist, employees need to enact specific other boundaries between the work and home role (Olson-Buchanan and Boswell, 2006). By advancing the terminology of Ashforth, Kreiner and Fugate (2000), we call these boundaries that employees may wish to build for separating work and home when being in the home domain "nano boundaries"[1] and the transitions between the respective roles

---

1   Ashforth, Kreiner and Fugate (2000) used the term "micro" role transitions to describe "frequent and usually recurring transitions, such as the commute between home and work" (472) – as opposed to "macro" role transitions such as a promotion or retirement. We refer to role transitions that happen at a much smaller scale, for instance, within the home domain when switching from a job-related mode to a non-job mode. Several small scale transitions are possible within a few minutes. To capture the small scale of these transitions, we use the term "nano boundaries."

"nano transitions". We suggest three types of nano boundaries: physical nano boundaries, temporal nano boundaries, and mental nano boundaries.

In traditional settings with highly segmented roles, physical boundaries play an important role: Work-role requirements are fulfilled in another physical location (i.e., in the office located in the company building) than the home-role requirements (e.g. in one's private home). In more integrated settings where work role requirements are completed when being in one's private home, such major physical boundaries loose their relevance. Instead, in order to help to disengage from work at least temporarily and to facilitate recovery, physical nano boundaries are needed. Such a physical nano boundary would imply to place and use one's smartphone or laptop computer only in clearly identified rooms. For instance, one might place and use the devices in one's home office or the living room, but not in one's bedroom or the children's room. Research on telework points into a similar direction: having a separate room for job-related work at home is associated with a lower degree of "spatial overlap" (247) between work and home life (Hartig, Johansson and Kylin, 2007; cf. also Hill, Hawkins and Miller, 1996).

Temporal boundaries refer to the time of the day and week when job-related tasks are completed. In very traditional settings, temporal boundaries are reflected in arrangements such as the nine-to-five workday. In more integrated settings, however, no such temporal boundaries do exist. Often, job-related tasks can be accomplished at any time. However, when job-related tasks may intrude into one's home domain at any time, mental disengagement from one's job becomes difficult. Therefore, employees might benefit from enacting temporal nano boundaries. For instance, they might want to decide not to take job-related phone calls after 9 pm, or to refrain from checking email on Saturday nights. Similarly, they might decide to refrain from completing other job-related tasks during specific times.

Setting physical and temporal boundaries might not be enough for detaching fully from work when being at home. Particularly when job-related information technology is used at home, deliberately setting mental boundaries might be necessary. Mental boundaries refer to cognitive strategies employees can use to disengage from work on a short-term basis. For instance, Mary might be checking her job-related emails at home at 8 pm. She answers some of these emails and looks at others, deciding that she will deal with them tomorrow. Although she will not look into the email mailbox later during the evening (temporal boundary) and puts her laptop in her bag (physical boundary), she might continue thinking about some of the emails she has received, making psychological detachment from her work impossible. In such a situation, it would help Mary if she could enact mental boundaries. For instance, she could deliberately tell herself that she is now at home, the emails do not refer to an urgent matter, and therefore, it is better to address them tomorrow. In addition, she could deliberately immerse herself fully in another activity and direct her whole concentration on this other activity and the people she is interacting with. Although setting physical and temporal boundaries for technology use might not be enough to enable detachment from work, these two facets of boundary management might help to set mental boundaries. Having the electronic device available all the time at any place might make it particularly difficult to enact a mental boundary because the device and the possibility that it could signal an incoming message is present all the time.

Using mental boundaries seems to be very similar to what Carver, Scheier and Weintraub (1989) described as "mental disengagement". Importantly, the mental boundary in our context refers to mentally disengaging from work during non-work time and not during working time. During work, it would not be adaptive to mentally disengage from one's momentary work. Creating a mental boundary for a limited amount of time could rather be seen as a self-regulatory skill. This skill helps to control one's work-related thoughts and associated emotions.

One could assume that people differ in their ability to set mental boundaries. For instance, people with a strong non-work role identity might find it easier to set such a boundary than do people with a stronger work role identity for whom their work is more salient all the time. Also one's general level of mindfulness (Brown and Ryan, 2003) might play a role. Being present at every moment might help employees to focus at the immediate (non-work) situation and to mentally disconnect from work.

Indirect evidence on the detrimental effects of not creating boundaries between job-related work and other at-home-activities comes from the Voydanoff's (2005) above cited study. Multitasking, i.e., doing job-related and home tasks at the same time, was found to be positively related to work–family-conflict and perceived stress. Clearly differentiating when and where to do which kind of tasks when being at home might make doing job-related tasks at home less stressful. Similarly, a study on telework showed that the more spatial (i.e., physical), temporal, and mental overlap people experienced between work and home, the more negative they evaluate this overlap (Hartig, Johansson and Kylin, 2007).

First more direct empirical evidence on the benefits of setting boundaries when using job-related information technology at home comes from a study by Park and Jex (2011). These authors found that creating boundaries around the use of work-related communication and information technology when being at home was negatively related to work-to-family interference. In other words, employees felt that their jobs interfered with home life when they did not create boundaries with respect to the use of technology at home. Unfortunately, this study did not differentiate between various types of boundaries.

New avenues for linking research on the work–family interface with research on recovery

At the beginning of the chapter, we have argued that lack of recovery will increase the experience of (WFC). More specifically, one would assume that particularly early recovery – that is, recovery shortly after the work has ended – will be most beneficial for reducing strain-based WFC, whereas recovery taking place later during the evening will be less effective for reducing strain-based WFC because then strains originating from one's job have already unfolded their negative impact on one's home life. Empirical studies could test this proposition by explicitly taking the timing of recovery activities and experiences into account. Such studies would require a relatively fine-grained experience sampling approach in which study participants report when they have pursued specific activities after leaving their workplace. An alternative would be to use an assessment tool for measuring peoples more general approaches of spending their time. In contrast to typical time-budget studies, it would be most important that this tool assesses the sequence in which activities are performed.

Experiencing that the demands at work do not leave enough time for meeting family demands is an important aspect of the WFC (time-base conflict). During recent years, it has been argued that in many employees' lives not only work and family compete for time, but also other areas require time investments, for instance learning (Butler, 2007). One can assume that when people face already problems in finding enough time for work, family, and other potentially important life areas, it will be difficult for them to devote sufficient time to recovery activities, such as a hobby or regular physical exercise. Also sleeping time might suffer. However, spending time on recovery is particularly important for people leading a stressful life – as it is typical when time-based WFC is high. One can assume that particularly time-consuming recovery activities are reduced when time-based WFC is high. Thus, time-based WFC makes recovery less likely. Lack of recovery, in turn, will impair health and well-being. It might be that under such circumstances, people turn to behaviors that are indicative of an unhealthy life-style (lack of exercise, eating unhealthy food, lack of sleep) in order to keep up with the time demands of work and family. These unhealthy behavior themselves will have long-term negative consequences. Thus, future studies may want to examine if lack of recovery activities mediates the relation between time-based WFC and impairments of employee health and well-being.

Furthermore, it would be interesting to examine how recovery more directly impacts on family processes. For instance, research summarized in this chapter has shown that when people feel recovered they feel more engaged at work and also perceive that they perform better (e.g. Binnewies, Sonnentag and Mojza, 2009; Sonnentag, 2003). Similarly, one could argue that being well recovered should also have benefits for family life. For instance, when recovered people are in a better mood what might help them to communicate more openly and more constructively with their partners and children. Recovery will replenish psychological resources that they can invest in their home life. For instance, they may have more resources to provide social support to other family members; self-regulatory resources may help to stay calm when conflicts occur.

In this chapter we have addressed constraints on recovery and have discussed how working at home and staying technically connected to one's job might impair recovery processes. In many cases, these constraints on recovery might not only have a negative effect on recuperation processes but also will negatively impact family life (e.g. Boswell and Olson-Buchanan, 2007). However, it should not be taken for granted that individual family members' attention to recovery may always increase the quality of family life. There might be also instances when time spent on individual recovery activities lacks for joint family time. Thus, future research might want to address how families as a whole and individual family members find a good balance between individual recovery and joint family activities.

Past work–family research addressed the topic at a rather abstract level (e.g. Maertz and Boyar, 2011) and did not pay much attention to routines and practices enacted within the families. Integrating research on recovery and the work–family interface may take a closer look at what is actually happening within the families, for instance with respect to (leisure) activities that contribute both to recovery from job stress (as well as stress at school) and to a cohesive family life.

With respect to the broader scope of our chapter, we suggest that future studies should pay more attention to recovery processes in contexts when people are facing recovery constraints, be it constraints from their families or from their jobs. For instance, how can employees initiate at least some energizing recovery processes when they are facing challenging care responsibilities at home or extremely high levels of workload on their jobs? Given the ongoing demographic changes in many Western countries with increased necessities for elderly care, it is particularly pressing to examine how employees can remain energetic, healthy, and committed to their jobs when at the same time they have to invest substantial amounts of time on the day of elder family member (Zacher, Jimmieson and Winter, in 2012).

Concluding remarks

As working life is becoming more and more challenging for many employees, recovery processes are increasingly important for maintaining health and well-being. There is broad evidence from empirical studies that psychologically detaching from work during non-work time is related to more favorable affective states in the short term and better well-being in the long term. Worrying about work is also reflected in strain indicators at the physiological level.

Although recovery is essential, many employees face constraints when it comes to planning and actually using time for recovery. Major constraints originate from duties related to housework and care, from actually working at home, and from staying electronically connected to the workplace when being at home. Although the use of job-related technology at home has advantages, it is a double-edged sword because mental disengagement from work most probably becomes more difficult and requires additional effort in term of boundary setting. In this chapter we have suggested that creating physical, temporal, and particularly mental boundaries is essential in order to protect the recovery potential that leisure time provides. More research is needed that identifies ways how people can create boundaries between work and home life. While strategies might be rather straightforward with respect to physical and temporal boundaries, the situation is more difficult with respect to mental boundaries. Moreover, it might even be that although setting mental boundaries seems to be generally important, it might not be equally important for everyone. There might be persons who enjoy quickly switching mentally between various life domains and who embrace multi-tasking.

We would like to add that most probably it is not the mere fact of working that is detrimental to recovery. Empirical studies suggest that – at least under some circumstances – volunteer work can be an activity that helps to recover from one's paid job. Mojza, Sonnentag and Bornemann (2011) reported that spending time on volunteer activities was related to lower levels of negative affect at work during the following day. Moreover, Mojza and Sonnentag (2010) found that job stressors had a less negative impact on employee affect after employees had engaged in some volunteer work during the preceding evening. More research is needed that examines in greater detail when voluntary work helps to replenish resources – as opposed to further depleting them.

When it comes to practical implications the research reviewed in this chapter suggests that it is crucial that employees find ways to recover on a regular basis. For some people recovery from family-related duties might be even a more pressing issue than recovering from job-related stress. It is difficult to recommend specific activities because individual preferences probably differ largely. But it is relatively safe to say that exercise and other physical activities have positive benefits for most people. In addition, full detachment from work from time to time seems to be crucial. Although more research is needed that sheds light on how this detachment can be achieved, full engagement in another activity (that is pleasurable at the same time) seems to be a promising way to forget about work for a limited amount of time. In addition, setting boundaries, particularly when doing job-related tasks also when being at home, seems to be necessary to create time and space that allows for optimal recovery.

In an ideal world, it would be easy to get enough recovery on a daily basis – if any recovery was needed at all! In many peoples' realities, however, numerous everyday-life constraints make recovery difficult. We find it important that people take these constraints into account when planning recovery – not in order to compromise on recovery but in order to make the best out of the time available, also when the amount of time might be very small in some instances.

References

American Psychological Association (2010). *Stress in America: Findings*. Washington, DC: American Psychological Association.

Ashforth, B.E., Kreiner, G.E. and Fugate, M. (2000). All in a day's work: Boundaries and micro role transitions. *Academy of Management Review* 25, 472–491.

Bakker, A.B., van Emmerik, I.H., Geurts, S.A.E. and Demerouti, E. (2008). Recovery turns job demands into challenges: A diary study on work engagement and performance. *Working paper. Erasmus University Rotterdam.*

Binnewies, C., Sonnentag, S. and Mojza, E.J. (2009). Daily performance at work: Feeling recovered in the morning as a predictor of day-level job performance. *Journal of Organizational Behavior* 30, 67–93.

—— (2010). Recovery during the weekend and fluctuations in weekly job performance: A four-week longitudinal study examining intra-individual relationships. *Journal of Occupational and Organizational Psychology* 83, 419–441.

Boswell, W.R. and Olson-Buchanan, J.B. (2007). The use of communications technologies after hours: The role of work attitudes and work-life conflict. *Journal of Management* 33, 592–610.

Brosschot, J.F., Pieper, S. and Thayer, J.F. (2005). Expanding stress theory: Prolonged activitation and perseverative cognition. *Psychoneuroendocrinology* 30, 1043–1049.

Brown, K.W. and Ryan, R.M. (2003). The benefits of being present: Mindfulness and its role in psychological well-being. *Journal of Personality and Social Psychology* 84, 822–848.

Butler, A.B. (2007). Job characteristics and college performance and attitudes: A model of work-school conflict and facilitation. *Journal of Applied Psychology* 92, 500–510.

Carver, C.S., Scheier, M.F. and Weintraub, J.K. (1989). Assessing coping strategies: A theoretically based approach. *Journal of Personality and Social Psychology* 56, 267–283.

Craig, A. and Cooper, R.E. (1992). Symptoms of acute and chronic fatigue. In A. P. Smith and D. M. Jones (eds) *Handbook of human performance* (Vol. 3, 289–339). London: Academic Press.

Cropley, M. and Millward-Purvis, L.J. (2003). Job strain and rumination about work issues during leisure time: A diary study. *European Journal of Work and Organizational Psychology* 12, 195–207.

Cropley, M., Dijk, D.J. and Stanley, N. (2006). Job strain, work rumination and sleep in school teachers. *European Journal of Work and Organizational Psychology* 15, 181–196.

Davidson, O.B., Eden, D., Westman, M., Cohen-Charash, Y., Hammer, L.B., Kluger, A.N., Krausz, M., Maslach, C., O'Driscoll, M., Perrewé, P. L., Quick, J. C., Rosenblatt, Z., & Spector, P.E. (2010). Sabbatical leave: Who gains and how much? *Journal of Applied Psychology* 95, 953–964.

Demerouti, E., Bakker, A.B., Sonnentag, S. and Fullagar, C. J. (2012). Work-related flow and energy at work and at home: A study on the role of daily recovery. *Journal of Organizational Behavior, 33*, 276–295.

Eng, W., Moore, S., Grunberg, L., Greenberg, E. and Sikora, P. (2010). What influences work-family conflict? The function of work support and working from home. *Current Psychology: Research & Reviews* 29, 104–120.

Fender, C.M. (2011). Electronic tethering: The impact of after-hours connectivity on work-to-family conflict and strain. *Paper presented at the Meeting of the Academy of Management, San Antonio TX, August 2011.*

Fenner, G.H. and Renn, R.W. (2010). Technology-assisted supplemental work and work-to-family conflict: The role of instrumentality beliefs, organizational expectations and time management. *Human Relations* 63, 63–82.

Fritz, C., Lam, C.F. and Spreitzer, G.M. (2011). It's the little things that matter: An examination of knowledge workers' energy management. *Academy of Management Perspectives.*

Fritz, C., Yankelevich, M., Zarubin, A. and Barger, P. (2010). Happy, healthy and productive: The role of detachment from work during nonwork time. *Journal of Applied Psychology* 95, 977–983.

Glavin, P., Schieman, S. and Reid, S. (2011). Boundary-spanning work demands and their consequences for guilt and psychological distress. *Journal of Health and Social Behavior* 52, 43–57.

Greenhaus, J.H. and Beutell, N.J. (1985). Sources of conflict between work and family roles. *Academy of Management Review* 10, 76–88.

Grzywacz, J.G., Almeida, D.M. and McDonald, D.A. (2002). Work-family spillover and daily reports of work and family stress in the adult labor force. *Family Relations* 51, 28–36.

Hartig, T., Johansson, G. and Kylin, C. (2007). The telework tradeoff: Stress mitigation vs. constrained restoration. *Applied Psychology: An International Review, 231–253.*

Hill, E. J., Hawkins, A.J. and Miller, B.C. (1996). Work and family in the virtual office: perceived influences of mobile telework. *Family relations* 45, 293–301.

Katz, D. and Kahn, R.L. (1978). *The social psychology of organizations* (2nd ed.). New York: Wiley.

Klumb, P., Hoppmann, C. and Staats, M. (2006). Work hours affect spouse's cortisol secretion. For better and for worse. *Psychosomatic Medicine* 68, 742–746.

Krajewski, J., Wieland, R. and Sauerland, M. (2010). Regulating strain states by using the recovery potential of lunch breaks. *Journal of Occupational Health Psychology* 15, 131–139.

Kühnel, J., Sonnentag, S. and Bledow, R. (2012). Resources and time pressure as day-level antecedents of work engagement. *Journal of Occupational and Organizational Psychology, 85,* 181–198.

Lundberg, U. and Frankenhaeuser, M. (1999). Stress and workload of men and women in high-ranking positions. *Journal of Occupational Health Psychology* 4, 142–151.

Maertz, C.P. and Boyar, S.L. (2011). Work-family conflict, enrichment, and balance under "levels" and "episodes" approaches. *Journal of Management* 37, 68–98.

Matthews, R.A. and Barnes-Farrell, J.L. (2010). Development and initial evaluation of an enhanced measure of boundary flexibility for the work and family domains. *Journal of Occupational Health Psychology* 15, 330–346.

Meijman, T.F. and Mulder, G. (1998). Psychological aspects of workload. In J. D. Drenth and H. Thierry (eds) *Handbook of work and organizational psychology, Vol. 2: Work psychology* (5–33). Hove, England: Psychology Press.

Mojza, E.J. and Sonnentag, S. (2010). Does volunteer work during leisure time buffer negative effects of job stressors? A diary study. *European Journal of Work and Organizational Psychology* 19, 231–252.

Mojza, E.J., Sonnentag, S. and Bornemann, C. (2011). Volunteer work as a valuable leisure time activity: A day-level study on volunteer work, non-work experiences, and well-being at work. *Journal of Occupational and Organizational Psychology* 84, 123–152.

Nippert, E.C. (1996). Calandars and keys: The classification of "home" and "work". *Sociological Forum* 11, 563–582.

Olson-Buchanan, J.B. and Boswell, W.R. (2006). Blurring boundaries: Correlates of integration and segmentation between work and nonwork. *Journal of Vocational Behavior* 68, 432–445.

Park, Y.A. and Jex, S.M. (2011). Work-home boundary management using communication and information technology. *International Journal of Stress Management* 18, 133–152.

Park, Y.A., Fritz, C. and Jex, S.M. (2011). Relationships between work-home segmentaiton and psychological detachment from work: The role of communication technology use at home. *Journal of Occupational Health Psychology* 16, 457–467.

Ragsdale, J.M., Beehr, T.A., Grebner, S. and Han, K. (2011). An integrated model of weekday stress and weekend recovery of students. *International Journal of Stress Management* 18, 153–180.

Reed, J. and Ones, D.S. (2006). The affect of acute aerobic exercise on positive activated affect: A meta-analysis. *Psychology of Sport and Exercise* 7, 477–514.

Rook, J.W. and Zijlstra, F.R.H. (2006). The contribution of various types of activities to recovery. *European Journal of Work and Organizational Psychology* 15, 218–240.

Rothbard, N.P., Philips, K.W. and Dumas, T.L. (2005). Managing multiple roles: Work-family policies and individuals' desires for segmentation. *Organization Science* 16, 243–258.

Rydstedt, L.W., Cropley, M. and Devereux, J. (2011). Long-term impact of role stress and cognitive rumination upon morning and evening saliva cortisol excretion. *Ergonomics* 54, 430–435.

Rydstedt, L.W., Cropley, M., Devereux, J.J. and Michalianou, G. (2009). The effects of gender, long-term need for recovery and trait inhibition-rumination on morning and evening saliva cortisol secretion. *Anxiety, Stress, and Coping* 22, 465–474.

Sanz-Vergel, A I., Demerouti, E., Bakker, A.B. and Moreno-Jiménez, B. (2011). Daily detachment from work and home: The moderating effect of role salience. *Human Relations* 64, 775–799.

Sanz-Vergel, A.I., Sebastián, J., Rodrígez-Munoz, A., Garrosa, E., Moreno-Jiménez, B. and Sonnentag, S. (2010). Adaptación del "Cuestionario de Experiencias de Recuperación" a una muestra espanola. *Psicothema* 22, 990–996.

Saxbe, D.E., Repetti, R.L. and Graesch, A. (2011). Time spent in housework and leisure: Links with parents' physiological recovery from work. *Journal of Family Psychology* 25, 271–281.

Sayer, L.C. (2007). More work for mothers? Trends and gender differences in multitasking. In T. van der Lippe and Peters (eds) *Time competition: disturbed balances and new options in work and care*: Edward Elgar.

Schieman, S., Milkie, M.A. and Glavin, P. (2009). When work interferes with life: work-nonwork interference and the influence of work-related demands and resources. *American Sociological Review* 74, 966–988.

Siltaloppi, M., Kinnunen, U. and Feldt, T. (2009). Recovery experiences as moderators between psychological work characteristics and occupational well-being. *Work & Stress* 23, 330–348.

Slatcher, R.B., Robles, T.F., Repetti, R.L. and Fellows, M.D. (2012). Momentary work worries, marital disclosure, and salivary cortisol among parents of young children. *Psychosomatic Medicine*, 72, 887–896.

Sonnentag, S. (2001). Work, recovery activities, and individual well-being: A diary study. *Journal of Occupational Health Psychology* 6, 196–210.

Sonnentag, S. (2003). Recovery, work engagement, and proactive behavior: A new look at the interface between non-work and work. *Journal of Applied Psychology* 88, 518–528.

Sonnentag, S. and Bayer, U.V. (2005). Switching off mentally: Predictors and consequences of psychological detachment from work during off-job time. *Journal of Occupational Health Psychology* 10, 393–414.

Sonnentag, S. and Fritz, C. (2007). The Recovery Experience Questionnaire: Development and validation of a measure assessing recuperation and unwinding from work. *Journal of Occupational Health Psychology* 12, 204–221.

Sonnentag, S. and Geurts, S.A.E. (2009). Methodological issues in recovery research. In S. Sonnentag, L. Perrewé and D.C. Ganster (eds) *Current perspectives on job-stress recovery. Research in occupatinal stress and well-being* (1–36). Emerald.

Sonnentag, S. and Natter, E. (2004). Flight attendants' daily recovery from work: Is there no place like home? *International Journal of Stress Management* 11, 366–391.

Sonnentag, S. and Niessen, C. (2008). Staying vigorous until work is over: The role of trait vigor, day-specific work experiences and recovery. *Journal of Occupational and Organizational Psychology* 81, 435–458.

Sonnentag, S. and Zijlstra, F.R.H. (2006). Job characteristics and off-job activities as predictors of need for recovery, well-being, and fatigue. *Journal of Applied Psychology* 91, 330–350.

Sonnentag, S., Binnewies, C. and Mojza, E.J. (2008). "Did you have a nice evening?" A day-level study on recovery experiences, sleep, and affect. *Journal of Applied Psychology* 93, 674–684.

—— (2010). Staying well and engaged when demands are high: The role of psychological detachment. *Journal of Applied Psychology* 95, 965–976.

Sonnentag, S., Kuttler, I. and Fritz, C. (2010). Job stressors, emotional exhaustion, and need for recovery: A multi-source study on the benefits of psychological detachment. *Journal of Vocational Behavior* 76, 355–365.

Sonnentag, S., Mojza, E.J., Binnewies, C. and Scholl, A. (2008). Being engaged at work and detached at home: A week-level study on work engagement, psychological detachment, and affect. *Work & Stress* 22, 257–276.

Towers, I., Duxbury, L., Higgins, C. and Thomas, J. (2006). Time thieves and space invaders: technology, work and the organization. *Journal of Organizational Change Management* 19, 593–618.

Trougakos, J.P., Hideg, I. and Cheng, B.H. (2011). Lunch breaks unpacked: The effect of daily lunch break activities and control over break on Fatigue. *Paper presented at the Meeting of the Academy of Management, San Antonio TX, August 2011.*

Trougakos, J.P., Beal, D.J., Green, S.G. and Weiss, H.M. (2008). Making the break count: An episodic examination of recovery activities, emotional experiences, and positive affective displays. *Academy of Management Journal* 51, 131–146.

van Hooff, M.L.M., Geurts, S.A.E., Beckers, D.G.J. and Kompier, M.A.J. (2011). Daily recovery from work: The role of activities, effort and pleasure. *Work & Stress* 25, 55–74.

von Thiele Schwarz, U. (2011). Inability to withdraw from work as related to poor next-day recovery and fatigue among women. *Applied Psychology: An International Review* 60, 377–396.

Voydanoff, (2005). Consequences of boundary-spanning demands and resources for work-to-family conflict an perceived stress. *Journal of Occupational Health Psychology* 10, 491–503.

Westman, M. and Eden, D. (1997). Effects of a respite from work on burnout: Vacation relief and fade-out. *Journal of Applied Psychology* 82, 516–527.

Zacher, H., Jimmieson, N.L. and Winter, G. (2012). Eldercare demands, mental health, and work performance: The moderating role of satisfaction with eldercare tasks. *Journal of Occupational Health Psychology, 17*, 52–64.

6   Consequences of combining work and family roles

A closer look at cross-domain versus within-domain relations

Maria C.W. Peeters, Lieke L. ten Brummelhuis and Elianne F. van Steenbergen

Introduction

Research on the work–family interface seems to pile up in pace with the ever increasing number of employees combining work and family roles. Two major developments in the work–family literature can be distinguished. First, over the past few decades, the focus in the literature has shifted from perceiving the combination of work and family roles as mainly problematic, resulting in conflict (Greenhaus and Beutell, 1985) to perceiving the combination of work and family roles also as possibly enriching (Greenhaus and Powell, 2006: Rothbard, 2001; Wayne *et al.*, 2007), hereby reflecting more adequately how work and family life may influence each other. Second, whereas early research assessed work–family conflict as a general concept, scholars now broadly agree that both conflict and enrichment are bi-directional in nature. That is, individuals can experience that their work conflicts with family life, and vice versa, that their family life conflicts with work (Gutek, Searle and Klepa, 1991). In the same vein, it can be experienced that work enriches family life, and that family life enriches work (Greenhaus and Powell, 2006). With regard to conflict, ample empirical evidence is supporting the notion that work-to-family conflict and family-to-work conflict are distinct experiences that each have their own causes in different domains. For instance, Mesmar-Magnus and Viswesveran (2005) performed a meta-analytic examination of the convergence of work-to-family and family-to-work conflict and concluded that – despite some overlap – the two concepts indeed are statistically distinct and have correlates in respectively the work and the family domain. With regard to enrichment, Carlson *et al.* (2006) developed and validated a questionnaire to measure both work-to-family enrichment and family-to-work enrichment. On the basis of their validation study in five different samples they concluded that enrichment is bi-directional too. Thus, both family-to-work and work-to-family conflict and enrichment are distinct processes as they seem to have their *causes* in different domains. However, it has to be noted that the above conclusions are mainly derived from cross-sectional studies indicating that reversed or reciprocal causal relationships cannot be ruled out.

The present chapter deals with the *consequences* of individuals' experiences of work–family and family–work conflict and enrichment. A thorough insight in the consequences is relevant for both theoretical and practical reasons. Let us first explain the theoretical relevance. As the current literature on consequences of the work–family interface is mainly characterized by cross-sectional studies, there still exists little knowledge about the causal relationships between experiences of conflict and enrichment on the one hand and their consequences on the other. For instance, does family-to-work conflict lead to decreased performance at work or is the other way around more plausible, namely that underperformers at work experience to a higher degree that their family life interferes with their work? Additionally, most studies do not make clear predictions about the domain in which they expect the outcomes of work-to-family and family-to-work conflict and enrichment. For instance, Allen *et al.* (2000) conclude on the basis of a systematic review of the literature that work-to-family conflict is associated with job, family and life attitudes, work behaviors and a variety of stress-related variables. In the present chapter, we argue that, if we are aiming for one overarching theoretical model about consequences of work–family interaction, it is critical to bring more clarity into the causal nature of conflict and enrichment experiences and to specify which changes are brought about in work and family outcomes. The latter purpose was also one of the aims of a very recent analysis of Amstad *et al.* (2011). They conducted a meta-analysis on the consequences of work-to-family conflict and family-to-work conflict with a special emphasis on cross-domain versus within-domain (or matching relationships as they label it) relationships. The results showed that work-to-family conflict and family-to-work conflict are consistently related to work-related, family-related and domain-unspecific outcomes. Both types of conflict showed stronger relationships to within-domain outcomes than to cross-domain outcomes. Thus, work-to-family conflict was more strongly associated with work-related than with family-related outcomes, and family-to-work conflict was more strongly associated with family-related than with work-related outcomes. These results strongly support our argument that it is important to take a closer look at cross-domain and within-domain relationships between work–family conflict and enrichment and their consequences. In this respect we theoretically challenge the traditional notion assuming that each direction of conflict and enrichment (from work to family and from family to work) is related to outcomes in the domain *receiving* the conflict or enrichment (so-called cross-domain relations). In this traditional view, the outcomes of work-to-family spillover are assumed to reside in the family domain only, whereas the outcomes of family-to-work are assumed to uniquely reside in the work domain (Ford, Heinen and Langkamer, 2007; Frone, Yardley and Markel, 1997). We will argue on the basis of the social exchange theory (Blau, 1964) that it is plausible that both domains will be (dis)advantaged when an employee experiences conflict or enrichment between the work and family role. Furthermore, in order to test our theoretical assumptions empirically, we will provide a selective overview of *longitudinal* studies on the consequences of work–family conflict and enrichment, hereby making a distinction between work related outcomes (e.g. task performance), non-work related outcomes (e.g. marital satisfaction) and health-related outcomes (e.g. exhaustion).

Insight in the consequences of work–family spillover is also highly relevant from a practical perspective. For instance, when employers seek to improve employee well-being, or when employees seek to improve family outcomes, it is important to know on what issues they should focus. Do work-to-family conflict and enrichment experiences only have consequences for the family domain or can outcomes in the work domain also be expected? Similarly, do individuals' experiences of family-to-work conflict or enrichment only influence their work outcomes? And what about health related outcomes? Are they specifically related to either one of the processes or can they be expected for both family-to-work as well as work-to-family processes. To sum up: we argue that work–family research will benefit from a more in-depth theoretical and empirical analysis of the potential consequences of combining work and family roles. In this chapter we will provide such an analysis by carefully considering the impact of work–family processes on work, non-work and health-related outcomes. Below, we first provide a brief overview of two theoretical approaches that have been leading in the work–family research field, the conflict and enrichment approach. Next, we build on social exchange theory to challenge the traditional assumptions that consequences of work-to-family processes occur only in the family domain and that consequences of family-to-work processes occur only in the work domain. Then, a literature overview of longitudinal studies follows. The chapter closes by drawing conclusions and providing future directions for work–family research.

Consequences of work–family conflict and enrichment from a theoretical perspective

The traditional view: cross domain consequences

Originally, the relationship between work and family was explained by the *scarcity theory on human energy* (Greenhaus and Beutell, 1985; Goode, 1960), which depicts role combination as a zero-sum game in which devoting attention to one role necessarily depletes the resources available to devote to other roles, assuming that time and energy are limited resources (Goode, 1960; Marks, 1977; Parasuraman and Greenhaus, 2002). In this tradition, many studies have examined processes of negative spillover. The term negative spillover describes the intra-individual process in which stress and strain from one life domain are transferred into another life domain, thus contributing to lowered satisfaction with and performance in that other domain (Bakker *et al.*, 2008; Rogers and May, 2003). Frone and colleagues (1992a) proposed a widely followed model to capture this process of negative spillover. In this model, stressors and demands within one role (e.g. work) create conflict with other roles (e.g. work-to-family conflict), which in turn reduces satisfaction with those latter roles (e.g. family roles). There is ample evidence in the literature showing that stressors and demands at work relate to enhanced work-to-family conflict (Byron, 2005), and that work-to-family conflict relates to decreased levels of marital and family satisfaction in individuals (Allen *et al.*, 2000). Moreover, consistent with Frone's model (1992a), a more recent meta-analysis which summarized 28 studies and over 7,000 individuals, showed that job-related stressors were related to decreased family satisfaction and that this association was indeed mediated by experienced WF conflict (Ford *et al.*, 2007).

The enrichment approach on the other hand stems from a positive perspective endorsed in the role accumulation theory (Sieber, 1974), the expansion approach (Marks, 1977), and the work of Edwards and Rothbard (2000). According to these theoretical notions, participating in several roles allows individuals to gain and invest in personal, energy, and support resources, which can lead to growth and fulfillment, and which may compensate for the increased demands that might arise over time. The main assumption of the enrichment perspective is that participation in one domain can result in gains or resources (e.g. skills, fulfillment, self-esteem) that can be utilized in the other domain (Greenhaus and Powell, 2006; Grzywacz and Marks, 2000; Wayne *et al.*, 2007). Again, a clear distinction is made between the domain that causes the experience of enrichment and the domain where the consequences of enrichment reside. This implies that gains acquired in a sending domain lead to change in the receiving domain via the experience of enrichment.

To conclude, although up-to-date most empirical studies are cross-sectional in nature, many scholars indeed seem to state that for both work–family conflict and work–family enrichment, the process starts in the sending domain, leading to change in the receiving domain, via the experience of conflict or enrichment. In this chapter we will challenge this idea, both theoretically and empirically.

Challenging the traditional view: consequences in the sending domain

Although it may seem intuitively plausible that work-to-family conflict and enrichment only have consequences in the family domain while the family-to-work direction uniquely causes effects in the work domain, a critical note can be made. Insights from the Social Exchange theory (Blau, 1964; Cropanzano and Mitchell, 2005) might help to see why it is questionable that for example experienced work–family conflict (e.g. feeling too exhausted from work to make a good contribution at home) only leads to diminished family outcomes, and not to deteriorated work outcomes.

The central assumption of social exchange theory is that individuals reciprocate the benefits they receive. In a social exchange, actor A trusts that his or her input will be returned by actor B at some point in the future, without specifying the future obligation (Blau, 1964; van Knippenberg, van Dick and Tavares, 2007). Wayne *et al.* (2007) applied the insights of social exchange to the work–family interface by suggesting that employees make positive cognitive attributions regarding the source of enrichment and generate positive attitudes and affects to that domain. For instance, if an employee feels well treated by the organization's work–life balance support which enables work-to-family enrichment, he or she becomes more satisfied with and committed to this organization in return and is more likely to put in extra effort to perform well (Carlson *et al.*, 2011; Muse *et al.*,

2008; Ryan and Kossek, 2008). Similarly, if an individual receives a benefit from his or her family life, he or she is likely to ascribe more positive cognitions to his/her family life, and reciprocate the received benefit by investing in this domain or evaluating this domain positively. For instance, if an employee feels energized and likes to go to work again on Monday because (s)he had a very pleasant weekend with the family (family-to-work enrichment), the employee is likely to evaluate the family relationships positively whereby relationship satisfaction increases. These examples show how family-to-work enrichment and work-to-family enrichment can increase both work and family outcomes. Or, in other words, a resource provided by the "sending" domain, increases not only outcomes in the "receiving" domain, but also in the "sending" domain, because of positive cognitive contributions (within-domain relationships). A similar argument can be made for the conflict approach. If high demands in one domain impede performance in the other domain, it is likely that the individual develops a more negative attitude towards the domain that causes conflict.

Recapitalizing, on the basis of social exchange theory it can be argued that consequences of work–family interaction can both be found in the "sending" (within-domain relations) and the "receiving" domain (cross-domain relations). Figure 6.1 depicts this new perspective on the work–family interface. As can be seen in this figure we identify also health outcomes. Earlier research has convincingly shown that combining work and non-work roles can also have mental and/or physical health consequences (Allen *et al.*, 2000; Carlson *et al.*, 2011). Because health outcomes are not particularly related to either the work or non-work domain, we placed them in a separate box.

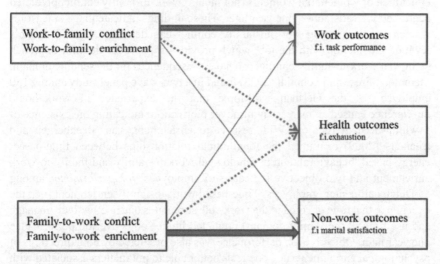

Figure 6.1 Integrative model of work–family consequences

Consequences of work–family conflict and enrichment from an empirical perspective

In this empirical part, we examine to what extent our theoretical assumptions hold empirically by presenting an overview of longitudinal studies that have considered the consequences of the conflict and/or enrichment in either directions (work-to-family or family-to-work) and in either a positive way (enrichment) or a negative way (conflict). We restrict our focus to longitudinal studies because cross-sectional studies inhibit us from drawing definitive conclusions about causality. As mentioned earlier we have categorized the outcomes of the work–family interface into three broad categories: (1) work related, (2) non-work related and (3) health related outcomes. In discussing the studies we specifically focus on the degree to which the studies provide empirical evidence for the 'traditional approach' (the cross-domain relations) and/or for the 'new approach' (the within-domain relations).

Work outcomes

To our knowledge, only four studies in the work–family literature have examined longitudinally how work–family experiences impact on work-related outcomes. Grandey, Cordeiro and Crouter (2005) examined among 201 working couples in the US whether family-to-work and work-to-family conflict experiences (as reported by the partner) predicted job satisfaction 1 year later (self-reports). In this study, family-to-work conflict did not longitudinally predict *job satisfaction* for either men or women, but women's (not men's) work-to-family conflict predicted decreased job satisfaction one year later. These findings indicate that – at least for women – experiencing work-to-family conflict can detrimentally affect one's level of satisfaction with the job, which provides support for the new approach being that work-to-family conflict can have consequences for the sending domain. Steinmetz, Frese and Schmidt (2008) found in a two-wave panel study among 130 employees of the German workforce that the experience of work–home interference caused an increase in turnover motivation, indicating the existence of a within-domain relation. With respect to enrichment, van Steenbergen and Ellemers (2009) examined the longitudinal relationships between time-based, energy-based, behavioral, and psychological work-to-family and family-to-work enrichment and two objective indicators of employees' *job performance* among 55 Dutch call-center employees. Time-based work-to-family enrichment (i.e., the experience that time devoted to the work-role stimulates one to effectively manage and use time in the family domain) predicted higher objective job performance one year later. Objective job performance was also predicted by both directions of psychological enrichment (i.e., one feels better able to put matters associated with one role into perspective by virtue of another role, which makes it easier to fulfill the requirements of the first role). Thus, increased job performance was predicted by work-to-family as well as family-to-work enrichment, which means that a positive outcome was observed in the receiving domain, but also in the so-called sending domain. Finally, in a recent 3-year cross-lagged panel study among 1632 Finnish dentists, Hakanen, Peeters and Perhoniemi (2011) found, for men and women, that work-to-family enrichment and *work engagement* reciprocally influenced each other over time. In this study, family-to-work enrichment did not predict work engagement. In sum, all four longitudinal studies falsify conventional thinking that only the family-to-work direction would predict work outcomes, as *work-to-family* conflict enrichment have been found to predict job satisfaction, job performance as well as employees' work engagement.

Non-work outcomes

Among the non-work related outcomes of combining work and family roles only marital satisfaction and parental stress were longitudinally examined. Of the four studies we detected, three studies focused on consequences of conflict between work and non-work and one study focused on consequences of enrichment between work and non-work. Leiter and Durup (1996) found in a study among 151 health care professionals that work-to-family conflict at time 1 was related to decreased *marital satisfaction* three month later. Family-to-work conflict was not longitudinally related to marital satisfaction. In a similar vein, O'Driscoll, Brough and Kalliath (2004) reported a significant negative impact of work-to-family conflict on *family satisfaction* (and not on job satisfaction) over a three month period. So, these studies seem to confirm the idea that the non-work related consequences of work–family conflict reside in the receiving domain. A study by Kinnunen, Geurts and Mauno (2004) revealed an interesting gender effect in this respect. They found that, among women, work-to-family conflict at Time 1 predicted *parental stress* one year later (and not marital satisfaction which was also included in the study), which again supports the idea that consequences will manifest predominantly in the receiving domain. Among men, a low level of marital satisfaction and a high level of parental stress functioned as precursors of work-to-family conflict a year later. Finally, up till now, a recent study by Hakanen *et al.* (2011) is the only study that longitudinally examined the consequences of the enriching linkage between work and family in relation to non-work consequences. In a 3-year cross-lagged panel study they found that family-to-work enrichment has a longitudinal effect in the originating domain, in this particular study *marital satisfaction*. In contrast, work-to-family enrichment was not related to marital satisfaction. In sum, all (but still few) studies examining the conflict approach longitudinally verify conventional thinking that family outcomes are best predicted by work-to-family conflict. The only study that focused on work–family enrichment revealed that marital satisfaction was best predicted by family-to-work enrichment hereby showing evidence for the new approach.

Health outcomes

As described earlier, in the work–family literature, both directions of conflict are assumed to relate to worsened scores on health outcomes whereas both directions of enrichment are assumed to relate to better scores on health (e.g. van Steenbergen and Ellemers, 2009, Allen *et al.* 2000). Our aim was to identify whether indeed both the work-to-family and family-to-work direction of conflict and enrichment prove to be important predictors, or whether either one of these directions is more important in predicting health related outcomes. We identified 13 studies that were designed to test the longitudinal relationships with health outcomes. Two of these studies examined the consequences of work–family experiences for employees' physical health and unhealthy behaviors, 10 studies examined the consequences for employees' mental health (i.e., emotional exhaustion or depression), and 1 study examined the consequences for mental as well as physical health.

In a sample of 58 call center employees, van Steenbergen and Ellemers (2009) examined whether time-based, energy-based, behavioral and psychological work-to-family and family-to-work enrichment longitudinally predicted employees' *cholesterol level* in the blood and their *Body Mass Index (BMI)* as assessed by medical assistants. Employees' time-based work-to-family enrichment (i.e., the time devoted to the work-role stimulates one to effectively manage and use the time in the family domain) predicted a lower, more healthy, BMI one year later and energy-based work-to-family enrichment (i.e., the feeling that work provides one with extra energy in the family domain) was a marginally significant predictor of a decreased cholesterol levels one year later. In addition, Frone, Russell and Cooper (1997) found in a 4-year follow up study that employees who experienced higher work-to-family conflict were more prone to *heavy alcohol consumption* 4 years later and that employees who experienced more family-to-work conflict were more likely to have developed *hypertension* (objectively assessed) and to rate their *physical health* as poorer.

In reviewing the studies that longitudinally examined the consequences for employees' mental health, one highly consistent empirical finding stands out: work-to-family conflict leads to *emotional exhaustion (burnout)*, which in turn predicts higher levels of work-to-family conflict, which indicates a "loss-spiral". Evidence for these reciprocal relationships between work-to-family conflict and emotional exhaustion over time was found across countries and in various occupational groups of employees. That is, except for two random samples of Finnish residents ($N = 365$, $N = 153$) in which no significant effects were found (Rantanen, Kinnunen and Pilkkinen, 2008), reciprocal relationships between work-to-family conflict and emotional exhaustion were found among 383 health care professionals in the Netherlands (Peeters *et al.*, 2004), among 335 employees of an employment agency in the Netherlands (Demerouti, Bakker and Bulters, 2004), in a sample of 257 Australian police officers (Hall *et al.*, 2010), among 151 female hospital workers in Canada (Leiter and Durup, 1996), and also in a sample of 2253 employees of different occupational groups in Norway (Innstrand *et al.*, 2008). Additionally, van Hooff and colleagues (2005) found these reciprocal relationships between strain-based work-to-family conflict and emotional exhaustion (not for time-based work-to-family conflict) in a sample of 730 police officers in the Netherlands. Notably, these results were obtained using different scales of work-to-family conflict and different longitudinal time intervals, namely

6 weeks (Demerouti *et al.*, 2004), 3 months (Leiter and Durup, 1996), 1 year (Peeters *et al.*, 2004; Hall *et al.*, 2005; van Hoof *et al.*, 2005), or 2 years (Innstrand *et al.*, 2008), which signifies the robustness of this finding. In addition to the effects on emotional exhaustion, van Hooff and colleagues (2005) also found in their sample of Dutch police officers that higher strain-based work-to-family conflict was related to more *depressive symptoms* one year later. Time-based conflict did not prove to predict depression (van Hoof *et al.*, 2005). Grant-Vallone and Donaldson (2001) demonstrated convincingly in a study among 342 non-professional employees that work–family conflict predicted employee well-being 6 months later, over and above social desirability bias. In addition, analyses were consistent when both self-reports and co-workers reports of employee well-being were used. Moreover, using a sample of 234 working couples in the United States, Hammer *et al.* (2005) examined whether conflict and enrichment (in both directions) were related to husbands' and wives own levels of depression one year later as well as their partners' depression (crossover). Interestingly, in this study, conflict and enrichment experiences did not predict one's own level of depression, but positive crossover effects to the other partner were found. Specifically, husbands' work-to-family enrichment predicted decreased depression in their wives one year later, and wives' family-to-work enrichment predicted decreased depression in their husbands one year later. Finally, in an interesting study among 179 American mothers who returned to their fulltime job after childbirth, Carlson and colleagues (2011) found that women's work-to-family enrichment (assessed at 4 months after childbirth) predicted better self-reported *physical health* 8 months after childbirth. Additionally, their reports of work-to-family conflict (at 4 months after childbirth) detrimentally predicted their *physical health* as well as *their mental health* (self-reports) 8 months after childbirth.

In sum, there is quite some longitudinal evidence supporting that work-to-family conflict leads to diminished health outcomes. In particular the effects on emotional exhaustion are well established. Moreover, emotional exhaustion in turn appeared to predict higher levels of work-to-family conflict, which is indicative of a "loss-spiral". Evidence for these reciprocal relationships between work-to-family conflict and emotional exhaustion over time was found across countries and in various occupational groups of employees. In contrast, there are only two studies in the literature that reported a significant longitudinal relationship between family-to-work conflict and health outcomes (Frone *et al.*, 1997; Hammer *et al.*, 2005). Although we couldn't identify many studies that examined the impact of employees' enrichment experiences on their health, the studies we did find show that both directions of enrichment predicted health outcomes. In total, this overview indicates that both directions of work–family conflict and enrichment significantly affect health outcomes.

Conclusions and directions for future research

The traditional assumption in work–family research is that work-to-family conflict and enrichment have consequences for the family domain, whereas family-to-work conflict and enrichment impact upon the work domain: the so-called cross-domain relations (Frone *et al.*, 1992a; Ford *et al.*, 2007). The purpose of this chapter was to challenge this traditional assumption. Based on the social exchange theory we argued that both directions of work–family conflict and enrichment can have consequences in both domains, the "sending" as well as the "receiving" domain. In line with Wayne *et al.* (2007), we reasoned that employees make cognitive attributions regarding the source of enrichment or conflict and generate positive or negative attitudes and feelings to that domain. For instance, when an employee feels that the work role builds his or her self- esteem and contributes to skills that benefit family life (work-to-family enrichment), he or she is likely to feel more satisfied with the work role and more motivated to work harder and perform well at work. We 'tested' both hypotheses against each other by reviewing empirical studies that took into account the causal direction of work–family relationships. In this section, we will for each dimension of the work–family interface, discuss in which domain(s) the consequences were mostly found. Next, we will draw some preliminary conclusions that give further direction to theory development in this area.

With respect to work-to-family conflict and enrichment this overview shows that when employees feel their work negatively interferes with their family lives *(work-to-family conflict)*, both the family domain as well as the work domain are likely to suffer and also employees' mental and physical health seem to get worse. So, in line with our predictions, consequences of work-to-family conflict can both be found in the sending and in the receiving domain and also health consequences of work-to-family conflict are to be expected. Surprisingly, when employees experience that their work is enriching their family life this has positive consequences for the work domain but not for the family domain. Apparently, when work for example enables an employee to develop skills that are also useful when managing household tasks (work-to-family enrichment), this will foster positive feelings and attitudes towards work. This finding falsifies the old approach and supports the new approach indicating that the positive consequences of work-to-family enrichment can also bounce back to the sending domain. In addition, employees' health (healthier BMI and decreased cholesterol level) will benefit from work-to-family enrichment.

With regard to the effects of experienced family-to-work conflict and enrichment, the results were less pronounced. Strikingly, when employees experience conflict from family to work *(family-to-work conflict)* it seems that only employees' health suffers. However, caution is in order regarding this latter conclusion because longitudinal research on this relationship is still scarce. More longitudinal studies are badly needed to examine the effect of family-to-work conflict on work outcomes as we could only identify one such study. Finally, *family-to-work enrichment* was both beneficial for the work domain as well as for the non-work domain. Again, this finding provides support for our prediction that family-to-work enrichment affects both the sending and the receiving domain.

Our overview gives rise to a few methodological conclusions. First, the number of longitudinal studies that we detected was very small. This is especially surprising because the work–family field is a very active and fast growing area of research. Second, the majority of studies focused on (mental) health related outcomes of work–family spillover, whereas only a few studies aimed at work-related consequences. The studies that included non-work related outcomes were most scarce and focused without exception on family outcomes, thus ignoring that combining multiple roles can also impact on how we evaluate our social lives, leisure time, possibilities for volunteer work or the degree to which combining roles leaves time for 'the self'. This lack of variety in possible consequences (especially non-work consequences) of combining multiple roles, provides new opportunities for future research. One could also argue that it is not surprising that health effects are most frequently reported, because these effects tend to be the strongest. Hence, it cannot be ruled out that work outcomes and non-work outcomes did not show significant relationships with work-to-family experiences and that researchers therefore decided not to report about these non-relationships. This so-called publication bias is undesirable as it obviously hampers the theoretical progression of this research area. Another remarkable issue was that most studies examined the consequences of work-to-family conflict or enrichment. The family-to-work direction was far less examined. As it is well-documented that work-to-family conflict is the most prevalent dimension of the work–family interaction (cf. Frone, Russell and Cooper, 1992b), publication bias can, also in this case, not be ruled out.

All in all, these observations emphasize the need for more longitudinal studies focusing on both directions of the work–family interface and on other non-work outcomes than family satisfaction. Such research will enable us to disentangle the intriguing connection between work and non-work life. Diary methods (Bolger, Davis and Rafaeli, 2003) can also be of great help in this respect. Diary studies enable researchers to depict within-person daily fluctuations in work–family conflict, work–family enrichment, and outcomes in both domains. Insight in these processes can provide insight in the changeability of these processes. For instance, to what extent can daily events in the work or non-work domain influence how one functions in either of the two domains? In addition, research that uses data that are collected from relevant others (e.g. partners and supervisors) is also very important in this respect. For instance, partner's reports of conflict and enrichment adds to our knowledge about the degree of subjectivity of the work–family interface. In the same vein, supervisor ratings of work performance add to the knowledge of the relationships between work–family spillover and both process and outcome performance. Finally, couple research can illuminate to what extent combining multiple roles has consequences for the spouses and/or children of the employee hereby shedding more light on crossover processes. In sum, we conclude in line with the review of Casper *et al.* (2007) that scholars publishing about the work–family interface could make greater use of longitudinal research designs, gather more multisource data, and include more concepts that capture the non-work domain.

Future directions

Both the theoretical expose as well as the overview of longitudinal studies has led to the conclusion that consequences of combining work and family roles can be found at work, in one's private life and in one's health. A next aim is now to unravel conditions that can predict in which domain(s) the consequences of work–family interference will occur. In other words: what determines which domain(s) is (are) affected by conflict and enrichment experiences between work and family? In order to find an answer to this question, it seems fruitful to take moderators into account. In this respect the social role-hypothesis might prove to be helpful. It can give direction to the question where the consequences of conflict and enrichment can be found. According to the social-role hypothesis, individuals differ in the value they attach to work and family roles (Voydanoff, 2002). This is also known as role salience, indicating the value, importance and commitment of an individual to a role (Cinamon and Rich, 2002; Pleck, 1977). The idea is that, if employees participate in two roles, they will find the role that is least important to them interfering with the domain that is important to them (Carlson and Kacmar, 2000; Ten Brummelhuis, van der Lippe, Kluwer and Flap, 2008). Extending this idea, it is arguable that individuals will try to prevent harmful effects on the domain that is most important to them. For example, when experiencing work-to-family conflict due to a high workload, employees who attach great value to their family-role might try harder to reduce any harmful consequences for their family lives. Role salience may also clarify in which domain additional resources are invested when employees experience work–family enrichment (Lobel and St. Clair, 1992; Wayne, Randel and Stevens, 2006). The domain to which the employee attaches greatest value is likely to benefit from enrichment, either directly, or via a feedback loop. Imagine, for example, an employee with high work-role salience who just got a work promotion. The promotion gives him or her energy and a good mood, which contributes to the atmosphere at home (work-to-family enrichment). At the same time, it is likely that the gained resources further motivate this employee to invest in work, as (s)he finds this domain most important. This may be expressed by showing up early at work on the next day, or helping colleagues. In conclusion, it is very plausible that role salience can predict to some extent in which domain consequences of combing work and non-work roles can be expected. It is a promising avenue for future research to illuminate more specifically how this process works. For instance, does work–family enrichment lead to more positive work outcomes for individuals with high family-role salience because they attribute the positive consequences to their work and in order to reciprocate they are motivated to work harder or like their work even more? Or does it work the other way around, that individuals with high family-role salience will invest the resources that are gained by work–family enrichment immediately in the family domain because this domain is more important to them?

Another suggestion for future research is to investigate the relative importance of enrichment versus conflict experiences in predicting consequences. Although it is evident that the work domain can create feelings of work-to-family enrichment as well as work-to-family conflict, and that these experiences can co-occur, it is still unknown whether or in what circumstances one of the two processes happens more frequently, or whether one process outweighs the other. For instance, a manager who has high job autonomy as well as a high workload can feel energized after a days work (work-to-family enrichment), but at the same time she may experience that there isn't enough time left to engage with the children (work-to-family conflict). In a similar vein, family life can include demanding aspects such as care for children or sleep deprivation which consume energy. However, support from the spouse, or quality time spent with family members, may counterbalance this drain in energy (Ten Brummelhuis, van der Lippe and Kluwer, 2010). It would be interesting to examine which process is decisive in its effect on work and family outcomes.

In addition, we want to put forward an alternative view that may simplify work–family research. The finding that the different work–family concepts do not clearly show an integrated picture may be an indication that a distinction in work-to-family and family-to-work processes does not help us gaining a better understanding of the work–family interface. Instead, it is possible that employees have a more integral perception of how they combine roles, whereby they simply consider whether they find a misfit or a balance between those roles (Clark, 2000; Frone, 2003). According to Frone (2003) balance occurs when an individual experiences low levels of interrole conflict in combination with high levels of interrole enrichment. So, Frone considers work–life balance primarily as the absence of conflict between the work and life domains. In contrast to this more traditional definition of work–life balance, newer conceptualizations have emerged. As a representative example of this, we present Voydanoff's (2005) definition that balance serves as "a global assessment that work resources meet family demands, and family resources meet work demands such that participation is effective in both domains" (825). Grywacz and Carlson (2007) expand this definition by stating that work–life balance is "the accomplishment of role-related expectations that are negotiated and shared between and individual and his or her role-related partners in work and family domains" (458). Clearly, the concept of work–life balance means different things to different people. Future research could scrutinize on the suitability of this concept for the study on consequences of combining work and non-work roles. It is plausible that in case of balance, employees will experience more positive outcomes, including work, non-work and health outcomes. Imbalance, by contrast, is then likely to go together with impaired outcomes in several life domains and in health. Thus, the concept of work–life balance or work–life harmony (McMillan, Morris and Atchley, 2011) may be a promising new avenue for work–family research. Moreover, if we want to contribute to closing the gap between theory and practice we should aim for simplicity whenever this is possible. Hence, HR interventions to build on work–life balance cannot be created, and culture changes cannot be facilitated, until organizations understand the nature and consequences of employees' work–life interface.

All in all, in order to fully grasp the cross-domain and within-domain consequences of conflicting and enriching relationships between work and family, a lot of work still needs to be done The integrative model of work–family consequences that we proposed may be a possible way to go. We hope that our analysis inspires others to further study the consequences of combining work and non-work roles in an innovative way and from a causal perspective.

References

Amstad, F.T., Meier, L.L., Fasel, U., Elfering, J. and Semmer, N.K. (2011). A Meta-Analysis of Work-family Conflict and Various Outcomes With a Special Emphasis on Cross-Domain Versus Matching-Domain Relations. *Journal of Occupational Health Psychology* 16, 151–169.

Allen, T.D., Herst, D.E., Bruck, C.S. and Sutton, M. (2000). Consequences associated with work to family conflict: A review and agenda for future research. *Journal of Occupational Health Psychology* 5, 278–308.

Bakker, A.B., Demerouti, E. and Dollard, M.F. (2008). How job demands affect partners' experience of exhaustion: Integrating work-family conflict and crossover theory. *Journal of Applied Psychology* 93, 901–911.

Blau, P.M. (1964). *Exchange and power in social life*. New York: Wiley.

Bolger, N., Davis, A. and Rafaeli, E. (2003). Diary methods: Capturing life as it is lived. *Annual Review of Psychology* 54, 579–616.

Byron, K. (2005). A meta-analytic review of work-family conflict and its antecedents. *Journal of Vocational Behavior* 67, 169–198.

Carlson, D.S. and Kacmar, K.M. (2000). Work-family conflict in the organization: Do life role values make a difference? *Journal of Management* 26, 1031–1054.

Carlson, D.S., Kacmar, K.M., Wayne, J.H. and Grzywacz, J.G. (2006). Measuring the positive side of the work-family interface: Development and validation of a work-family enrichment scale. *Journal of Vocational Behavior* 68, 131–164.

Carlson, D.S., Grzywacz, J.G., Ferguson, M., Hunter, E.M., Clinch, C.R. and Arcury, T.A. (2011). Health and turnover of working mothers after childbirth via the work-family interface: An analysis across time. *Journal of Applied Psychology* 96, 1045–1054.

Casper, W.J., Eby, L.T., Bordeaux, C., Lockwood, A. and Lambert, D. (2007). A review of research methods in IO/OB work-family research. *Journal of Applied Psychology* 92, 28–43.

Clark, S.C. (2000). Work/family border theory: a new theory of work/family balance. *Human Relations* 53, 747–770.

Cinamon, R.G. and Rich, Y. (2002). Gender differences in the importance of work and family roles: implications for work-family conflict. *Sex Roles* 47, 531–541.

Cropanzano, R. and Mitchell, M.S. (2005). Social exchange theory: An interdisciplinary review. *Journal of Management* 31, 874–900.

Demerouti, E., Bakker, A.B. and Bulters, A.J. (2004). The loss spiral of work pressure, work-home interference and exhaustion: Reciprocal relations in a three-wave study. *Journal of Vocational Behavior* 64, 131–149.

Edwards, J.R. and Rothbard, N.P. (2000). Mechanisms linking work and family: Clarifying the relationsip between work and family constructs. *Academy of Management Review* 25: 178–199.

Ford, M.T., Heinen, B.A. and Langkamer, K.L. (2007). Work and family satisfaction and conflict: A meta-analysis of cross-domain relations. *Journal of Applied Psychology* 92, 57–80.

Frone, M.R. (2003). Work-family balance. In J.C. Quick and L.E. Tetrick (eds) *Handbook of occupational health psychology* (143–162). Washington, DC: American Psychological Association.

Frone, M.R., Russell, M. and Cooper, M.L. (1992a). Antecedents and outcomes of work-family conflict: Testing a model of the work-family interface. *Journal of Applied Psychology* 77, 65–78.

—— (1992b). Prevalence of work-family conflict: Are work and family boundaries asymmetrically permeable? *Journal of Organizational Behavior* 13, 723–729.

—— (1997). Relation of work-family conflict to health outcomes: A four-year longitudinal study of employed parents. *Journal of Occupational and Organizational Psychology* 70, 325–335

Frone, M.R., Yardley, J.K. and Markel, K.S. (1997). Developing and testing an integrative model of the work-family interface. *Journal of Vocational Behavior* 50, 145–167.

Goode, W.J. (1960). A theory of strain. *American Sociological Review* 25, 483–496.

Grandey, A.A., Cordeiro, B.L. and Crouter, A.C. (2005). A longitudinal and multi-source test of the work-family conflict and job satisfaction relationship. *Journal of Occupational and Organizational Psychology* 78, 305–232.

Grant-Vallone E.J. and Donaldson S.I. (2001). Consequences of work-family conflict on employee well-being over time. *Work & Stress* 15, 214–226.

Greenhaus, J.H. and Beutell, N.J. (1985). Sources of conflict between work and family roles. *Academy of Management Review* 10, 76–88.

Greenhaus, J.H. and Powell, G.N. (2006). When work and family are allies: A theory of work-family enrichment. *Academy of Management Review* 31, 72–92.

Greenhaus, J.H., Collins, K.M. and Shaw, J.D. (2003). The relations between work-family balance and quality of life. *Journal of Vocational Behavior* 63, 510–531.

Grzywacz, J.G. and Carlson, D.S. (2007). Conceptualizing work-family balance: Implications for practice and research. *Advances in Developing Human Resources* 9, 455–471.

Grzywacz, J.G. and Marks, N.F. (2000). Reconceptualizing the work-family interface: An ecological perspective on the correlates of positive and negative spillover between work and family. *Journal of Occupational Health Psychology* 5, 111–126.

Gutek, B.A., Searle, S. and Klepa, L. (1991). Rational versus gender role explanations for work-family conflict. *Journal of Applied Psychology* 76, 560–568.

Hakanen, J.J., Peeters, M.C.W. and Perhoniemi, R. (2011). Enrichment processes and gain spirals at work and at home: A 3-year cross-lagged panel study. *Journal of Occupational and Organizational Psychology* 84, 8–30.

Hall, G.B., Dollard, M.F., Tuckey, M.R., Winefield, A.H. and Thompson, B.M. (2010). Job demands, work-family conflict, and emotional exhaustion in police officers: A longitudinal test of competing theories. *Journal of Occupational and Organizational Psychology* 83, 237–250.

Hammer, L.B., Cullen, J.C., Neal, M.B., Sinclair, R.R. and Shafiro, M.V. (2005). The longitudinal effects of work-family conflict and positive spillover on depressive symptoms among dual-earner couples. *Journal of Occupational Health Psychology* 10, 138–154.

Innstrand, S.T., Langballe, E.M., Espnes, G.A., Falkum, E. and Aasland, O.G. (2008). Positive and negative work-family interaction and burnout: A longitudinal study of reciprocal relations. *Work & Stress* 22, 1–15.

Kinnunen, U., Geurts, S. and Mauno, S. (2004). Work-to-family conflict and its relationship with satisfaction and well-being: a one-year longitudinal study on gender differences. *Work & Stress* 18, 1–22.

Leiter, M.P. and Durup, M.J. (1996). Work, home, and in-between: A longitudinal study of spillover. *Journal of Applied Behavioral Science* 32, 29–47.

Lobel, S.A. and St. Clair, L. (1992). Effects of family responsibilities, gender and career identity salience on performance outcomes. *Academy of Management Journal* 35, 1057–1069.

Marks, S.R. (1977). Multiple roles and role strain: Some notes on human energy, time and commitment. *American Sociological Review* 42, 921–936.

McMillan, H.S., Morris, M.J. and Atchley, E.K. (2011). Constructs of the work/life interface: A synthesis of the literature and introduction of the concept of work/life harmony. Human Resource Development Review 10, 6–25.

Mesmar-Magnus, J.R. and Viswesveran, C. (2005). Convergence between measures of work-to-family and family-to-work conflict: A meta-analytic examination. *Journal of Vocational Behavior* 67, 215–232.

Muse, L., Harris, S.G., Giles, W.F. and Feild, H.S. (2008). Work-life benefits and positive organizational behavior: Is there a connection? *Journal of Organizational Behavior* 29, 171–192.

O'Driscoll, M., Brough, P. and Kalliath T.J. (2004). Work/family conflict, psychological well-being, satisfaction and social support: A longitudinal study in New Zealand. *Equal opportunities International* 23, 36–56.

Parasuraman, S. and Greenhaus, J.H. (2002). Toward reducing some critical gaps in work-family research. *Human Resource Management Review* 12, 299–312.

Peeters, M.C.W., de Jonge, J. Janssen, P.P.M. and van der Linden, S. (2004). Work-home interference, job stressors and employee health in a longitudinal perspective. *International Journal of Stress Management* 11, 305–322.

Pleck, J.H. (1977). The work-family role system. *Social Problems* 24, 417–427.

Rantanen, J., Kinnunen, U., Feldt, T. and Pulkkinen, L. (2008). Work-family conflict and psychological well-being: Stability and cross-lagged relations within one- and six-year follow-ups. *Journal of Vocational Behavior* 73, 37–51.

Rothbard, N. P.(2001). Enriching or depleting? The dynamics of engagement in work and family roles. *Administrative Science Quarterly* 46, 655–684.

Rogers, S.J. and May, D.C. (2003). Spillover between marital quality and job satisfaction: Long-term patterns and gender differences. *Journal of Marriage and the Family* 65, 482–495.

Ryan, A.M. and Kossek, E.E. (2008). Work-life policy implementation: Breaking down or creating barriers to inclusiveness? *Human Resource Management* 47, 295–310.

Sieber, S.D. (1974). Toward a theory of role accumulation. *American Sociological Review* 39, 567–578.

Steinmetz, H., Frese, M. and Schmidt, P. (2008). A longitudinal study on antecedents and outcomes of work-home interference. *Journal of Vocational Behavior* 13, 231–241

Ten Brummelhuis, L.L., van der Lippe, T. and Kluwer, E.S. (2010). Family involvement and helping behavior in teams. *Journal of Management* 36, 1406–1431.

Ten Brummelhuis, L.L., van der Lippe, T., Kluwer, E.S. and Flap, H. (2008). Positive and negative effects of family involvement on work-related burnout. *Journal of Vocational Behavior* 73, 387–396.

van Knippenberg, D., van Dick, R. and Tavares, S. (2007). Social identity and social exchange: Identification, support, and withdrawal from the job. *Journal of Applied Social Psychology* 37, 457–477.

van Hooff, M.L.M., Geurts, S.A.E., Taris, T.W., Kompier, M.A.J., Dikkers, J.S.E., Houtman, I.L.D. and van den Heuvel, F.M.M. (2005). Disentangling the causal relationships between work-home interference and employee health. *Scandinavian Journal of Work, Environmental & Health* 31, 15–29.

van Steenbergen, E.F. and Ellemers, N. (2009). Is managing the work-family interface worthwhile? Benefits for employee health and performance. *Journal of Organizational Behavior* 30, 617–642.

Voydanoff, P. (2002). Linkages between the work family-interface and work, family and individual outcomes: An integrative model. *Journal of Family Issues* 23, 138–164.

—— (2005). The effects of community demands, resources, and strategies on the nature and consequence of the work-family interface: An agenda for future research. *Family Relations* 54, 583–595.

Wayne, J.H., Randel, A.E. and Stevens, J. (2006). The role of identity and work-family support in work-family enrichment and its work-related consequences. *Journal of Vocational Behavior* 69, 445–461.

Wayne, J.H., Grzywacz, J.G., Carlson, D.S. and Kacmar, K.M. (2007). Work-family facilitation: A theoretical explanation and model of primary antecedents and consequences. *Human Resource Management Review* 17, 63–76.

7 A primer on sampling

Joseph G. Grzywacz, Dawn S. Carlson and
Beth A. Reboussin

Introduction

The utility of any research fundamentally comes down to two main elements: sampling and measurement. In the domain of work and family a substantial literature has amassed on the later topic. Researchers have introduced several measures of key concepts in the work–family literature, such as work–family conflict (Carlson, Kacmar and Williams, 2000; Kopelman, Greenhaus and Connolly, 1983; Netermeyer, Boles and McMurrian 1996), work–family enrichment (Carlson *et al.*, 2006), positive spillover (Hanson, Hammer and Colton 2006), role balance (Marks and MacDermid, 1996), work- and family-role salience (Amatea *et al.*, 1986), and work–family balance (Carlson, Grzywacz and Zivnuska, 2009). Several chapters have characterized and critiqued measures available to work and family researchers (Bellavia and Frone, 2005; Carlson and Grzywacz, 2008; MacDermid, 2005). Against this backdrop, comparatively little research attention has been given to sampling in the work and family literature. Where attention to measurement is essential for validly assessing key concepts, attention to sampling is essential for choosing appropriate analysis techniques and for making generalizations beyond study samples (Kalton, 1983).

The relative inattention to sampling (vis-à-vis measurement) in the work and family literature is problematic. One problem is the appearance of inconsistent results. Several reviewers of the literature have, for example, commented on inconsistent gender differences in core concepts in the literature, like work–family conflict (Bellavia and Frone, 2005; Eby *et al.*, 2005). While a portion of the inconsistent gender effect may be attributed to measurement problems (Carlson and Grzywacz, 2008; Eby *et al.*, 2005), another portion of the inconsistency may be due to sampling error. Sampling error reflects deviation in the traits, experiences or behaviors in the study sample compared to the broader population the sample was selected from (Dodge, 2003). Another problem resulting from inattention to sampling is ambiguity surrounding what is known. In the absence of a coherent body of research studies using samples that are representative of a circumscribed population, describing what we "know" is challenging. Ambiguity about what we "know" and "don't know," in turn, undermines the creation of effective programs and interventions to enhance daily work and family life.

The overall goal of this chapter is to enable and motivate work and family researchers to more thoroughly consider sampling issues when designing their research. This consideration is essential for advancing theory and for designing research that will produce results with strong practical application. To accomplish this goal, this chapter will provide a basic overview of sampling, including key definitions and an overview of common types of sample designs. We then illustrate why careful attention to sampling is important when designing work and family research. We then provide an overview of the sampling strategies used in contemporary work and family research, and we conclude with recommendations and guidelines for future work and family research.

Sampling basics

Basic overview

All approaches to sampling require understanding two interrelated concepts that cannot be defined apart from each other: *element* and *population* (Frankel, 1983). An element is an object of study. In the work and family literature elements are typically individuals' experiences (e.g. episodes of work–family conflict), behaviors (e.g. turnover intentions, organizational citizenship behaviors) or consequences (e.g. poor health, burnout); however, elements can also take other forms (e.g. marital dyads, supervisor-subordinate pairs). The element is also the unit of analysis. A population is defined as a discrete set of elements. Common examples of populations in work and family research include all employees of Company A (Hill *et al.*, 2001), all working mothers of infants under the age of one year in County Y (Carlson *et al.*, 2011), or all married individuals in Branch B of the military who were relocated in 2010. An element and population are jointly defined, in that elements are the basic building blocks of a population while a population is the sum total of all possible elements (Frankel, 1983).

Researchers typically collect data from a subset of the population, or a sample. The motivation for collecting data from a sample is largely practical: it is typically not possible to study an entire population either because of inadequate financial, temporal or human resources. However, the value of the data obtained from the sample and subsequent analytic results is determined by the sample design, or the rules and procedures used to obtain the sample (Frankel, 1983). The relative strength of a sample design depends on several factors, particularly the appropriate coverage of the population (i.e., no elements of the population are systematically excluded). Additionally, however, the strength of the sample design is influenced by the soundness of the theoretically or empirically justified rules for including or excluding elements from the sample, completeness of procedures for pursuing elements selected for inclusion, and documentation of the final disposition of all elements selected for inclusion.

Sampling strategies

There are two main classes of sampling strategies. Probability sampling, the first main class, refers to strategies where every element of a population has a known non-zero probability of being selected for inclusion in the sample (Frankel, 1983; Kalton, 1983). The second class of sampling strategies use non-probability methods and is characterized by an unknown probability of being selected for inclusion into the study sample. Probability samples are the only type of sample for which population inferences can be drawn, either in terms of generating prevalence estimates or for characterizing associations among concepts at the level of a population.

Probability sample designs

Probability samples share a common feature: they all require an explicit articulation of a set of rules for defining the study population. An example set of rules for studying the potential benefits of flextime policies for a specific employer might be something like "all full-time wage or salary employees of *Company A*". Notice that this study population does not include part-time employees, temporary workers, or independent contractors performing work for *Company A*. A more population-based example of rules defining a study population can be seen in the National Study of the Changing Workforce (NSCW), that is, people who; 1) worked at a paid job or operated an income-producing business, 2) were 18 years or older, 3) were in the civilian labor force, 4) resided in the contiguous 48 states, and 5) lived in a non-institutional residence, i.e. household, with a telephone (Keene and Quadagno, 2004). In both the illustrative example of "all full-time wage or salary employees of *Company A*" and the more concrete example provided by the NSCW, it is possible to create a list of all the possible elements of the study population. This list of elements is sometimes referred to as the sampling frame (Kalton, 1983).

Once the sampling frame has been created, researchers can use a variety of methods to obtain a probability sample. The most straightforward method for individual researchers is simple random sampling. In *simple random sampling* each element has an equal probability of being selected for potential participation in the research. Simple random sampling can occur through sophisticated procedures like enumerating each element in the sample frame and using a list of random numbers to select elements for recruitment, or through uncomplicated procedures like putting the name of every element in a hat and drawing names to be recruited.

More complex methods for obtaining probability samples are stratified random sampling and random cluster sampling. In the case of *stratified random sampling*, the researcher groups elements of the sample frame based on one or more characteristics of interest (e.g. gender, supervisor versus subordinate, wage versus salary) before sampling. Once elements have been grouped, the researcher can use simple random sampling procedures to select elements from each group for potential recruitment and participation. Stratified random sampling ensures that estimates can be made with equal accuracy in different subgroups (e.g. men and women) and that comparisons of groups can be made with adequate statistical power (e.g. whether women and men experience differential rates of work–family conflict).

Random cluster sampling is used when "natural" groups exist in a population (e.g. units or divisions within an organization, different neighborhoods within a city). Sampling essentially involves a three stage process: the first is the disaggregation of the theoretical population into discrete groups or clusters, the second stage is the random selection of clusters, and the third stage is the random selection of elements within clusters. Cluster sampling generally provides less precision than stratified random sampling; the main objective is practicality and reduced costs. Cluster sampling is typically used when the researcher cannot obtain a complete list of the members of the population they wish to study but can get a complete list of groups or "clusters" of the population or when a random sample would produce a list of subjects so widely scattered that surveying them would be cost prohibitive. Although most researchers are equipped to design and implement a simple random sampling procedure, researchers should seek the advice and guidance of sampling methodologists to appropriately design and implement other methods of constructing a probability sample.

Non-probability sample designs

The probability of any given element in a population of being selected for inclusion in the study is unknown in non-probability sample designs. Perhaps the best example of a non-probability sample design is the *convenience* sample. In this case, study participants are identified and recruited largely out of ease of access rather than any substantive consideration arising from the research question of interest. *Purposive sampling*, by contrast, is a non-probability sampling strategy where individuals are identified and selected because of one or more known attributes of interest to the research question. For example, researchers are increasingly interested in managers' and supervisors' attitudes about work–life issues because they are gatekeepers of information. To study these attitudes, a researcher may use a listserv for a professional organization to advertise a study about manager attitudes about work–life, and explicitly describe inclusion criteria (e.g. eligible participants must manage or supervise 2 or more subordinates). The sample resulting from this procedure would be classified as "non-probability" because some individuals meeting the inclusion criterion may not be members of the professional organization, whereas others may not receive the email because of faulty address: in both cases the probability of selection of individual elements is unknown. However, it is not a "convenience" sample because the sample was constructed to capture the unique experiences of current managers and supervisors.

A final common non-probability sample design is a *quota sample*. In a quota sample a researcher identifies a specific number of individuals to be recruited to the study, frequently in specific groups. To follow the previous example, the researcher might hypothesize that the gender of the manager is an important attribute, so the interviewer is told to sample a fixed number of male managers and a fixed number of female managers. The interviewer may then use either convenience or judgment sampling to choose managers from each subset (e.g. those that seem most helpful or are closest geographically). The resultant sample is, again, a non-probability sample for the reasons identified above.

Problems arising from inadequate sampling

Precise estimation of work and family experiences

While an estimator of work and family experiences may give the true value on average, estimates obtained from different samples within the same population may vary substantially in value; this is referred to as precision. The challenge of obtaining a precise estimate can be illustrated using generated data of self-reported levels of work–family conflict among a population of six employees (Table 7.1). The population average is 2.9. Implementation of a simple design where $n=3$ from the population is randomly selected (50 per cent random sample) illustrates substantial variation from the population average for specific samples randomly drawn from the population. As shown in Table 7.2, the population estimate would be 2.1 if sample 19, containing elements 3, 5 and 6, were randomly selected. By contrast, the population estimate would be 3.9 if sample 2 containing elements 1, 2 and 4 were randomly selected. Even though all of the samples were randomly selected from the same population, you wouldn't expect that all samples would yield the exact same estimate. They would differ just due to the random "luck of the draw" or to the natural fluctuations of drawing a sample. One way to characterize this sampling imprecision is to estimate the standard deviation of the samples' means (i.e., the standard error). As the sample size increases, the precision or standard error of an estimate decreases. The degree of sampling imprecision in the work and family conflict literature could see major reductions if larger samples were more widely employed (Shen et al., 2011). Imprecision can also result if the response of interest (e.g. work and family conflict) varies greatly between subgroups but sampling is not stratified by design. Simple random sampling in this situation could result in large disparities in sample size among the groups which reduces precision.

Table 7.1 Generated data of the reported work–family conflict (WFC) in a population of six workers

Worker	WFC
1	4.3
2	3.0
3	1.5
4	4.0
5	2.7
6	2.1
Average	2.9

Table 7.2 Estimated means from an exhaustive list of possible simple random samples of n=3 from a population of six workers

Sample Number	Population Elements in the Sample	Variable Values for the Sample Elements			Sample Mean
1	1, 2, 3	4.3	3.0	1.5	2.9
2	1, 2, 4	4.3	3.0	4.3	3.9
3	1, 2, 5	4.3	3.0	2.7	3.3
4	1, 2, 6	4.3	3.0	2.1	3.1
5	1, 3, 4	4.3	1.5	4.3	3.4
6	1, 3, 5	4.3	1.5	2.7	2.8
7	1, 3, 6	4.3	1.5	2.1	2.6
8	1, 4, 5	4.3	4.0	2.7	3.7
9	1, 4, 6	4.3	4.0	2.1	3.5
10	1, 5, 6	4.3	2.7	2.1	3.0
11	2, 3, 4	3.0	1.5	4.3	2.9
12	2, 3, 5	3.0	1.5	2.7	2.4
13	2, 3, 6	3.0	1.5	2.1	2.2
14	2, 4, 5	3.0	4.0	2.7	3.2
15	2, 4, 6	3.0	4.0	2.1	3.0
16	2, 5, 6	3.0	2.7	2.1	2.6
17	3, 4, 5	1.5	4.0	2.7	2.7
18	3, 4, 6	1.5	4.0	2.1	2.5
19	3, 5, 6	1.5	2.7	2.1	2.1
20	4, 5, 6	4.0	2.7	2.1	2.9
Average					2.9

Returning to Table 7.2, if these estimates were obtained from Carlson and colleagues (2000) measure of work–family conflict, researchers would conclude from sample 19 that the average worker "disagrees" that work conflicts with family, while the conclusion from sample 2 is that the average worker "agrees" that work conflicts with family (Carlson, Kacmar and Williams, 2000). If a frequency based response scale is used (e.g. Grzywacz and Marks, 2000), the conclusion from sample 19 is that work and family "rarely" conflict with each other, while the conclusion from sample 2 is that work and family "usually" conflict with each other. The divergent conclusions that would be drawn from this simple illustration highlight the importance of careful sample selection if the goal of the study is to make inferences about a broader population, be it a population of workers in a company or a broader population such as community or national populations.

Biased estimates of association

A biased estimator is one that, on average, over- or underestimates the quantity of interest. It is a systematic error which can result from not selecting a truly random sample which is representative of the larger population. Another problem that may occur from inadequate attention to sampling is bias in estimation of association. We use an inconsistency found in work and family research to illustrate these effects. Specifically, as previously discussed, there is substantial interest in whether work–family experiences differ between women and men, but qualitative reviews of the literature cite substantial inconsistency in reported differences in work–family experiences (Eby *et al.*, 2005). We performed a series of simulations to demonstrate the potential consequences that overrepresentation of women in these studies may have.

The simulations focus on two basic questions; that is, are there gender differences in work–family experiences and are work–family experiences associated with mental health outcomes. Although our illustration focuses on gender, identical issues arise for a myriad of other concepts and constructs when studying work and family.

Simulation 1: Gender Differences in Negative Spillover from Work to Family

We generated 1,000 random samples of size N=10,000. For each random sample, gender (x) was generated to produce a 50:50 distribution. Given an individual's gender x, the dependent variable of interest (y) representing negative spillover from work to family was generated from a normal distribution with standard deviation 2.85 and mean 10.07 for females and $10.07 + \beta_1$ for males where β_1 is the gender difference in negative spillover from work to family. We considered small, moderate and large effect sizes for the gender difference β_1. The standard deviation and the mean negative spillover from work to family for females were based on data from the 2004 National Survey of Midlife Development in the United States (MIDUS).

For each of the simulated samples, the relationship between negative spillover from work to family and gender in the full population (N=10,000) was estimated with linear regression using the equation $y = \beta_0 + \beta_1 x + \varepsilon_y$ where $\beta_0 = 10.07$ and ε_y is the error-term. Random samples of size n=1000, n=500 and n=250 were then drawn from the population with no oversampling and oversampling of females at rates of 20 per cent, 40 per cent, 60 per cent and 80 per cent, and the relationship between negative spillover from work to family and gender re-estimated. This process was repeated for each scenario 1,000 times. We calculated two statistics to summarize the simulation results. The mean absolute per cent error is the average absolute difference between the sample estimate and the true (population) value relative to the true (population) value x 100. This measure gives an indicator of how close the estimated sample value is to the true population value. The false negative rate is the probability of failing to reject the null hypothesis that there are no gender differences when there are gender differences.

The results of our simulation indicate non-trivial, sometimes substantial, biases in estimated gender differences in negative spillover from work to family resulting from over-representation of women in a study sample relative to the population (Table 7.3). Not surprising, the level of bias depends on both the sample size and the magnitude of the gender difference. The average bias in large samples (n=1,000) when gender differences were large (d=0.5) as measured by the mean absolute per cent error ranged from roughly 5 per cent to 8 per cent for modest and extreme oversampling of women. However, when effect sizes are modest (d=0.1), estimated gender differences from large samples were biased by 30–50 per cent, whereas estimated gender differences were biased by 40–70 per cent and 56–95 per cent in medium and small samples, respectively.

The ability to draw correct conclusions about gender differences is also influenced by sample characteristics (Table 7.3). Regardless of sample size, failing to detect a gender difference in negative spillover from work to family (false negative rate) is generally uncommon when effect sizes are medium (d=0.3) or large (d=0.5). The lone exception is small samples (n=250) with heavy over-representation of women: there is a 32 per cent probability of failing to detecting a medium size (d=0.3) gender difference in negative spillover from work to family when the sample has 80 per cent more women than the population. However, when the effect size is small (d=0.1), the false negative rate is substantial. In large samples (n=1,000) there is a 30 per cent probability of failing to detect a gender difference if the sample over-represents women by 40 per cent. In small samples (n=250) the probability of failing to detect a gender difference in negative spillover from work to family ranges from 56 per cent to 95 per cent, depending upon the level of over-representation of women in the sample.

Simulation 2: Association of negative spillover from work to family with mental health

Beyond delineating basic differences in work and family experiences, such as gender differences in negative spillover from work to family or work–family conflict, appropriate sampling also has implications for studying hypothesized associations of work and family experiences with presumed antecedents and consequences. Figure 7.1 illustrates this issue using hypothetical data of the association of negative spillover from work to family (a common measure of work and family experience) and negative affect (a common measure of mental health).

The black and grey dots illustrated in Figure 7.1 show observations from a full population (N=500). In this population, negative spillover from work to family is positively related to negative affect; the association based on a simple regression is represented by the dashed line. The black dots in Figure 7.1 represent a sample (n=100) that was drawn from the full population, but was based on a third variable that is correlated with both negative spillover from work to family and negative affect: gender. In this population women have higher levels of negative affect and lower levels of negative spillover from work to family than men. In this illustration, women were oversampled at a rate of 80 per cent to produce a gender composition of 80 women and 20 men. Whereas the population had a 50:50 gender composition, the sample had an 80:20 composition of women to men. Thus, the sample contains 60 per cent ((80:50)/50=60 per cent) more women than the population it was intended to represent. The solid line shows the estimated relationship between negative spillover from work to family and negative affect in this systematically biased sample. The coefficient estimate in the (biased) sample is stronger (further from zero) than the 'true' coefficient in the full population with a 50:50 gender distribution.

Table 7.3 Mean absolute per cent error and false negative rates for estimating gender differences in levels of negative work-to-family spillover by level of over-representation of women in analytic samples relative to the population, effect size and sample size

Oversampling Rate %	Sample Size (#females, #males)	Effect Size = 0.1		Effect Size = 0.3		Effect Size = 0.5	
		Mean Absolute % Error	False Negative Rate	Mean Absolute % Error	False Negative Rate	Mean Absolute % Error	False Negative Rate
0	(500, 500)	26.3	15.5	8.7	0.0	4.4	0.0
20	(600, 400)	29.4	20.9	9.7	0.0	4.8	0.0
40	(700, 300)	32.2	29.2	10.6	0.0	5.3	0.0
60	(800, 200)	35.5	40.7	11.6	0.0	5.8	0.0
80	(900, 100)	48.5	59.9	15.9	0.1	7.9	0.0
0	(250, 250)	41.0	49.0	13.5	0.0	6.8	0.0
20	(300, 200)	42.1	52.6	13.9	0.0	6.9	0.0
40	(350, 150)	44.3	52.8	14.6	0.0	7.3	0.0
60	(400, 100)	50.0	63.5	16.5	4.0	8.2	0.0
80	(450, 50)	69.8	77.2	23.0	8.0	11.5	0.0
0	(125, 125)	57.9	71.1	19.0	1.3	9.5	0.0
20	(150, 100)	56.3	72.0	18.6	1.6	9.3	0.0
40	(175, 75)	63.1	76.0	20.8	3.3	10.4	0.0
60	(200, 50)	70.9	81.2	23.3	8.0	11.6	0.0
80	(225, 25)	94.5	87.5	31.2	31.5	15.6	0.0

Simulation parameter assumptions:

1 Gender distribution in the population is 50:50 with population size = 10,000

2 Negative work-to-family spillover (NWTF) is normally distributed with standard deviation 2.85 and the mean NWTF score is assumed to be 10.07 among females (based on MIDUS data)

3 The regression equation is (NWTF) = $10.07 + b_1 X_1 + e$ where $X_1 = 1$ for males and 0 for females and $b_1 = 0.5$ for a small effect size, $b_1 = 1.5$ for a moderate effect size and $b_1 = 3.0$ for a large effect size.

4 1000 datasets were simulated with sample sizes of n = 1000, 500 and 250 drawn from the population of size 10,000.

Mean Absolute per cent Error = the average absolute difference between the sample estimate and the true (population) value relative to the true (population) value X 100. The estimate in this case is the regression coefficient for gender which is the difference in negative work to family spillover between males and females. This measure gives an indicator of how close the estimated value is to the true value.

False negative rate = the probability of failing to reject the null hypothesis when the alternative is true. In this case, the null hypothesis is that there are no gender differences and the alternative is that there are gender differences. Therefore, the false negative rate is the probability of failing to detect a difference when there is one.

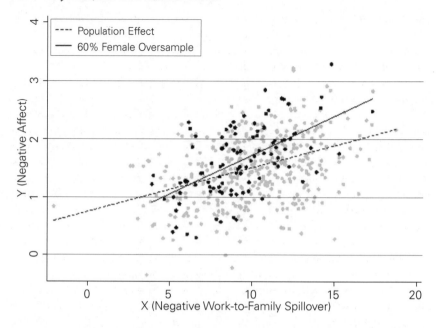

Figure 7.1 Illustration of the biased estimates of association from sample wherein a factor associated with both the dependent and independent variables (i.e., gender) was over-represented in the sample relative to the population

Next, we performed a simulation study to systematically evaluate the effect displayed in Figure 7.1. Similar to our earlier simulation, a total of 1,000 random samples of size 10,000 were generated. For each random sample, ten thousand observations x_1, representing negative spillover from work to family they were generated from a normal distribution with mean 10.08 and standard deviation 2.85. The same number of observations ε_y and ε_x^* from normal distributions with means 0 and standard deviations 0.533 and 1.0, respectively were generated. Given x_1 and ε_y, the dependent variable of interest y = negative affect was generated with the function $y = \beta_0 + \beta_1 x_1 + \varepsilon_y$ where $\beta_0 = 0.88$ and $\beta_1 = 0.06$. The standard deviations for x and error-term ε_y and the regression coefficients β_0 and β_1 were based on estimates from the MIDUS dataset and represent a moderate effect size. The probability to be male was generated with the probit function $x_2^* = \alpha_0 + \alpha_1 x_1 + \alpha_2 y + \varepsilon_x^*$.

Small, moderate and large effect sizes were considered for the coefficients α_0, α_1, and α_2 representing the strength of the relationship between gender and the two variables of interest. The coefficient α_1 was always set to positive and α_2 negative to indicate that greater negative spillover from work to family was associated with a higher probability of being male and higher negative affect with a lower probability. The binary variable x_2 was set equal to 1 if $x_2^* > 0$ and 0 otherwise where $x_2 = 1$ was male. For each of the simulated samples, the relationship between negative affect and negative spillover from work to family in the full population of size 10,000 was estimated with linear regression. Random samples of size 250 were then drawn from the full-population of size 10,000 with no oversampling, and with oversampling of females at rates of 20 per cent, 40 per cent, 60 per cent and 80 per cent. In each random sample the relationship between negative affect and work-to-family conflict was re-estimated. This process was repeated for each scenario 1,000 times.

As with our first simulation, two statistics were calculated. The first statistic, the mean absolute per cent error, was described previously; however, in this case the estimate of interest is the regression coefficient for work-to-family conflict (i.e., β_1). The second statistic reported is the per cent relative bias for β_1, which is the average difference between the sample estimate and the population value, relative to the population value x 100. This measure gives an average estimate of bias in the association of negative spillover from work to family with negative affect.

The consequence of oversampling women in samples studying the association of negative spillover from work to family with negative affect depends on both the magnitude of the oversampling, and the size of the gender effect (Table 7.4). Estimated associations of negative spillover from work to family with negative affect are generally robust to modest oversampling of women (i.e., ≤ 40 per cent), regardless of gender effect: the relative bias of the estimated association of work-to-family conflict is less than 11 per cent. Further, for small and medium gender effects (i.e., d=0.1 and d=0.3, respectively) the average absolute per cent error in the association of negative spillover from work to family with negative affect is generally comparable to the per cent error obtained from samples whose gender composition matches the population. However, biases resulting from moderate to large oversampling of women (i.e., 60–80 per cent) are non-negligible when the gender effect is large (i.e., d=0.5). Paralleling the hypothetical results illustrated in Figure 7.1, when samples over-represent women by 60 per cent, estimated associations between negative spillover from work to family and negative affect are biased by 24.7 per cent, on average, and the estimate departs from the true association by 26.4 per cent. When samples over-represent women by 80 per cent relative to the population, both the per cent relative bias and the average absolute per cent error approach 50 per cent.

Sampling strategies used in work and family research

In the previous sections we described basic features of sampling, including providing a description of alternative sampling strategies, and attempted to demonstrate the importance of purposeful and diligent sampling in work and family research. Using both hypothetical data and results obtained from simulations of real data we illustrated how poor sampling can contribute to notably different conclusions and biased estimates of association. With this background in place, this section describes the sampling strategies previously used in work and family research.

Table 7.4 Relative bias and mean absolute per cent error when estimating the relationship between negative affect and negative work-to-family spillover in the presence of gender selection bias by level of over-representation of women in analytic samples relative to the population, effect size and sample size

Oversampling Rate %	Sample Size (#females, #males)	Gender Effect 0.1		Gender Effect 0.3		Gender Effect 0.5	
		% Relative Bias	Mean Absolute % Error	% Relative Bias	Mean Absolute % Error	% Relative Bias	Mean Absolute % Error
0	(125, 125)	0.02	16.0	0.4	15.3	−1.0	15.4
20	(150, 100)	0.4	15.8	1.6	15.5	2.4	16.0
40	(175, 75)	1.2	14.9	3.9	15.8	10.7	18.2
60	(200, 50)	1.3	15.4	8.6	16.7	24.7	26.4
80	(225, 25)	1.7	15.7	15.5	20.1	46.8	46.9

Simulation parameter assumptions:

1 Gender distribution in the population is 50:50
2 The dependent variable is negative affect (NAF) with standard deviation 0.533 (based on MIDUS data).
3 Negative work-to-family spillover (NWTF) is normally distributed with standard deviation 2.85 and the mean 10.08 (based on MIDUS data)
4 The regression equation of interest is $NAF = a_0 + a_1 NWTF + e$, where $a_0 = 0.88$ and $a_1 = 0.06$ from the MIDUS data. This represents an effect size of 0.3.
5 Gender is related to both NAF and NWTF through the probit regression equation $Prob(male) = b_0 + b_1 NAF + b_2 NWTF + e_2$. We consider three scenarios where both predictors have effect sizes of 0.1, 0.3 and 0.5 on the probability of being male.
6 The population size is N=10,000 and 1000 datasets were simulated with a sample sizes of n= 250 drawn from the population.

Mean Absolute per cent Error = the average absolute difference between the sample estimate and the true (population) value relative to the true (population) value X 100. The estimate in this case is the regression coefficient for gender which is the difference in negative work to family spillover between males and females. This measure gives an indicator of how close the estimated value is to the true value.

Per cent Relative bias = the average difference between the sample estimate and the population value (sample estimate − population estimate) relative to the population value X 100. The estimate in this case is the estimated regression coefficient a_1.

Method

Articles published from 2005–2010 were identified via computer databases using manual searches with the following search terms: work–family, work–life, work–nonwork, work and family, family friendly, family and policy, work schedules and family, family–work relationship, and workplace flexibility. We focused on seven journals: three top IO/OB journals (*Journal of Applied Psychology, Journal of Vocational Behavior, Journal of Occupational Health Psychology*), two top family journals (*Journal of Marriage and Family, Family Relations*) and two multidisciplinary journals (*Human Relations, Community, Work, and Family*). We excluded meta-analyses and literature reviews focusing on empirical studies including a key work and family domain variable. We found 73 articles, 4 of which have multiple studies and each study was coded separately, thus a total of 77 studies were analyzed.

For each of the articles identified the article was reviewed to gather information from the method section. First, the location of the data was coded. Then we coded if the author(s) specified a target population to whom the research question was being asked. We then noted if an explicit description of the targeted sample to be accrued was provided. Next, we looked to see if author(s) provided an explicit identification of sampling method. If so the sample method was categorized such that we could categorize the method as census, probability sampling, or various form of non-probability sampling. Finally, for each of these studies the response rate was recorded, if provided.

Results

Of the studies examined, 58 (75 per cent) reported where the sample was obtained; of those who reported where the sample was obtained, half were conducted on US-based samples while 40 per cent were based on non-US samples. Turning to indicators that explicit methods were used to guide the identification and accrual of research samples, we first examined whether researchers articulated a specific target population for whom a research question was being asked (Table 7.5). In most cases (n=67/73=92 per cent) researchers identified a target population; general populations were most frequently (n=35, 45 per cent) identified, and included populations like "...parents living with children younger than 18..." (Milkie *et al.*, 2010), or "...MBA and undergraduate students at four universities in the US" (Hunter *et al.*, 2010). Nearly one-in-five studies (17 per cent) targeted a population comprised of multiple units from multiple organizations, such as "...full-time employees from five companies in Beijing." (Wang *et al.*, 2010) or "...workers employed in large Canadian organizations, married, dual-earner, with child or elderly dependents at home" (Higgins, Duxbury and Lyons, 2010).

Many published studies did not use sampling strategies to guide identification and accrual of study participants (Table 7.5). A census approach, whereby everyone in the population was invited to participate, was used in 28 studies (36 per cent). Of these 28 studies, 4 (14 per cent) did not report a response rate, and

Table 7.5. Methods used to identify and accrue study samples in work and family research published from 2005 to 2010 in seven core journals

	Number of Studies	*Per cent of total†*
No method described	8	10
Census	28	36
Sampling		
Probability	18	23
Non-Probability		
Convenience	16	21
Quota	1	1
Purposeful	4	5
Snowball	2	3
Total non-probability	23	30

†73 published articles. Four articles included data from multiple samples using different sampling methods, resulting in n=77 distinct sampling strategies

published response rates for the remaining studies ranged from 4 per cent to 95 per cent, with a median response rate of 56 per cent. Fully 10 per cent of the studies (n=8) provided no method description for identifying and accruing the study sample.

The remaining 41 studies (53 per cent) used some type of sampling procedure to identify and accrue a study sample. Researchers provided an explicit description of the targeted sample to be accrued in 32 of these 41 studies (78 per cent). Probability methods of sample identification and accrual were reported in 18 of the 41 sampling studies (44 per cent). Among the 18 studies where probability sampling methods were used, 8 (44 per cent) did not report a response rate, and published response rates for the remaining studies ranged from 36 per cent to 84 per cent, with a median response rate of 61 per cent. Non-probability methods were reported in 23 of the 41 studies using sampling (56 per cent). Convenience sampling was the single most common non-probability method; it was used in 16 studies. Response rates provide little practical value in non-probability samples; nevertheless, they were reported in 8 (35 per cent) of the studies.

Conclusions

As speculated in our introduction, sampling is an issue that is given little thoughtful deliberation in work and family research. Probability methods for identifying and accruing samples representative of the target population were reported in nearly one-quarter of the published studies, most of these articles were based on analyses of existing data sources such as the National Study of the Changing Workforce (Thompson and Prottas, 2005), or the General Social Survey (Dierdorff and Ellington, 2008). Although they are excellent sources of data, these national studies were not designed to specifically study work and family. Consequently, the main conclusion of this content analysis is that work and family researchers are frequently interested in answering population-level questions, but studies designed to answer these questions typically do not put rules into place to make sure recruited samples reflect the population from which it was drawn.

Recommendations and guidelines for research

Like measurement, sampling of observations is a central part of research. Unfortunately, sampling is typically given short-shrift in work and family research. The general absence of deliberate sampling procedures to ensure study samples accurately reflects populations of interest creates impediments to advancing both the science and practice of minimizing the work–family challenge confronted by many workers. As we have demonstrated, inattentiveness to sampling contributes to imprecise estimates of the prevalence of work and family experiences, it can produce biased estimates of association, and it can result in concluding that no association exists even when it does. We suspect that poor consideration of sampling contributes to specific problems in the work and family literature, such as inconsistent findings that work and family experiences differ by gender, and that it may undermine the identification of viable targets or strategies for helping working families.

The primary recommendation of this chapter is for the Work and Family research community to give sampling greater attention when designing, implementing, reporting, and reviewing research. In this section we outline a set of recommendations for each phase of the research enterprise. We also provide guidelines for researchers to implement these recommendations. Readers need to recognize that these guidelines are not definitive nor are they exhaustive: sampling is a major domain of research methodology that cannot be summarized in a single chapter.

Recommendations during research design

Define the sample needed to answer the research question

Just as study design, measurement selection, and analytic technique each follow from the research question: the study sample should be appropriate for the research question. Although not discussed here, one aspect of sample design that receives frequent attention is sample size (Shen et al., 2011): researchers will frequently determine the sample size needed to have sufficient analytic power. However, less common is a well defined articulation of what the final sample should "look like" to enable answering the research question.

Researchers should follow two basic guidelines as they attempt to implement this recommendation. First, define the sample based on key concepts in the posed research question(s) or study hypothesis(es). A simple illustration is the necessity of having a sample with both women and men to answer questions about gender differences in work and family experiences. Similarly, if a researcher is interested in the health-related consequences of flexible work arrangements: a sample containing variability in both health status and use of flexible work arrangements is needed. Second, researchers also need to identify key concepts that threaten the ability to answer the research question(s) or test the study hypothesis(es). For example, at the population level, women and men tend to hold very different jobs (Hanson, Schaub and Baker, 1996). Similarly, within any given organization women and men can hold different types of jobs (McKay, 2006), and the design of identical jobs can differ for women and men (Nordander *et al.*, 1999). Consequently, the researcher interested in answering questions about gender differences in work and family experiences needs to acknowledge these realities to understand how they bear on the research question, and then design a study sample able to answer the research question.

Identify inclusion and exclusion criterion needed to achieve the defined sample

Operationalizing some attributes of interest in work and family research is relatively straightforward. Gender differences research requires a sample with both women and men; flexible work arrangements can be defined in terms of access to specific types of flexibility (e.g. schedule flexibility, remote work arrangements), use of these types of flexibility, or self-appraisals of flexibility. Other attributes of interest in work and family research are more challenging to operationalize. Operationalizing "work–family conflict" from a sampling perspective can be challenging. Proxies such as age of youngest child or number of required work hours per week offer some potential to introduce variability into the sample, but they are imperfect.

The primary guideline for implementing this recommendation is having a clear vision of the study's primary aims. Discern concepts that are essential to the study (either because they reflect core concepts of interest, or because they pose significant threats to the research) from more marginal concepts. Engaging colleagues from other disciplines or academic perspectives is an excellent way of discerning essential concepts from those that are more marginal. Essential concepts are translated into inclusion/exclusion criterion, whereas more marginal concepts can be allowed to vary in the sample, but then statistically controlled. However, another salient guideline is the "keep it simple" principal. Inclusion/ exclusion protocols can easily become overly burdensome and potentially impractical in many field settings: keep them focused on the essential concepts of the research project.

Determine the most appropriate sampling strategy for the study

Every researcher grapples with the problem of limited resources. The use of sophisticated probability sampling methods requires substantial financial, human and technological resources. Further, some research questions require access and entrée to specific types of samples. For example, researchers may be interested in the work and family experiences of inter-racial couples, or those of "hidden populations" such as undocumented immigrants, women who have been abused, or formerly incarcerated individuals. With these types of populations, clearly delineated sample frames are often not available, thereby impeding the use of probability methods.

A set of questions can guide researchers in implementing this recommendation. First, and most salient, what is the goal; that is, what is the level of inference the researcher seeks from the study? If an investigator is primarily interested in testing basic associations, as might be the case if the study focuses on a novel area of inquiry, then samples can be designed less stringently. However, if the primary goal of the study is draw inferences about some population of interest (e.g. employees in company X generally think Y, or women employed in the services industry experience different levels of X than men), then the sample design needs to enable that level of inference. Second, and more practically, what resources are needed to make the level of inference desired? Researchers should critically evaluate the financial, human and technological resources available to conduct the research. Considerations such as the availability of lists of potential study participants and the degree and adequacy to which those lists cover the population of interest are fundamental to individuals interested in conducting population research. However, even if population inference is not a primary objective, researchers need to consider the resources needed to implement a proposed study. For example, minimizing threats to biases within the sample may require the use of human resources to screen every potential study participant to ensure inclusion/ exclusion criterion are met. Finally, how available resources can be used to design the most rigorous study possible? Just as researchers frequently select key measures based both on what is necessary (what do I want to measure?) and what is feasible (e.g. how many items will my survey tolerate?); likewise, researchers need to select a sampling strategy that aligns with the overall goal, while also remaining attentive to the constraints of the researcher and the study environment.

Create a specific plan for accruing the study sample

Think through each stage of the sampling and recruitment component of the project and critically evaluate alternatives. Start with the sample frame and decide the best way to construct it. Occasionally, researchers may have access to lists (e.g. employee lists within an organization, marketing lists of households in a census block group), but several factors can influence the quality and acceptability of these lists. Intra-organizational lists such as those from a Human Resources department may be lacking based on how frequently core databases are updated or technical differences in how "employee" is defined. Similarly, marketing lists that can be purchased by researchers can be problematic because telephone numbers or addresses are out of date. Researchers might be able to create their own sample frame by conducting their own census of an organization/unit or geographic region, but this requires time, human resources and both access to and familiarity with the unit. Once available strategies for defining the sample frame have been identified, the researcher needs to select the sample frame most consistent with the research question.

Next, the researcher needs to identify a sampling strategy. Of primary interest is whether a probability method will be used. If a probability method is used, the researcher will need to design the parameters surrounding selection (e.g. simple random selection, stratified random, etc.) and how that will be implemented. If a non-probability method will be used, the researcher needs to articulate steps to minimize the threat of potential sampling biases. In both cases, articulation inclusion/exclusion criterion is vitally important. Finally, the researcher needs to identify a recruitment strategy. If probability methods are used, the researchers will use "active" recruitment methods, meaning that members of the study actively pursue individuals identified as potentially study eligible. If non-probability methods are used, the researcher will need to decide if active methods will be used, or if more passive forms will be used (e.g. flyers posted in public spaces, Facebook posts to groups). Again, the sampling strategy and the recruitment method should be purposefully selected to align with the overall goal of the study.

Recommendations for reporting research

Transparency in all aspects of sampling is the primary recommendation for researchers when reporting the results of their research. Of course, transparency is far from a new idea, rather it is the fundamental goal of every research report. Ideas need to be conveyed clearly and in a way that allows replication. There are several guidelines for transparent reporting of sampling issues. First, researchers should explicitly report the size and structure of the sample frame from which the study sample was obtained. The primary objective leading the description of the sample frame is to enable readers to critically evaluate whether the selected sample frame "represents" the intended population of interest. Next, authors need to report how prospective study participants were selected for potential recruitment and the procedures used to recruit study participants. Authors are encouraged to explicitly state if probability methods were used, and, if so, how those probability methods were implemented. Likewise, researchers should explicitly report if non-probability methods were used. Response rates should be reported when a denominator can be identified.

As important to transparency of reporting, is frank acknowledgement of study limitations. Researchers are encouraged to thoughtfully reflect on how sampling issues may bear on study results. If probability methods are used, researchers should remind readers of the population from which the results are relevant, and differentiate that population from other populations of potential interest. National probability samples are valuable, but they are not the definitive sources of data. For example, many national probability samples including the National Study of the Changing Workforce and the National Study of Midlife Development in the United States use sampling procedures wherein most participants are obtained from large metropolitan areas (e.g. New York, Chicago, Los Angeles): findings from these samples may not represent more discrete metropolitan areas or non-metropolitan areas that also grapple with work and family issues. If non-probability methods are used, researchers need to discuss how sample characteristics may bear on results and generalizability. For example, the results from our simulations clearly suggest that results from study samples that over-represent women relative to the population from which they are drawn can lead to falsely concluding gender differences in work–family conflict and biased estimates of association between work–family conflict and mental health. Finally, researchers are encouraged to limit discussions of study implications to points supported by the collected data. Avoid population inferences if non-probability methods are used, and clearly identify speculative inferences beyond the data if they are made.

Recommendations for reviewing research

The primary recommendation for reviewers is attentiveness to sample design when evaluating research manuscripts for potential publication. This recommendation is made with some trepidation, because it is a criterion that can be misused if one standard is viewed as the "gold standard" for all research. Clearly, all things equal, research designs that use probability methods of selecting prospective study participants are better than non-probability methods. However, "all things equal' is a rare scenario given the myriad of factors shaping the overall quality of research. Does the use of probability methods counter-balance a biased sample frame? Can researchers make reasonable population inferences from a study with a definitive sample frame, even if non-probability methods are used? Questions like these are provided to illustrate that reality that fact that there are no "perfect" studies.

In the absence of perfection, reviewers are encouraged to be attentive to sampling issues within the context of what the study was designed to do, not some external gold standard. When reviewing the manuscript, evaluate the clarity of the description of the sample frame and the extent to which the sample frame is free of bias threats. Discern whether the reported sample design and sampling strategy align with the goals of the study, and whether they are described in a manner that enables replication. Finally, evaluate the acknowledged limitations of the sample, and the extent to which the researchers reporting the results are making appropriate inferences. In short, be attentive to sampling when reviewing research manuscripts, but recognize that it is one element (albeit an important element) of research design that shapes the overall contribution of study results to the advancement of science. Small or highly specific samples can have substantial scientific value.

Conclusion

The overall goal of this chapter was to enable and motivate work and family researchers to more thoroughly consider sampling issues when designing their research. The basic overview of sampling concepts and procedures provided in this chapter should provide a starting point for enabling work and family researchers to use more rigorous sampling strategies in their study designs. Moreover, the recommendations and guidelines provided in this chapter can enable researchers to implement strategies that minimize potential sampling biases. The results of our simulations showed how sampling biases can lead to false conclusions will likely motivate work and family researchers to be more attentive to sampling when designing theoretical or applied research. As implied by the use of "a primer" in the title, we did not expect to cover the entire and complex domain of sampling. Rather, we wanted to whet work and family researchers' appetites to recognize the importance of sampling, and to elevate it as an important methodological feature for advancing work and family research and practice.

Acknowledgements

This research was supported by grants from the Eunice Kennedy Schriver National Institute for Child Health and Development (R01HD061010 and R01HD056360).

References

Allen, N.J., Stanley, D.J., Williams, H.M. and Ross, S.L. (2007). Assessing the impact of nonresponse on work group diversity effects. *Organizational Research Methods* 10, 262–286.

Amatea, E.S., Cross, E.G. Clark, J. and Bobby, C.L. (1986). Assessing the work and family role expectations of career-oriented men and women: The life role salience scales. *Journal of Marriage and Family* 48, 831–838.

Assael, H. and Keon, J. (1982). Nonsampling vs. sampling errors in survey research. *Journal of Marketing* 46, 114–123.

Baruch, Y. (1999). Response rate in academic studies – A comparative analysis. *Human Relations* 52, 421–438.

Bellavia, G. and Frone, M. R. (2005). Work-family conflict. In J. Barling, E.K. Kelloway and M.R. Frone (eds) *Handbook of Work Stress*. Thousand Oaks, CA: Sage.

Carlson, D.S. and Grzywacz, J.G. (2008). Reflections and future directions on measurement in work-family research. In K. Korabik, D.S. Lero and D.L. Whitehead (eds.) *Handbook of work-family integration: Research, theory and best practices* (57–73). San Diego, CA: Elsevier.

Carlson, D.S., Grzywacz, J.G. and Zivnuska, S. (2009). Work-family balance: Is balance more than conflict and enrichment? *Human Relations* 20, 1–28.

Carlson, D.S., Kacmar, K.M., Wayne, J.H. and Grzywacz, J.G. (2006). Measuring the positive side of the work-family interface: Development and validation of a work-family enrichment scale. *Journal of Vocational Behavior* 68, 131–164.

Carlson, D.S., Kacmar, K.M. and Williams, L.J. (2000). Construction and initial validation of a multidimensional measure of work-family conflict. *Journal of Vocational Behavior* 56, 249–276.

Carlson, D.S., Grzywacz, J.G., Ferguson, M., Hunter, E.M., Clinch, C.R. and Arcury, T.A. (2011). Health and turnover of working mothers after childbirth via the work-family interface: An analysis across time. *Journal of Applied Psychology* 96, 1045–1054.

Connelly, N. A., Brown, T.L. and Decker, D.J. (2003). Factors affecting response rates to natural resource focused mail surveys: Empirical evidence of declining rates over time. *Society and Natural Resources* 16, 541–549.

Dierdorff, E.C. and Ellington, J.K. (2008). It's the nature of the work: Examining behavior-based sources of work-family conflict across occupations. *Journal of Applied Psychology* 93, 883–892.

Dodge, Y. (Ed). (2003). *The Oxford Dictionary of Statistical Terms*. New York: Oxford University Press.

Eby, L.T., Casper, W.J., Lockwood, A., Bordeaux, C. and Brinley, A. (2005). Work and family research in IO/OB: Content analysis and review of the literature (1980–2002). *Journal of Vocational Behavior* 66, 124–197.

Frankel, M. (1983). Sampling Theory. In Rossi P.H., Wright, J.D. and Anderson, A.B. (Eds.), *Handbook of survey research*. New York: Academic Press.

Grzywacz, J.G. and Marks, N.F. (2000). Reconceptualizing the work-family interface: An ecological perspective on the correlates of positive and negative spillover between work and family. *Journal of Occupational Health Psychology* 5, 111–126.

Hall, C.Hall, C.L. (1997). Cultural malpractice: The growing obsolescence of psychology with the changing US population. *American Psychologist* 52, 642–651.

Hanson, G.C., Hammer, L.B and Colton, C.L. (2006). Development and validation of a multidimensional scale of perceived work-family positive spillover. *Journal of Occupational Health Psychology* 11, 249–265.

Hanson, S.L., Schaub, M. and Baker, D.P. (1996). Gender stratification in the science pipeline: a comparative analysis of seven countries. *Gender & Society* 10, 271–290.

Higgins, C.A., Duxbury, L.E. and Lyons, S.T. (2010). Coping with overload and stress: Men and women in dual-earner families. *Journal of Marriage and Family* 72, 847–859.

Hill, E.J., Hawkins, A.J., Ferris, M. and Weitzman, M. (2001). Finding and extra day a week: The positive influence of perceived job flexibility on work and family life balance. *Family Relations* 50, 49–58.

Hoonakker, P. and Carayon, P. (2009). Questionnaire survey nonresponse: A comparison of postal mail and internet surveys. *International Journal of Human-Computer Interaction* 25, 348–373.

Hunter, E.M., Perry, S.J., Carlson, D.S. and Smith, S.A. (2010). Linking team resources to work-family enrichment and satisfaction. *Journal of Vocational Behavior* 77, 304–312

Kalton, G. (1983). *Introduction to survey sampling*. Beverly Hills: Sage Publications.

Keene, J.R. and Quadagno, J. (2004). Predictors of perceived work-family balance: Gender difference or gender similarity. *Sociological Perspectives* 47, 1–23.

Kopelman, R.E., Greenhaus, J.H. and Connolly, T.F. (1983). A model of work, family, and interrole confl ict: A construct validation study. *Organizational Behavior and Human Performance* 32, 198–215.

MacDermid, S.M. (2005). (Re)Considering conflict between work and family. In E.E. Kossek and S. Lambert (eds) *Work and family integration in organizations: New directions for theory and practice* (19–40). Mahwah, NJ: Lawrence Earlbaum Associates.

McKay, S.C. (2006). Hard drives and glass ceilings: gender stratification in high-tech production. *Gender & Society* 20, 207–235.

Marks, S.R. and MacDermid, S.M. (1996). Multiple roles and the self: A theory of role balance. *Journal of Marriage and the Family* 58, 417–432.

Milkie, M.A., Kendig, S.M., Nomaguchi, K.M. and Denny, K.E. (2010). Time with children, children's well-being, and work-family balance among employed parents. *Journal of Marriage and Family* 72, 1329–1343.

Netemeyer, R.G., Boles, J.S. and McMurrian, R. (1996). Development and validation of work-family conflict and family-work conflict scales. *Journal of Applied Psychology* 81, 400–410.

Nordander, C., Ohlsson, K., Balogh, I., Rylander, L., Palsson, B. and Skerfving, S. (1999). Fish processing work: The impact of two sex dependent exposure profiles on musculoskeletal health. *Occupational & Environmental Medicine* 56, 256–264.

Peterson, R.A. and Brown, S.P. (2005). On the use of beta coefficients in meta-analysis. *Journal of Applied Psychology* 90, 175–181.

Rogelberg, S. and Stanton, J.M. (2007). Understanding and dealing with organizational survey nonresponse. *Organizational Research Methods* 10, 195–209.

Roth, P.L. and BeVier, C.A. (1998). Response rates in HRM/OB survey research: Norms and correlates, 1990–1994. *Journal of Management* 24, 97–117.

Shen, W., Kiger, T.B., Davies, S.E., Rasch, R.L., Simon, K.M. & Ones, D.S. (2011). Samples in applied psychology: Over a decade of research in review. *Journal of Applied Psychology*, 96, 1055-1064.

Thompson, C.A. and Prottas, D.J. (2005). Relationships among organizational family support, job autonomy, perceived control, and employee well-being, *Journal of Occupational Health Psychology* 10, 100–118.

Wang, M., Liu, S., Zhan, Y. and Shi, J. (2010). Daily work-family conflict and alcohol use: testing the cross-level moderation effects of peer drinking norms and social support. *Journal of Applied Psychology* 95, 377–386.

8 Experience sampling methods for work–family research

A review and research agenda

Adam Butler, Zhaoli Song and Remus Ilies

We need not conduct an empirical study to know that individuals' work and family experiences are considerably dynamic. Family life can intrude on work without notice, and a difficult event at work can later strain relationships at home. Researchers seeking to understand this complexity can employ a data collection method, referred to as experience sampling (ESM), which captures frequent observations of phenomena, sometimes as they are happening. As a result, the data provide a rich picture of role experiences over time, and the method overcomes some of the limitations of cross-sectional survey research.

In this chapter, we enthusiastically endorse the use of ESM by work–family researchers. We describe the different sampling techniques that are available and advance several arguments for the superiority of ESM over other methods. Key studies are reviewed, and we identify gaps in our knowledge, suggesting research areas that may be particularly valuable for the development of theory, policy, and practice.

Experience sampling methods

ESM refers to a set of survey techniques that repeatedly sample participants' behaviors and experiences at moments within their natural life settings. In the literature, it is also sometimes called the diary method (Bolger, Davis and Rafaeli, 2003) or ecological momentary assessment (EMA; Shiffman, Stone and Hufford, 2008). In an invaluable historical review of ESM, Wheeler and Reiss (1991) classified the different methods of sampling into three broad categories. The first and most widely used ESM in work–family research is interval-contingent recording. With this method, participants respond to survey items at fixed, predetermined intervals, such as at the end of the day. For example, Butler *et al.* (2005) solicited end of day reports from non-professional couples using personal digital assistants or PDAs (e.g. Palm Pilot). More recently, researchers have used interval-contingent methods that require multiple reports per day. For example, Ilies, Wilson and Wagner (2009) had university staff complete internet-based surveys in the morning and afternoon and paper surveys at the end of each day. The employees' spouses also completed a telephone survey at the end of each day. The commonality among these studies is that participants responded at a relatively fixed time each day of the study.

A second type of response methodology, called signal-contingent recording, requires participants to report their experiences at a signal controlled by the researcher. In early signal-contingent recording studies, a phone call, an alarm watch, or beeper made the signal. In their seminal study of work and family role juggling, Williams *et al.* (1991) used wrist watches that signaled participants to report their activities, role juggling, and affect eight times per day for eight days. The signal schedule was generated randomly and varied each day of the study. More recent studies have used cell phones to signal respondents (Rönkä *et al.*, 2010; Song, Foo and Uy, 2008). Often, signal-contingent studies will require more reports over the course of a day than interval contingent studies.

The third type of response methodology, event-contingent recording, requires participants to record their experiences after the occurrence of a specified event. As noted by others (Beal and Weiss, 2003), this approach is well suited for studying dynamic phenomena that may have a low base rate and, therefore, might fail to be captured by interval or signal contingent methods. We are not aware of any work–family research using event-contingent recording.

The case for experience sampling methods in work–family research

In reviewing work–family research published between 1980 and 2003 in IO-OB journals, Casper *et al.* (2007) found that 89 per cent of the studies used a cross-sectional research design. Only one of the studies in their review used an ESM design. Using somewhat restrictive criteria, we identified 15 additional ESM studies published since their review; yet, the standard design in work–family research remains cross-sectional. Though we would not go so far as to suggest that work–family researchers abandon cross-sectional designs, there are significant limitations associated with the design that constrain or obfuscate our understanding of work–family experiences. In this section, we highlight some significant gaps in the work–family nomological network, identify problems associated with cross-sectional work–family research, and illustrate how ESM studies can overcome these limitations.

Work–family research gaps

We think there are two significant gaps in work–family research that could be bridged by studies using ESM designs. First, from a theoretical standpoint, ESM could help explain the boundary transition processes that occur between roles. Second, from a practical standpoint, ESM studies could be used to provide more rigorous evaluations of interventions designed to enhance role balance. We also believe that these two research areas are linked. That is, as we better understand role transition processes, we gain more insights into the types of interventions that are likely to be effective.

Boundary theory (Ashforth, Kreiner and Fugate, 2000; Nippert-Eng, 1996) proposes that individuals construct idiosyncratic boundaries between work and family and that the nature of these constructions affects role transition processes.

Importantly for the application of ESM, theorists assume that these transitions are frequent and recurring. Moreover, features of the role boundary, notably its degree of segmentation or integration, are predicted to affect the frequency and character of role transitions. For example, Ashforth, Kreiner and Fugate (2000) proposed that the affective impact of interrole conflict is weakened when role integration is greater.

As we will make clear in the next section of our chapter, because of inferential problems and reporting biases, it is simply not possible to examine role transition processes using cross-sectional study designs. A study by Ilies, Wilson and Wagner (2009) nicely illustrates the potential for boundary transition research using ESM. They found that employees reported higher marital satisfaction on days when their job satisfaction was higher. Job satisfaction at the end of the workday also influenced positive and negative affect experienced later at home (positively and negatively, respectively). Finally, they found that the tendency to integrate work and family roles strengthened the links between work and family, such that job satisfaction more strongly influenced employee affect expression at home as rated by spouses.

A second prominent research gap that could be filled by ESM studies concerns the evaluation of interventions designed to promote the effective management of multiple role demands. Although Kossek, Blates and Matthews (2011) recently offered suggestions to close what they called the "implementation gap," their recommendations, and those within the commentaries that followed, largely neglected methodological concerns (see *Industrial and Organizational Psychology: Perspectives on Science and Practice* 4(3), 2011). Yet, the practical implications of our findings must lay within-person, necessitating the use of designs such as ESM for intervention research.

Consider flexible workplace arrangements, an increasingly popular family-friendly benefit allowing employees to modify when and where work is accomplished. Although several recent policy reports have touted the business benefits of workplace flexibility (e.g. American Psychological Association, 2004; US Council of Economic Advisors, 2010), we are not aware of any ESM studies examining within-person associations between program use and individual outcomes. The absence of such studies is particularly notable given the variability in effect sizes found in meta-analyses of between-person associations (e.g. Gajendran and Harrison, 2007). We simply do not know whether individuals experience reduced work–family conflict when they have flexibility than when they do not. In short, our confidence in the supposed benefits of flexible arrangements ought to be lower than it is given the quality of the empirical evidence (cf. Allen and Shockley, 2009).

Inferential errors

Often, researchers use the results of between-person analyses to make within-person inferences regarding work–family associations. For example, a positive between-person association between a particular coping mechanism and some work–family outcome is commonly interpreted to mean that an individual will fare better should he or she increase use of that particular coping method. However, making that sort of within-person inference minimally requires a longitudinal design. Moreover, since coping is known to vary daily, the longitudinal design ought to consist of brief inter-observational periods. Yet, as far as we know, there are no daily studies of coping and work–family experiences.

The inferential problem arises because within-person correlations can differ in both magnitude and direction from between-person correlations. As noted by Kenny, Bolger and Kashy (2002), it is possible to obtain a significant between-person correlation even though no one in the sample shows a significant within-person association. Indeed, we have observed differences between within-person and between-person associations in our own work–family studies. In a daily study of non-professional couples, Bass *et al.* (2009b) found significant within-person and between-person associations between women's work hours and leisure time spent with children. The within-person association was negative, indicating that on days when wives worked more, they spent less time in leisure with their children. However, the between-person association was positive, indicating that wives who worked more hours also reported spending more time in leisure with their kids. It would clearly be an error to conclude from the between-person association that increases in a woman's work hours are related to increases in her leisure time with children. No one, for example, would recommend that women could enjoy more quality time with their children by working more. The correct inference is that women who worked more hours overall also spent more time in leisure with children, but these women spent less time in leisure with children on *days* when they worked more hours.

Retrospective reporting biases

Cross-sectional studies of work and family consist entirely of retrospective reports on distal personal experiences. Consider the following item from a popular measure of work–family conflict (Netemeyer, Boles and McMurrian, 1996): "Things I want to do at home do not get done because of the demands my job puts on me." In order to accurately respond to the item, an individual must recall past instances of disruption that would be stored as episodic long-term memories. Ample experimental research indicates that memories of this type are loosely organized, subject to rapid forgetting, and biased by several recall processes (Kahneman, 1999; Robinson and Clore, 2002a; Ross, 1989).

Reporting accurately on distal work–family experiences also requires the individual to aggregate across relevant episodes over time. As the time frame for these reports increase, the recall of work–family experiences is likely to be based to a greater extent on one's beliefs rather than the actual episodes (Robinson and Clore, 2002a). In a study of emotional recall, Robinson and Clore (2002b) found that response latency for emotion judgments increased linearly as the reporting time frame increased from now, to hours, days, and weeks, suggesting that individuals were attempting to access emotional episodes in memory. However, as the time frame moved beyond weeks to months, years, and "in general," response latencies did not increase, suggesting recall on the basis of more general beliefs. Although work–family experiences are not affective responses per se, they are strongly associated with daily affect, would be similarly stored in memory, and presumably would be subject to belief based recall (e.g. Ilies *et al.*, 2007; Song, Foo and Uy, 2008).

Although the types of reports solicited in experience sampling studies are also retrospective, the temporal distance between the experience and report is relatively short. As a result, it's reasonable to assume that individuals are able to access these episodic memories. In experience sampling studies using a signal-contingent method, the report may be so close in time to the experience that it is directly accessible as experienced. As the time frame for experience sampling increases, individuals may be forced to rely on episodic memories of their experiences, and some recall bias may influence the reporting. Nevertheless, the standard end-of-day recall used in interval contingent studies is likely to be more closely based on actual experiences than the general experience reports solicited in cross-sectional studies.

Within-person variability

There can be no doubt that individuals' work–family experiences vary throughout the day. As an illustration, Figure 8.1 shows the self-reported levels of work–family conflict by two individuals who participated in a 14-day daily study (Butler *et al.*, 2005). Substantial within-person variability is actually predicted by several theories relevant to the study of the work–family interface. For example, conservation of resources theory (Hobfoll, 1988, 1989) predicts that environmental resource loss predicts strain. To the extent that relevant environmental features,

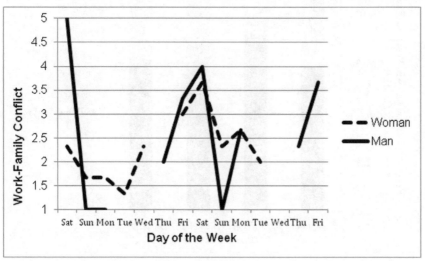

Figure 8.1 Illustration of dynamic work–family experiences for two individuals

such as job demands, show significant daily variability (Butler *et al.*, 2005), then work–family conflict should similarly be variable. However, some of that dynamism may be eliminated by resource investment, such as a family supportive organizational culture, that can protect against resource loss. Thus, COR theory would predict less daily variability in work–family conflict for individuals with greater coping resources. Other theories, such as boundary theory, similarly predict variability in work–family experiences (Ashforth, Kreiner and Fugate, 2000; Nippert-Eng, 1996). For example, individuals with greater boundary flexibility and permeability could be expected to also show greater daily variability in work–family experiences as boundary theory predicts that both factors increase role intrusions.

Substantial within-person variability in work–family experiences poses a problem for cross-sectional studies because it is not clear what work–family constructs measured at a single point in time or "in general" represent. Although longitudinal data from panel designs can capture within-person variability, these studies often involve long time lags. There is no theoretical basis for determining the appropriate time lag between the measurement of modeled work–family variables, but we argue that frequent observations such as those made possible by experience sampling designs provide the most ecologically valid view of individuals' work–family experiences.

A substantial number of studies, reviewed below, indicate that work–family experiences vary significantly from day-to-day. As shown in Figure 8.2, estimates of within-person variability in work-to-family conflict, expressed as a percentage

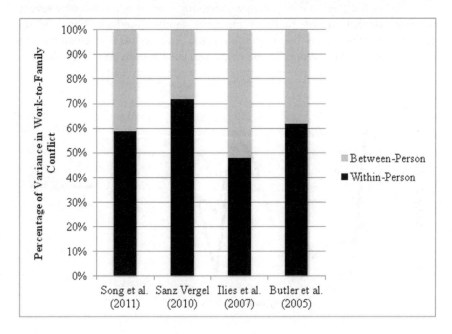

Figure 8.2 Reported variance for "null" models of work-to-family conflict

of total variance, range from 48 per cent (Ilies *et al.*, 2007) to 72 per cent (Sanz-Vergel *et al.*, 2010). Although fewer in number, studies also find substantial within-person variability in family-to-work conflict and work-to-family facilitation (Butler *et al.*, 2005; Song *et al.*, 2011). We should note that estimates of within-person variance in work–family experiences confound true variance in those experiences with variance due to measurement error. At best, we can say that estimates of within-person variability in sampled experiences overestimate the true variability, but it is not known by how much.

Review of work–family experience sampling studies

We conducted a search of the published research literature and attempted to identify all of the studies examining linkages between work and family using ESM. We restricted our review to studies that reported within-person relationships between work and family. That is, both the predictor and criterion had to be measured within-person (i.e., at Level-1 in HLM terms). In addition, we restricted our review to studies examining direct, spillover, or crossover effects from work to family (or vice versa) and to studies that examined variables that were clearly work or family based. Our review did not include the experience sampling research on recovery, reviewed elsewhere in this volume (Sonnentag). We summarize a few of the key studies below, but a comprehensive table reviewing this literature, editable by anyone, may be found at "http://goo.gl/UVU9F".

Spillover and direct work–family influences

The term spillover refers to influences among work and family that generate similarities between the two domains (Edwards and Rothbard, 2000). In the most restrictive sense, spillover has been used to describe a process by which the same construct (e.g. positive affect) spills over from one role to another, thus linking the two roles (Edwards and Rothbard, 2000; Judge and Ilies, 2004). As Edwards and Rothbard (2000) explain in their seminal paper on mechanisms linking work and family, a second type of work–family spillover refers to effects from one domain to another that link distinct yet related constructs (e.g. job satisfaction and marital satisfaction; Ilies, Wilson and Wagner, 2009). Below we review key within-individual studies concerning the second type of spillover because the first type involves, by definition, constructs that are not specific to either work or family roles (e.g. positive affect). We also review some of the key studies of direct within-individual influences between work and family that may not meet the strict definition of spillover per se.

In perhaps the first within-individual work–family study, Repetti (1989) examined how workload impacted withdrawal and emotions at home in a sample of 33 air traffic controllers. Results generally supported the hypothesized negative effects of workload on family life, although only subjective workload had an effect on marital withdrawal. Even though this study involved only one daily survey, a major strength of its design involves the use of both employee and spouse reports, as well as objective measures of workload, which eliminates common rater bias as an explanation for the observed associations. In a follow-up study, Repetti (1993) examined the within-individual associations between several work characteristics and health complaints and mood at home. The findings from this second study showed that workload and negative social interactions increased health complaints and were associated with more negative moods at home, although only subjective workload was related to health complaints.

In another important early work–family study that adopted an experience-sampling methodology, Williams *et al.* (1991) conceptualized work–family conflict as juggling between the two roles and found that juggling work and family roles resulted in higher negative affect and lower task enjoyment in a sample of working mothers. In a follow-up study of 41 working parents, Williams and Alliger (1994) found that multiple role juggling, task demands, personal control and goal progress predicted mood in both work and family roles, and that moods, role juggling and role involvement predicted work–family conflict. These two studies by Williams and colleagues are important because they specifically addressed work–family conflict and also because their design separated predictor and criterion variables in time (i.e., lagged effects) within each day of the study.

Butler *et al.* (2005) also specifically addressed work–family conflict in a study of 91 parents. These authors found a positive within-individual relationship between job demands and work–family conflict across the 14 days of the study, but did not find support for the buffering hypothesis of the demands-control model (Karasek, 1979) that predicts a dampening effect of job control on the strength of the relationship between demands and work–family conflict. In fact, the results concerning the interaction between demands and control were opposite from the demands-control prediction.

Also examining how job demands influence family life, Ilies *et al.* (2007) employed a sophisticated experience-sampling design by surveying employees twice at work (via the Internet) and once at home (on paper surveys that were mailed each morning) on each of the 10 days of the study. Importantly, in this study spouses were also interviewed daily by a survey research organization employed by these researchers. The results of this study supported a model by which workload decreased employees' engagement in family social activities by increasing work–family conflict. This study also validated the subjective measurement of work–family conflict at the daily level by finding a negative within-individual association of work–family conflict with social behavior at home (importantly, these two constructs were measured from different sources). In another study examining the effects of job demands on employees' family lives, Bass et al. (2009) showed that work hours were negatively related to time spent in childcare and leisure with children.

Crossover between work and family

In contrast to the direct effects of spillover, crossover occurs when one person's experiences influence another family member's experiences through a transmission process (Westman, 2001). Marital and family research suggests crossover effects occur due to the interconnection of family members and the intimate nature of their relationships (Larson and Almeida, 1999). The examination of crossover effects is underrepresented generally in work–family research, including among studies using ESM. This may be because of the difficulty in collecting simultaneous, matched reports from multiple family members. Due to the lack of studies on crossover from family to work, our review was limited to studies in which one family member's work experience influenced the family experience of a spouse or significant other. Other related research on distress crossover between spouses is not reviewed here because it may not strictly represent work–family linkages, but this is included in our linked table (Song *et al.*, 2011).

The ESM studies of this phenomenon have demonstrated crossover from one person's work experience to both marital and parenting experiences of his or her spouse. For example, in a 42 day interval contingent (end of day) study of 49 couples with children, Doumas, Margolin and John (2003) found that husband's work hours were negatively related to both marital warmth and marital conflict reported by their wives. Also, wives worked more hours when their husband's experienced less marital warmth on the previous day. In a 14 day end of day study of 46 non-professional couples with children, Bass *et al.* (2009) found that greater daily job demands for wives were positively associated with husband's reports of spending leisure time with children.

Conclusion

The studies reviewed above dismantle any notion that work and family experiences are separate and independent. Moreover, the findings illuminate the risks of particular daily work experiences to individual well-being (e.g. mood) and family functioning (e.g. child and marital relationships). These within-person relationships provide more compelling evidence of the link between work and family than between-person results, some of which may be discounted because of third-variable confounds. However, the existing ESM studies are not without limitations – they focus on putative antecedents at work and outcomes at home and exclusively examine affective transmission mechanisms. To overcome these limitations and research gaps we identified earlier, we highlight some directions for future research in the following section.

Future directions in work–family experience sampling research

In the following section, we propose several promising avenues for future work–family ESM research. We should note that the relative lack of studies using ESM means that there are a multitude of important, unanswered research questions. Moreover, given that within-person findings may not correspond with between-person findings, there is a need for work–family researchers to attempt to replicate cross-sectional studies using ESM.

Family-to-work relationships

As we noted in our review of the literature, nearly all of the extant work–family ESM studies examine the impact of work on putative family outcomes. This is a particularly glaring gap in the research because it reinforces conventional notions that what happens in one's family ought to be irrelevant to performance at work. A recent study designed to address this concern, by Ilies, Keeney and Scott (2011), examined how sharing positive experiences about the workday at home influence evaluations of work. In this study, employees were asked to describe their most positive work experience of the day and rate it on several characteristics for a period of three weeks. Then for about half of these experiences (chosen randomly), they were instructed to share them with their spouses at home. The results indicated that the simple fact of sharing positive work experiences at home – what the authors termed *work–family interpersonal capitalization*, increased job satisfaction, controlling for how positive the experience was and for other positive events/experiences. This study provides a nice model for future research in this area addressing the general question of how family processes influence individuals at work.

Mechanisms linking work and family

Although the affective mechanisms linking work and family are fairly well understood, other potential linking mechanisms have largely been unexamined. This has constrained our understanding of the within-person mechanisms that allow work to affect family and vice versa. Recently, Repetti, Wang and Saxbe (2009) suggested two additional mechanisms of spillover between work and family roles, cognitive and physiological. We add to that list a behavioral linking mechanism, cross-boundary behaviors. Below, we detail some of the mechanisms that could be explored in future research. Given that these mechanisms may be correlated with affect, researchers should specify multiple mediation models to identify the unique effects of each potential mechanism.

Physiological mechanisms

One potential physiological mechanism that has recently been explored is cortisol, a hormone that is released in response to stress. Saxbe and Repetti (2010) reported a study that collected mood and cortisol information 4 times a day for three days from 30 couples. They found that smilar to negative mood, salivary cortisol levels of husbands and wives were positively correlated. The strength of the relationship was stronger when couples were at home in the morning and evening, which suggests that the physiological synchrony between spouses emerges from shared life experiences.

Cardiovascular indicators may also provide physiological evidence of the link between work and family. In a study with a complex experience-sampling design, Ilies, Dimotakis and De Pater (2010) surveyed employees at work three times a day randomly within 2-hour blocks, once a day at the end of work, and another time at home, using Palm Pilots. Along with the at work and end-of-work surveys, employees also took their blood pressure using semi-automated monitors that recorded the time and day of the measurement so they could be matched with the subjective response data. Relevant for work and family, the results of this study showed that even though high work demands increased both subjective (affective) distress and systolic blood pressure, the negative effects of high work demands on well-being at home were realized primarily through a subjective mechanism. That is, the indirect effect through subjective distress was much stronger than the one through blood pressure.

Cognitive mechanisms

Cognition is a common psychological pathway for spillover between work and family. As individuals are engaged in work or family roles, thoughts about alternative role demands or experiences may intrude. Although cognitive processes linking work and family have largely been ignored by researchers, there is empirical evidence from an ESM study that cognitions are important in the spillover process. Cropley and Purvis (2003) had schoolteachers in the U.K. complete an hourly report of their cognitions on one mid-week evening. They found that teachers who were classified on the basis of a baseline survey as having high job strain had more ruminative thoughts about work than teachers with low strain. Interestingly, there were no differences in rumination between the two groups early in the evening, but as the evening wore on, rumination declined much more sharply for the low strain teachers. Overall, rumination tended to be lower when the teachers were with family or friends, suggesting that the mere presence of significant others may aid in the recovery process from work.

Cross-boundary behaviors

Another potential research focus for linking mechanisms between work and family is behavior. Role behaviors in one life domain (either work or family) can permeate the work–family boundary to manifest themselves in the other life domain (family or work). Greenhaus and Beutell (1985) classified behavior-based as one of three sources of conflict between work and family. Two particularly salient cross-boundary behaviors are overtime work and working from home. We are not aware of any ESM studies on these behaviors, but believe such work is warranted given their commonness.

First, working increasingly long hours, often at the expense of family, has been a relentless trend since the early 1970s (Schor, 1991). Second, with the increase of flexibility and portability of work, workers can request to work from home instead of at their office. The most well-studied issue in the literature on work location is telecommuting or telework, defined as work conducted from home that is supported by telecommunications technology and organizational formal policy (Kossek, Lautsch and Eaton, 2006). As one of the flexible work practices, working from home is viewed as a partial solution to ameliorate the clash between work and family demands (Hill *et al.*, 2001). Overtime work and working from home indicate that work has permeated the work–family boundary into the individual's non-work domain. To recover a lagging work schedule, employees may stay overtime at the office, therefore borrowing from home time; alternatively, he or she may take the uncompleted work back home to do, thereby allowing work to invade home space.

Making a business case for work–family balance

Some might argue from a business perspective that organizations only incur responsibility for helping employees better manage the intersection of work and family if a firm link is established between work–family experiences and valued organizational outcomes. ESM would provide a rigorous test of these questions because of their ability to examine within-person relationships over time. Unfortunately, outcomes that might be considered directly relevant to bottom-line concerns in business are rare to absent in work–family ESM studies. We think there are two promising avenues for future research in this area: exploring business outcomes and examining the impact of workplace flexibility programs.

Business outcomes

It's difficult to precisely define what constitutes a relevant business outcome, but three constructs with a seemingly more direct connection to business profits are performance, health, and withdrawal. Among all of the constructs investigated by organizational behavior researchers, few are more central to bottom-line concerns in business than job performance; yet, there is not a single experience sampling study examining the link between work–family experiences and job performance. These methods are well-suited for studying this question because there is empirical evidence that job performance is a dynamic phenomenon (e.g. Hofman, Jacobs and Baratta, 1993). Moreover, results from cross-sectional studies indicate that work–family conflict is related to both job performance and organizational citizenship behavior (Bragger *et al.*, 2005; Witt and Carlson, 2006). An end of workday study including performance information from supervisors, peers, or objective sources would be particularly beneficial because it would expand the number of studies with multi-sourced data.

Withdrawal behaviors such as tardiness and absence pose a challenge for ESM because they tend to occur at a low base rate. One solution to this problem is to use event contingent sampling, where individuals provide reports only when a withdrawal event occurs. An alternative approach is to use an interval contingent method over a very long time period, an approach used by Hackett, Bycio and Guion (1989) in a study of absence in nurses. Over four to five months, they provided paper surveys to nurses with the instruction to complete them after every scheduled shift, whether they worked the shift or not. They found that work interference with family was positively related to the desire to miss work, but was not related to actual absence. Other factors, such as death of a family member or friend, were positively related to absence.

Health outcomes could be considered an important business outcome because organizations may bear the costs of poor health either directly, through higher health insurance or provider costs, or indirectly through absence and performance. There is a large body of cross-sectional studies indicating a link between work–family experiences and health (Greenhaus, Allen and Spector, 2006), yet there are very few similar experience sampling studies. Recently, Wang *et al.* (2010) examined the daily relationship between work–family conflict and alcohol use, an indicator of behavioral health. Chinese workers responded to a telephone survey every evening for 35 consecutive days about their level of work-to-family and family-to-work conflict and their alcohol use on the previous day. Daily work-to-family but not family-to-work conflict was related to alcohol use, and the significant relationship was moderated by peer alcohol norms, worker support, and family support, all of which were measured on a baseline survey (i.e., level-2). Focusing on other health behaviors, such as diet and exercise, is a promising direction for future ESM studies because health behaviors are likely to show greater daily variability than physical or mental illness.

Using mobile technology to sample experiences

Mobile phones represent one of the newest alternative platforms survey researchers can adopt. Modern mobile phones have several unique technical features that are particularly suitable for ESM research. First, the phones are programmable and responses are captured, stored, and transferred in electronic formats. Furthermore, wireless technology allows instant transference of survey data. This technical feature is preferred when the survey demands immediate response or follow-up interactions need to be incorporated. Second, a mobile phone is a highly portable device that is carried wherever its owner goes. Survey questions can be delivered to participants who can respond by themselves with little time and location constraints. Moreover, the penetration rate of mobile phones is very high which provides the potential to reach a large population without the need to purchase the technology.

Phone capabilities have greatly expanded over the past decades, from simple voice communication to include data and multimedia functions. Almost all mobile phones can send SMS (Short Message Service) messages and make phone calls. More advanced phones can send MMS (multimedia message service) messages, access the internet, shoot photos, and record videos. These different functionalities allow different mobile survey modes. There are four basic modes of mobile surveys that can be delivered through mobile phone: SMS surveys, MMS surveys, application-based surveys, and mobile web surveys (Townsend, 2005; Li and Townsend, 2008). The last two modes have larger capacity to accommodate multi-item surveys than the first two; thus, they have been more often used in survey research.

We have identified two published work–family experience sampling research studies that used mobile survey techniques. In a study of married couples and their children in Finland, Rönkä and her associates used a variation of the SMS survey design (Rönkä *et al.*, 2010). They mailed to each participant a diary booklet including reporting times, instructions, and diary questions. Participants were asked to answer the survey three times a day using their own mobile phones for a period of one week. They were asked to input their answer to survey questions in one SMS message in pre-described order and format. Since this study used both paper-and-pencil and mobile techniques, it can be categorized as a fusion method, combining features of the two approaches, but eliminating the principal drawback of paper that the time of response is unknowable.

Another study used the application-based survey mode (i.e., surveys are programmed as downloadable applications or software that can be installed and run on clients' mobile phones.) to collect diary survey responses from 50 married couples in Singapore (Song, Foo and Uy, 2008). The application was J2ME based (a Java platform for mobile devices) and pre-installed into participants' mobile phones. Participants were reminded with SMSs 4 times a day for a period of 8 days. The survey had 15 items (the work version) or 17 items (the home version) depending on participants' reported life situation (work vs. home). More than half of surveys were collected within 2 minutes of sending the SMS reminders.

In short, the accessibility of participants "anywhere and anytime" enabled by mobile technology means researchers can capture time-sensitive and location-sensitive information from individuals, which are features particularly suitable for ESM research. Moreover, given the widespread use of mobile phones and the availability of free SMS services (e.g. Google voice), the startup costs for good experience sampling technology have been greatly diminished. We expect more and more work–family studies will use mobile phones rather than other platforms to collect diary survey data.

Conclusion

Experience sampling methods provide a unique way for researchers to capture dynamic work–family experiences, enabling them to explore within-person relationships while minimizing memory biases inherent to self-reported survey data. Although the work–family literature has expanded greatly in the last two decades, relatively few studies have employed ESM. As a result, there are many unanswered questions about within-person work–family relationships, some of which we addressed in this chapter. Fortunately for researchers, new technologies have reduced the costs of answering these questions. We greatly encourage new and established work–family researchers to consider ESM for their next research project.

References

Allen, T.D. and Shockley, K.M. (2009). Flexible work arrangments: Help or hype? In D.R. Crane and E.J. Hill (eds) *Handbook of families and work: Interdisciplinary perspectives* (265–284). Lanham, MD: University Press of America.

American Psychological Association. (2004). *Public policy, work, and families: The report of the APA presidential initiative on work and families.* Washington, DC: Author.

Ashforth, B.E., Kreiner, G.E. and Fugate, M. (2000). All in a day's work: Boundaries and micro role transitions. *Academy of Management Review* 25, 472–491.

Bass, B.L., Butler, A.B., Grzywacz, J.G. and Linney, K.D. (2009a). Work-family conflict and job satisfaction: Family resources as a buffer. *Journal of Family and Consumer Sciences* 100, 24–30.

—— (2009b). Do job demands undermine parenting? A daily analysis of spillover and crossover effects. *Family Relations* 58, 201–215.

Beal, D.J. and Weiss, H.M. (2003). Methods of ecological momentary assessment in organizational research. *Organizational Research Methods* 6, 440–464.

Bolger, N., Davis, A. and Rafaeli, E. (2003). Diary methods: Capturing life as it is lived. *Annual Review Psychology* 54, 579–616

Bragger, J.D., Rodriguez-Srednicki, O., Kutcher, E.J., Indovino, L. and Rosner, E. (2005). Work-family conflict, work-family culture, and organizational citizenship behavior among teachers. *Journal of Business and Psychology* 20, 303–324.

Butler, A.B., Grzywacz, J.G., Bass, B.L. and Linney, K.D. (2005). Extending the demands-control model: A daily diary study of job characteristics, work-family conflict, and work-family facilitation. *Journal of Occupational and Organizational Psychology* 78, 155–169.

Casper, W.J., Eby, L.T., Bordeaux, C., Lockwood, A. and Lambert, D. (2007). A review of research methods in IO/OB work-family research. *Journal of Applied Psychology* 92, 28–43.

Cropley, M. and Purvis, L.J.M. (2003). Job strain and rumination about work issues during leisure time: A diary study. *European Journal of Work and Organizational Psychology* 12, 195–207.

Doumas, D.M., Margolin, G. and John, R.S. (2003). The relationship between daily marital interaction, work, and health-promoting behaviors in dual-earner couples: An extension of the work-family spillover model. *Journal of Family Issues* 24, 3–20.

Edwards, J.R. and Rothbard, N.P. (2000). Mechanisms linking work and family: Clarifying the relationship between work and family constructs. *Academy of Management Review* 25, 178–199.

Executive Office of the President, Council of Economic Advisors. (2010). *Work-life balance and the economics of workplace flexibility.* Washington, DC: Author.

Gajendran, R.S. and Harrison, D.A. (2007). The good, the bad, and the unknown about telecommuting: Meta-analysis of psychological mediators and individual consequences. *Journal of Applied Psychology* 92, 1524–1541.

Greenhaus, J.H. and Beutell, N.J. (1985). Sources of conflict between work and family roles. *Academy of Management Review* 10, 76–88.

Greenhaus, J.H., Allen, T.D. and Spector, P.E. (2006). Health consequences of work-family conflict: The dark side of the work-family interface. In. P.L. Perrewe and D.C. Ganster (eds) *Research in Occupational Stress and Well-Being: Vol 5. Employee health, coping, and methodologies* (61–98). Amsterdam: JAI Press: Elsevier.

Hackett, R.D., Bycio, P. and Guion, R.M. (1989). Absenteeism among hospital nurses: An idiographic-longitudinal analysis. *Academy of Management Journal* 32, 424–453.

Hill, E.J., Hawkins, A.J., Ferris, M. and Weitzman, M. (2001). Finding an extra day a week: The positive influence of perceived job flexibility on work and family life balance. *Family Relations* 50, 49–58.

Hobfoll, S.E. (1988). *The Ecology of Stress.* New York: Hemisphere.

—— (1989). Conservation of resources: A new attempt at conceptualizing stress. *American Psychologist* 44, 513–524.

Hofmann, D.A., Jacobs, R. and Baratta, J.E. (1993). Dynamic criteria and the measurement of change. *Journal of Applied Psychology* 78, 194–204.

Ilies, R., Dimotakis, N. and De Pater, I.E. (2010). Psychological and physiological reactions to high workloads: Implications for well-being. *Personnel Psychology* 63, 407–436.

Ilies, R., Keeney, J. and Scott, B.A. (2011). Work-family interpersonal capitalization: Sharing positive work events at home. *Organizational Behavior and Human Decision Processes* 114, 115–126.

Ilies, R., Wilson, K.S. and Wagner, D.T. (2009). The spillover of job satisfaction onto employees' family lives: The facilitating role of work-family integration. *Academy of Management Journal* 52, 87–102.

Ilies, R., Schwind, K.M., Wagner, D.T., Johnson, M.D., DeRue, D.S. and Ilgen, D.R. (2007). When can employees have a family life? The effects of daily workload and affect on work-family conflict and social activities at home. *Journal of Applied Psychology* 92, 1368–1379.

Judge, T.A. and Ilies, R. (2004). Affect and job satisfaction: A study of their relationship at work and at home. *Journal of Applied Psychology* 89, 661–673.

Kahneman, D. (1999). Objective happiness. In D. Kahneman, E. Diener and N. Schwarz (eds) *Well-being: The foundations of hedonic psychology* (85–105). New York: Russell Sage Foundation.

Karasek, R.A. (1979). Job demands, job decision latitude, and mental strain: Implications for job redesign. *Administrative Science Quarterly* 24, 285–308.

Kenny, D.A., Bolger, N. and Kashy, D.A. (2002). Traditional methods for estimating multilevel models. In D.S. Moskowitz and S.L. Hershberger (eds) *Modeling intraindividual variability with repeated measures data: Methods and applications* (1–24). Mahwah, NJ: Lawrence Erlbaum Associates.

Kossek, E.E., Baltes, B.B. and Matthews, R.A. (2011). How work-family research can finally have an impact in organizations. *Industrial and Organizational Psychology: Perspectives on Science and Practice* 4, 352–369.

Kossek, E.E., Lautsch, B.A. and Eaton, S.C. (2006). Telecommuting, control, and boundary management: Correlates of policy use and practice, job control and work-family effectiveness. *Journal of Vocational Behavior* 68, 347–367.

Larson, R.W. and Almeida, D.M. (1999). Emotional transmission in the daily lives of families: A new paradigm for studying family process. *Journal of Marriage and the Family* 61, 5–20.

Li, H. and Townsend, L. (2008). Mobile research in marketing: Design and implementation issues. *International Journal of Mobile Marketing* 3, 32–40.

Netemeyer, R.G., Boles, J.S. and McMurrian, R. (1996). Development and validation of work-family conflict and family-work conflict scales. *Journal of Applied Psychology* 81, 400–410.

Nippert-Eng, C.E. (1996). *Home and work: Negotiating Boundaries through Everyday Life*. Chicago, IL: University of Chicago Press.

Repetti, R.L. (1989). Effects of daily workload on subsequent behavior during marital interaction: The roles of social withdrawal and spouse support. *Journal of Personality and Social Psychology* 57, 651–659.

—— (1993). Short-term effects of occupational stressors on daily mood and health complaints. *Health Psychology* 12, 125–131.

Repetti, R., Wang, S. and Saxbe, D. (2009). Bringing it all back home: How outside stressors shape families' everyday lives. *Current Directions in Psychological Science* 18, 106–111.

Robinson, M.D. and Clore, G.L. (2002a). Belief and feeling: Evidence for an accessibility model of emotional self-report. *Psychological Bulletin* 128, 934–960.

—— (2002b). Episodic and semantic knowledge in emotional self-report: Evidence for two judgment processes. *Journal of Personality and Social Psychology* 83, 198–215.

Rönkä, A., Malinen, K., Kinnunen, U., Tolvanen, A. and Lämsä, T. (2010). Capturing daily family dynamics via text messages: Development of the mobile diary. *Community, Work, & Family* 13, 5–21.

Ross, M. (1989). Relation of implicit theories to the construction of personal histories. *Psychological Review* 96, 341–357.

Sanz-Vergel, A.I., Demerouti, E., Moreno-Jimenez, B. and Mayo, M. (2010). Work-family balance and energy: A day-level study on recovery conditions. *Journal of Vocational Behavior* 76, 118–130.

Saxbe, D. and Repetti, R.L. (2010). For better or worse? Coregulation of couples' cortisol levels. *Journal of Personality and Social Psychology* 98, 92–103.

Schor, J. (1991). *The overworked American: the unexpected decline of leisure*. New York: Basic Books.

Shiffman, S., Stone, A.A. and Hufford, M.R. (2008). Ecological momentary assessment. *Annual Review of Clinical Psychology* 4, *1–32*.

Song, Z., Foo, M.D. and Uy, M.A. (2008). Mood spillover and crossover among dual-earner couples: A cell phone event sampling study. *Journal of Applied Psychology* 93, 443–452.

Song, Z., Foo, M.D., Uy, M.A. and Sun, S. (2011). Unraveling the daily stress crossover between unemployed individuals and their employed spouses. *Journal of Applied Psychology* 96, 151–168.

Townsend, L. (2005). The status of wireless survey solutions: The emerging "power of the thumb." *Journal of Interactive Advertising* 6, 40–45.

Wang, M., Liu, S., Zhan, Y. and Shi, J. (2010). Daily work-family conflict and alcohol use: Testing the cross-level moderation effects of peer drinking norms and social support. *Journal of Applied Psychology* 95, 377–386.

US Council of Economic Advisors (2010). *Work-life balance and the economics of workplace flexibility*. Washington, DC: Author.

Westman, M. (2001). Stress and strain crossover. *Human Relations* 54, 717–752.

Wheeler, L. and Reis, H.T. (1991). Self-recording of everyday life events: Origins, types, and uses. *Journal of Personality* 59, 339–354.

Williams, K.J. and Alliger, G.M. (1994). Role stressors, mood spillover, and perceptions of work-family conflict in employed parents. *Academy of Management Journal* 37, 837–868.

Williams, K.J., Suls, J., Alliger, G.M., Learner, S.M. and Wan, C.K. (1991). Multiple role juggling and daily mood states in working mothers: An experience sampling study. *Journal of Applied Psychology* 76, 664–674.

Witt, L.A. and Carlson, D.S. (2006). The work family interface and job performance: Moderating effects of conscientiousness and perceived organizational support. *Journal of Occupational Health Psychology* 11, 343–357.

9 Chains of events in work–family research

Fabienne T. Amstad and Norbert K. Semmer

Work–family interference is a widely discussed phenomenon (Frone, 2003; Geurts and Demeouti, 2003; Greenhaus and Allen, 2011). But we know rather little about specific mechanisms involved. How does work interfere with family life in everyday situations? Are there specific family situations that have a negative impact on work life? What, specifically, does it look like when work negatively affects family life, or family negatively affects work? This chapter focuses on specific events in the work and family domains and the mechanisms linking these discrete events. We focus on how specific events in one domain trigger further events in the other domain, leading to (more or less typical) event-chains. We introduce a particular study design, the case-crossover design, which is well suited for identifying the triggers for specific outcomes. Finally, we present a study that tries to identify prototypical chains of events.

Mechanisms of the work–family interface

Conditions at work and in the family can be analyzed on at least two different levels: a general level and a specific level. Maertz and Boyar (2011) likewise recognize these two levels although they refer to "levels" as a general condition, whereas they refer to "episodes" as specific conditions. Studying the interface between work and family on a general level focuses on the typical or normative experience, and is assessed using averages or percentages. For instance, researchers assess the amount of stress and resources in one life domain, the number of important events, or the frequency of work–family conflict. Such conditions are averaged and analyzed with regard to their associations with potential outcomes, such as well-being, health, productivity, or satisfaction with life domains. Psychology in general, and also work–family research, has traditionally focused on this general level, asking question like "Is work–family conflict associated with less work satisfaction?" (cf. meta-analyses by Allen *et al.*, 2000; Amstad *et al.*, 2011; Byron, 2005; Ford, Heinen and Langkamer, 2007; Kossek and Ozeki, 1998; Michel *et al.*, 2011), including possible mediators and moderators (e.g. Kossek *et al.*, 2011; Michel *et al.*, 2009).

Increasingly, however, studies are focusing on a more specific level (cf. Bolger, Davis and Rafaeli, 2003). Rather than analyzing averages over long periods of time, they focus on short-term developments, such as daily events and conditions that may change rapidly over time. Such studies ask questions like "Is work stress during the day associated with less enthusiasm for household chores in the evening?" (e.g. Repetti and Wood, 1997). Furthermore, studies have started to investigate the impact of specific daily activities on well-being at home (e.g. Sonnentag and Zijlstra, 2006) and of day-specific variables, such as daily time pressure or working hours, on well-being (Sonnentag and Bayer, 2005).

All these studies have led to important insights. What is missing, however, is a focus on specific events (Maertz and Boyar, 2011). What characterizes events at work that do, or do not, have an impact on family life, and vice versa? Furthermore, we might ask how these impacts on the respective other domain unfold: Events often do not have a "direct" impact on the respective other domain; rather they trigger behaviors, or other events, which, in turn, impact the other domain. For instance, a failure at work may trigger rumination that is carried over into the family domain, where it may trigger additional problems. However, the failure experience might also trigger successful problem-solving, leading to less rumination about the failure, or even to a positive spillover in terms of sharing one's success. Finally, the type of impact may be quite specific as well, involving, for instance, distancing, sharing, seeking support, or seeking distraction. Our aim, therefore, is to have a closer look at event-characteristics, and to discuss how such an event-based approach may contribute to work–family research.

An event-related approach in work–family research

Affective event theory defines an event as "something that occurs in a certain place during a particular period of time. Implied [...] is the idea of change, a change in circumstances, a change in what one is currently experiencing" (Weiss and Cropanzano, 1996: 31). Some, but not all, events have an affective significance in that they create emotional reactions or mood change in individuals. Work and family life experiences often have an affective quality. Not only major life events like promotion, career change, divorce, or childbirth, but also day-to-day experiences like going for a bike-ride with one's children, or being able to help a coworker, may trigger affective reactions (Eby, Maher and Butts, 2010; cf. Kanner *et al.*, 1981). Affective reactions in turn influence behavior (Stanley and Burrows, 2001; Weiss and Cropanazano, 1996), which then triggers further reactions, both by the focal person and by others involved.

Specific events have occasionally been studied in research in work and family research (e.g. Pearlin and McCall, 1990). However, if (a) events influence affect, and (b) affect influences behavior, which then (c) triggers new events, we are dealing with chains of events. Relating one element of that chain (e.g. the failure experience at work) to a later one (e.g. strain-related spillover into family life) neglects the fact that any intermediate element of the event-chain may enhance, or diminish, the chances of a specific outcome (in this case: strain-related spillover) occurring. Refining the study of work and family experiences by focusing on the intermediate events would likely enhance our understanding of how things unfold over time. Therefore, we feel it is important to study not only events but also chains of events.

An Event-Chain Framework (ECF) for Studying the Work–family Interface

Amstad and Semmer (2009) developed a framework for studying chains of events at the work–family interface. The framework applies to both positive (uplifts) and negative events (hassles), and to both directions of the work–family process (work-to-family and family-to-work). The framework contains four stages of successive events (see Figure 9.1):

(1) An event occurs in life domain one (work or family); it can be either positive or negative. For instance: Your students are not attentive in your class on the day your supervisor monitors your teaching. If the event is negative, as the example would suggest, (2) the person is likely to cope with the situation in the same life domain in which the event occurred (e.g. try to get the class's attention back, avoid your supervisor right after the class finishes, etc.; see Zohar, 1999). Note that coping, by the most common definition (e.g. Lazarus, 1999) does not imply that these attempts have to be successful. The framework then focuses on the person entering the second life domain, which, in our example, is the family. Before examining the impact of the event on the second life domain, (3) the specific condition of this second domain are considered. For instance, it should matter whether the momentary circumstances are "as usual" or not. With regard to our example, the moment you arrive at home and your spouse gives you some flowers, you might forget about your stressful work day. Conversely, if a child is ill, you may put your experience at work into perspective. But if it is an evening like any other, there is enough room for the negative work event to intrude your family life. (4) Finally, like the event itself, its impact on the affected life domain can be either positive or negative. In our example the impact is likely to be negative. Coming home in the evening, you may not be in the mood to play with your children, because your thoughts are still circling around the turbulence in the class or around the supervisor; as a consequence, your children may be disappointed. An important feature of this sequence is that the triggering event in

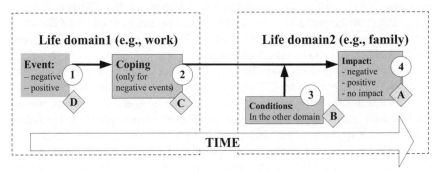

Figure 9.1 Framework for studying chains of events at the work–family interface

the first life domain (in our example the work domain) does not deterministically impact the second life domain (e.g. family). Coping attempts at work may have been successful; positive events at work, such as a positive feedback about your last class, may have compensated for it (cf. Gross *et al.*, 2011), or you might have calmed down on your way home and not be bothered by the incident any more by the time you enter your home (cf. the concept of boundary management; Kreiner, Hollensbe and Sheep, 2009). Furthermore, the framework simplifies things, as there may be many more events that come into play between the original event and the potential impact in the other life domain (e.g. having an argument with a colleague may lead to you being inattentive at a meeting, causing further problems and conflicts).

Examples of studies consistent with the proposed framework

Studies that have tried to investigate chains of events are quite rare. Usually, they focus on parts of the framework. A few empirical studies have analyzed the relationship between mood and daily hassles at home or at work, such as overload, or arguments with the spouse, children, or co-workers (Bolger, Kessler and Schilling, 1989; Bolger *et al.*, 1990; DeLongis, Folkman and Lazarus, 1988). Evidence for spillover effects on mood (in both directions, that is, work-to-family and family-to-work) has been found; however, the effects were much stronger for negative than for positive mood (Williams and Alliger, 1994). Mood has also been found to mediate between job and marital daily satisfaction (Heller and Watson, 2005). In several of these studies stressful events were assessed in detail (e.g. argument with spouse or coworkers), but the potential outcome was assessed in much more general terms, that is, mood. These studies, therefore, do not tell us much about the specific impact the events had in the other life domain

Conversely, some studies focused on a specific kind of impact, but remained rather general with regard to triggers. Thus, studies investigated the relationship between experienced distress at work and social support (Pearlin and McCall, 1990), social withdrawal (Repetti, 1992; Repetti and Wood, 1997), and the involvement in various activities (Crouter *et al.*, 1989) at home, such as parenting behavior. In this research, the nature of the stressful events in the other life domain was not specified. Moreover, processes were described with regard to one direction only, that is, for work-to-family conflicts.

Micro process designs to study chains of events

In the following, we would like to have a closer look to different possibilities to study such chains of events. Considering our framework there are two possibilities to study chains of events. One approach starts with a triggering event (No. 1 in Figure 9.1) and its consequences throughout the day, including consequences in the other life-domain. For instance, one would follow an individual's day from the inattentive class through the escape from the supervisor after class to the "usual" evening at home, where the individual is not in the mood to play with the children.

The other approach starts with a specific event that is analyzed as outcome, and goes backward to see what could have lead to this event (case-crossover design: see characters A-D in Figure 9.1). In our example, we would start with the fact that our focal person is not in the mood to play with the children, trying to find out why he/she is not in a playing mood by going back.

Both approaches can shed light on how conflict or facilitation between life domains unfolds throughout a day, or from day to day. The case-crossover design is especially strong in terms of causal inferences. Our event-chain approach informs about typical constellations and sequences. Neither approach has been used much in work–family research. We will first discuss the case-crossover design and then present a study illustrating our event-chain approach.

Case-crossover design

Case-crossover designs are often used in epidemiological research, particularly with "rare event" types of conditions such as heart attack. The basic question is: "Did something different happen on the day of the heart attack that may have triggered this outcome? For instance, Mittleman and colleagues (1993) studied physical exertion and found that heavy physical exertion can trigger the onset of myocardial infarction (i.e., heart attack), especially among individuals who are typically sedentary. In a similar vein, Möller *et al.* (1999) and Mittleman *et al.* (1995) demonstrated that anger episodes can trigger myocardial infarction.

An important aspect of a case-crossover design is that participants serve as their own control. Specifically, the time before the event is compared to another time for the same participant. For instance, participants might be interviewed with regard to events that immediately preceded the outcome of interest. Then it is determined if a specific trigger (e.g. an anger episode) was also present in an earlier, comparable time period (e.g. the same time the day before). If it was present less frequently during control periods (i.e., non-myocardial infarction days) than during hazard periods (i.e., myocardial infarction days) in a representative sample of individuals and observation days, the researcher would conclude the hypothesized trigger is, indeed, a risk factor for the event. However, if the trigger was frequently present during control periods (e.g. participants report being angry shortly before the onset of myocardial infarction but also report to have been angry frequently during the control time, when no myocardial infarction occurred), then anger could not be regarded as a trigger. Case-crossover designs have the unique advantage of having perfect control of all possible confounders because the individual serves as his or her own control. Moreover, strong individual-difference variables, such as hostility or other elements of personal, can be analyzed as moderators. This possibility has been illustrated in research indicating that the effect of acute anger on myocardial infarction is stronger among individuals who typically display nonhostile behavior (Möller *et al.*, 1999).

Case-crossover designs are suited for events that have an abrupt onset. Cumulative risks, such as myocardial infarction after years of exposure to aversive conditions, cannot be analyzed by way of case-crossover designs. Furthermore, the effect period, that is, the time during which the trigger shows its effect, should not be too long. Thus MI occurring long after an angering event, due to prolonged rumination, is more difficult to analyze with a case-crossover design, because many other things could have happened between the triggering event and the outcome event as the time period gets longer, and one would have to control for a number of potential other triggers.

How could such a design be used in work–family research? In our framework (Figure 9.1) a specific event in one life domain would be in the focus of attention (A), and we ask what happened just before. This may be in the same life domain (B) or in the respective other life domain (C and D). Then one would ask about a comparable time period (e.g. the night before) or about an average of a longer preceding period (e.g. the last few months) where the outcome in question did not occur (control period), and determine whether the potential trigger was present or not. If we return to the example of the stressed professor with the inattentive class, we would look at other days on which the focal person was not in the mood to play with the children in the evening and investigate if this evening also was preceded by an inattentive class. The more often evenings with a "non-playing mood" were preceded by an inattentive class across participants, the more likely the inattentive class would be classified as a "trigger" for subsequent withdrawal in the family domain.

In this way, specific triggers for events that characterize spillover and crossover between the domains of work and family could be determined. On the negative side, one could try to identify, for instance, events at work (in the family) that precede conflict in the other domain. On the positive side, one could study the precursors for sharing work (private) experiences with the family (with colleagues). One could also study events that are likely to disrupt a spiral that is developing (e.g. conflict escalation), thus investigating the "triggers" of a non-event where normally an event would be expected; applying boundary work tactics (Kreiner, Hollensbe and Sheep, 2009) would be candidates for such "antidotes" for negative spillover. Furthermore, one could study the immediate triggers of making a decision, which might have been contemplated for some time. For instance, one might try to identify what triggers the decision to quit one's job, to move, to look for a job after having a child, etc. Such changes often are discussed for quite some time, and then a specific event may trigger "crossing the Rubicon", as when a performance evaluation that is considered unfair triggers the decision to quit one's job. Thus, the case-crossover design might be used to establish the predictive power of "shocks" that are considered an important trigger for quitting in the unfolding model of employee turnover (Lee and Mitchell, 1994; Holtom *et al.*, 2005, cf. Holtom *et al.*, 2008). Employing the case-crossover design in this way might advance our understanding of the characteristics of triggers for important events, both at work and in the family.

The chain-of-events approach

Our own approach shares many features with the case-crossover design. It is also oriented towards identifying the characteristics of events, or behaviors that trigger further events and behaviors. It is less stringent, however, with regard to causal inferences, and it focuses not on single triggers but on event chains. Following Figure 9.1, the basic idea is to investigate how an experience (event) in one life domain influences a person in the respective other life domain. Hence, a triggering event (positive or negative) of one life domain is followed through into another domain to explore the social consequence of the event and individuals' reactions to it (e.g. mood, rumination, behavior). In contrast to the case-crossover design, we do not ask backward (what happened before Y occurred), but rather forward (what happened after X occurred). This study design is especially appropriate to study daily events, because individuals tend to remember events in a successive way. It includes both qualitative and quantitative aspects, a feature that may contribute to a deeper understanding of the processes involved (cf. Grzywacz *et al.*, 2007). Examples of such daily events in the family and the work domain are arguments with one's spouse or with one's co-workers.

This type of data allows going beyond analyzing if, and to what extent, events at work and in the family have an impact on the respective other domain. Since we ask about specific events, we can get a clearer, qualitatively rich and vivid picture of the type of events that trigger such a spillover, and of the type of impact they have. At the same time, the type of data allows for quantification. Furthermore, whereas previous studies were confined to the combination of specific triggers, such as work overload, with unspecific impacts, like distress (Bolger *et al.*, 1990; 1989; Williams and Alliger, 1994) or to the combination of unspecific events with specific impacts, such as social withdrawal (Repetti and Wood, 1997; Repetti, 1992; Pearlin and McCall, 1990), our method of assessment, allows combining events with impacts at several levels of specificity or generality. The approach has similarities with the critical incident approach (see p.139), except that we are not trying to elicit characteristics of good vs. poor performance, but to elicit sequential triggers that lead to (or prevent) spillover into the respective other domain.

Empirical study

We would like to present a study conducted according to our Chain-of-Events approach. Our basic question was whether specific constellations of events can be identified that tend to lead to spillover between life domains, both in terms of the characteristics and the sequence of the events. More specifically, we asked if specific events in one domain, both positive and negative, triggered specific outcomes in the respective other domain. For negative events, we also asked about coping and about the specific constellation in the impact domain as potential modifiers of the unfolding sequence.

Methods

Sample

Interviews were conducted with 58 Swiss couples. Because interviews were carried out with each partner separately, there are a total of 116 participants, of which 112 interviews were suitable for analysis. To be eligible, our interview partners had to meet the following criteria: Both partners had to work at least 16 hours a week, corresponding to a 40 per cent full time equivalent, in order to make sure that they were involved enough in their work domain. Because having children under 13 seems to be particularly demanding (Higgins, Duxbury and Lee, 1994), participants had to be parents of at least one child in this age group. The sample was highly educated, with 71.2 per cent holding at least a Bachelor's degree. Mean age was 38.37 years. Men worked more paid hours than women.

The interview

The interviews were semi-structured. They were conducted according to the Behavioral Event Interview by L. Spencer and S. Spencer (1993), which is based on the Critical Incident Technique by Flanagan (1954). Participants were asked to report four concrete events that had occurred during the previous two weeks. The short time frame was chosen in order to minimize retrospection bias (Schwartz, 1990). We wanted to include both directions and both qualities of events, and therefore asked participants to report a negative and a positive situation for both the work and the family domain. We asked in detail about what had happened, and about participants' thoughts and feelings. Reconstructing the event in a very detailed manner should further minimize retrospection bias, which may be expected to be stronger when people report general evaluations (cf. L. Spencer and S. Spencer, 1993). The questions were identical for each of the four situations, and they followed our framework (1–4) depicted in Figure 9.1.

Data analysis

The procedure of analyzing and quantifying the interview data included a number of steps. First, we developed categories concerning event characteristics (e.g. overload/underload [qualitative and quantitative], demands on emotion regulation, etc.). Typically, an event is characterized by several such characteristics. The interviews were coded according to these characteristics by two coders, yielding very satisfying reliability (kappa; Cohen, 1960; Fassnacht, 1982; Fleiss, 1975). These categories were then subjected to cluster analysis to determine in what way they combined into types of events. Hierarchical cluster analysis groups "objects" (usually people, in our case events) by searching the greatest possible resemblance according to pre-defined variables, which in our case were the characteristics coded (cf. Romesburg, 1984). Based on this analysis, we could develop a typology of events. For instance, one cluster refers to "problems in the organization of work", involving such characteristics as low control, lack of information, role conflict and role ambiguity (see Table 9.1). Finally, we looked for prototypical chains of event, testing if specific types of events tended to co-occur with specific types of coping (for negative events) only, to a specific state of the "other" domain, and to specific impacts.

Results

Tables 9.1 and 9.2 show the types of events, coping strategies, and impacts that resulted from cluster analysis. We will first describe types and frequencies of each step for the negative process, and then for the positive process.

Table 9.1 Frequencies of categories of the negative processes

Process stage	Category	Frequency	
		work-to-family	*family-to-work*
Negative event [a]	Organizational work problems	36 (36.8)	37 (36.2)
	Task-related stressors	14 (12.6)	11(12.4)
	Social stressors	35(37.3)	39 (36.7)
	Conflicts about task or organisation	13(10.1)	7 (9.9)
	Conflict between work and family	8 (8.6)	9 (8.4)
	Miscellaneous	4 (4.5)	5 (4.5)
Coping with negative event [b]	Focus on venting emotions	10 (20.6)**	31 (20.4)**
	Immediately problem focused	15 (16.1)	17 (15.9)
	Restraint coping	5 (5.5)	6 (5.5)
	Emotional supportive interaction	12 (8.5)	5 (8.5)
	Escape	13 (11.6)	10 (11.4)
	Acceptance	11 (14.1)	17 (13.9)
	Instrumental social support	18 (15.6)	13 (15.4)
	Planning	22 (14.1)**	6 (13.9)**
Impact of negative event [c]	tiredness / contemplation	13 (18.8)*	14 (8.2)**
	Telling	22 (16)*	1 (7)**
	seeking social support	24 (23.7)	10 (10.3)
	Interaction with bad mood	16 (12.5)	2 (5.5)*
	organization / task	3 (7)*	7 (3)**

Note: Numbers in parentheses are the expected frequencies. Significant deviation between observed frequency and expected frequency is marked by asterisks. [a] χ^2 (5, N=218) = 2.54, n.s.; [b] χ^2 (7,N=211) = 25.48**; [c] χ^2 (4,N=112) = 23.86** . * p<.05 **p<.01 (one-tailed)

Negative process

Triggering events

With regard to triggering events, it is notable that social stressors and disruptions to routines or expectations were most frequent, and this applies both to events originating in the family and to events originating at work (e.g. time pressure, lack of control, problems with coordination/cooperation). That social stressors are frequent in general is not surprising, given the importance of social relations for individual well-being (Baumeister and Leary, 1995; Cohen, 2004). What was

Table 9.2 Frequencies of categories of the positive processes

Process stage	Category	Frequency	
		work-to-family	family-to-work
Positive event[a]	Task & organization	41 (25.4)**	10 (25.6)**
	Having a good time with domain members	8 (41.8)**	76 (42.2)**
	Receiving social support	9 (9.5)	10 (9.5)
	Feedback & appreciation	53 (34.3)**	16 (34.7)**
Impact of positive event[b]	Factual report	11 (10.2)	7 (7.8)
	Being full of energy	10 (10.7)	9 (8.3)
	Sharing joy	12 (7.4)*	1 (5.6)**
	Telling	22 (15.3)*	5 (11.7)**
	Interaction with domain members	7 (5.1)	2 (3.9)
	Task-related impact	3 (13)**	20 (10)**
	Contemplation	4 (6.2)	7 (4.8)
	Good mood (without any other aspect mentioned)	13 (14.1)	12 (10.9)

Note: Numbers in parentheses are the expected frequencies. Significant deviation between observed frequency and expected frequency is marked by asterisks. [a] χ^2 (3,N=223) = 93.78**; [b] χ^2 (7,N=145) = 35.27**; * p<.05 **p<.01 (one-tailed)

surprising though was that social events were not more frequent in the family than at work, given that the family is, almost by definition, mostly a social group, whereas work is more defined by issues of task fulfillment. It seems that social stressors at work deserve more attention than they have been receiving (Dormann and Zapf, 1999, 2002; Spector and Jex, 1998; cf. Semmer, McGrath and Beehr, 2005). Conversely, the extent to which families, especially families with children, are systems that have tasks to fulfill, may have been underestimated (Resch, 1999), as indicated by the high frequency of problems of (house)work organization, not only at work but also in the family.

Overall, no differences in the frequency of negative events were reported with regard to work versus family. The following example refers to a stressful event at work, which was coded as social:

> *Interviewee*: It was a problem of competence and responsibility, especially, because we usually come up with different ways of solving a problem. I thought, what he [colleague] did was rubbish and he thought, what I did was rubbish, and then, we had a bit of a fight. (female, 32)

Coping

In contrast to negative events, the overall frequency of coping strategies does differ according to the origin of the triggering event. More specifically, venting of emotions is more typical for family events, whereas planning is more typical for events originating at work. Partly, this may be due to the fact that the family

Box 9.1 Extract of an interview demonstrating the process prototypes: problem of work organization–tiredness/rumination

---

Interviewee: I had a meeting lasting all day. I am self-employed, but I work together with other people in a kind of network. And the situation was that we didn't have enough time to discuss everything we had to discuss (…).

Interviewer: And when you recognized that you didn't have enough time, what was your reaction in this specific moment?" (…)

Interviewee: It was like a feeling of exhaustion and also… hmm, I'd have preferred to, how should I say this, I'd have preferred to leave, to escape (…)

Interviewer: And with these feelings, how did you cope with these feelings in this situation?

Interviewee: We planned the day in a more structured way, and structured the work we had to do. This gave us the opportunity to manage the time pressure.

Interviewer: And this strategy did it change something about the situation?

Interviewee: Yes, yes.

Interviewer: What exactly?

Interviewee: The pressure got smaller and, how should I say, manageable.(…)

Interviewer: And in the evening, did it have any impact on your family?

Interviewee: Yes, I was exhausted, and this had an impact.

Interviewer: Which kind of impact?

Interviewee: I said to my daughter, she is 4, that I was very tired and that we would be going to bed at the same time. (female, 37)

---

system, being the more intimate one, induces especially strong emotions. Partly it may due to a higher threshold for venting emotions at work than in the family (cf. Argyle and Henderson, 1986; Perrez, Schoebi and Wilhelm, 2000).

Impact

Not surprisingly, events occurring in the work domain have an impact on the family domain more often than vice versa. This was true for both positive and negative events. However, the difference was more pronounced for negative events. It is interesting that the tendency to "leave our private life behind us" is more pronounced when private difficulties (i.e., negative events) are concerned. Perhaps this is the case because we want to protect the privacy of our family life. Furthermore, work requirements demand full concentration, and letting private problems intrude our mind may endanger performance. Positive things, on the other hand, are unlikely to be associated with feelings that we often do not want to share, such as shame, guilt, or fear of losing reputation; furthermore, they are likely to enhance, rather than hinder, performance on many tasks (Lyubomirsky, King and Diener, 2005), and so our efforts to ward off private intrusions may not be necessary for the positive case

(Grzywacz and Marks, 2000). Altogether, positive events had a higher chance to have an impact than negative events, (71 per cent vs. 57 per cent), and this difference is mainly attributable to the low number of negative family events having an impact on work (only 13 per cent of all events that had an impact were negative and originating in the family). This overall pattern confirms the often-found asymmetrical permeability of the work–family interface (Eagle, Miles and Icenogle, 1997, Frone, Russel and Cooper, 1992).

However, we were interested not only in which types of events had an impact in the respective other domain but also in differences in impact in each of the two domains. Our results do indicate such differences. Family events tend to impact work in a way that is less explicitly social: Fatigue and rumination, and problems with organizing one's work characterize the impact of family events on the work domain (cf. Demerouti, Taris and Bakker, 2007). Events originating at work have an impact on family life in a different way, which is characterized by talking about the work event and by displaying a bad mood when interacting with family members. These different characteristics of the respective impact correspond well with the task-focus of the work domain and the social focus of the family domain. It is the core aspect of each domain that typically is affected by negative events from the respective other domain.

One interviewee told us:

> *Interviewee:* If there is something in my office that is really upsetting me, I take it home with me [in my mind]. I have noticed that when I come home from my office, I cannot really bear my children for the moment... (female, 43)

Positive process

With regard to positive events, the social vs. task distinction between the two domains seems especially clear. There is a significant overall difference in the requency of particular types of positive events originating at work vs. in the family. Positive events at work tend to originate in successes with regard to the organization of one's work and completion of tasks. Furthermore, feedback and appreciation are reported frequently; these are, of course, social events, but they are tied to task-related successes, and thus the core aspect of work, to a considerable degree (Grebner, Elfering and Semmer, 2010). Conversely, just having a good time, without any necessary connection to a task, is typical for the family.

The impact of positive events in some way mirrors that of negative events. Again, permeability is asymmetric, with work impacting the family more than vice versa. It seems that people are not too open about their private life when at work, whereas sharing experiences, including work experiences, is one of the key features of family life. This is seen very clearly in the distribution of "sharing joy" and "telling", which are much more typical for work-to-family than vice versa. And, again, the impact of family on work results in tasks being carried out differently; work seems to become easier and more joyful when backed up by good experiences from home. The following is an example for 'sharing joy' at home:

Interviewee: As soon as I was in the door I started telling what had happened. I just couldn't wait to start talking about it.

Interviewer: And how did your family members react?

Interviewee: My wife was happy as well, praised me, and said 'Wow, you see, you did a good job'. She is supportive, constructive, and shared the joy. (…) That's chicken soup for the soul. (male, 34)

Prototypical chains of events

Analyses so far referred to elements of the proposed framework. The following analyses focus on chains of events: Are there typical constellations of triggering events, coping, state of the impact domain, and the type of impact?

To label a process as a 'prototypical chain', two requirements had to be fulfilled: (1) The relationship between the type of event and the type of impact had to be significant, as indicated by chi-square analysis. (2) The minimal frequency of the process prototype had to be three. Analyses were run separately for positive and negative processes. The condition in the impact domain was assessed with regard to a rather basic distinction, that is, whether things were "as usual" vs. unusual.

Negative events

With regard to negative events, two specific process types could be identified. The first begins with organizational stressors and leads to 'tiredness and rumination in the other domain (see Figure 9.2). Interestingly, this process prototype was only found in one direction, work-to-family. Six participants reported this process prototype.

In-depth analyses yielded an interesting picture about the second process step, this is coping strategies. All participants who reported this specific process prototype adopted a problem-focused strategy to cope with the stressful situation. It is generally accepted that a problem-focused way of coping is more effective than an emotion-focused way (Carver, Scheier and Weintraub, 1989). However, this process prototype illustrates that problem-focused coping may be more successful, but still has its costs (Schönpflug and Battmann, 1988); these costs, in our case, refer to fatigue and lower well-being. This process prototype was not associated with any specific conditions in the impact domain, that is, the connection between problems at work, problem-focused coping, and fatigue/rumination held regardless of whether the condition at home was as usual or not. This finding may be related to the type of impact, which has an internal experience at its core.

The second process prototype begins with social stressors, mostly conflicts and a lack of appreciation, as the triggering event, which leads to 'seeking social support' as the impact on the other life domain (see Figure 9.3). Eleven people reported such a process prototype from work-to-family, and 3 participants reported the same prototype from family-to-work.

Box 9.2 Extract of an interview demonstrating the process prototypes: social stressor-seeking for social support

> *Interviewee:* We had a big discussion, and I tried to explain my side of the story. And then she simply said 'that's not true', and when you're trying to explain something, she says 'don't interrupt me!' and in a very snide tone… I wouldn't even talk to my children like this.
>
> *Interviewer:* And then, when she was saying those things, what did you think?
>
> *Interviewee:* Is it worth all this? The whole effort I put in to organize childcare for my children during my working days. Is it worth it, and then I have to listen to such things. This was what I thought.
>
> *Interviewer:* And what were your feelings?
>
> *Interviewee:* I was completely disappointed, totally disappointed.
>
> *Interviewer:* And what did you do in this moment?
>
> *Interviewee:* I said nothing. I said nothing and walked away afterwards. (…)
>
> *Interviewer:* And afterwards, when you went home, did this event have any impact on the family?
>
> *Interviewee:* Hmm, I have to think about it. I was happy that I could go back home to my family. And I talked with my husband, and then everything wasn't so bad.
>
> *Interviewer:* How did your husband react to your story?
>
> *Interviewee:* He also thought that what had been happening with that person was absolutely inappropriate. And he also knows everything about this power struggle. And sometimes he gives me examples from himself, from the industry, and then you can see that it's the same everywhere (laughs). (female, 35)

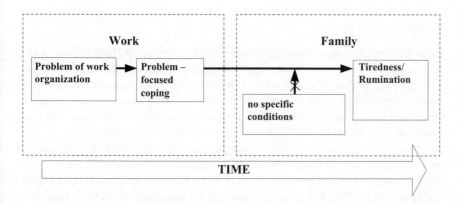

Figure 9.2 Specific process prototypes: problem of work organization–tiredness/rumination

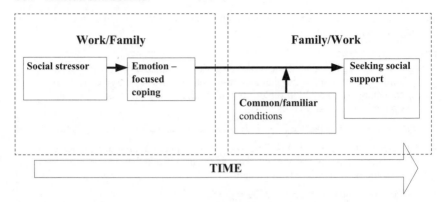

Figure 9.3 Specific process prototype: social stressor-seeking for social support

Most people who reported this kind of process prototype stated that they had first coped in an emotion-focused way (venting emotions, restraint coping, emotional supportive interaction, escape or acceptance). Later, these participants sought social support in the other life domain. It seems that, after having experienced a situation in which they feel attacked or degraded, people look for appreciation to restore a positive self-image. A good way to meet this need is asking for support from others. In particular, emotional support has this connotation of appreciation (Sarason *et al.*, 1996; see Semmer et al., 2007). In contrast to the first process prototype, however, the momentary condition of the other life domain was important. Specifically, there was enough space to seek/give social support only if the condition of the other life domain was basically "as usual". Unusual conditions, on the other hand, may well "overrule" the need for support and fail to provide the opportunity for a supporting exchange.

Positive events

In the positive case, no relationships between positive events and their impacts were found, and this was true both for work-to-family and for family-to-work processes. This is a very interesting result, which cannot be attributed to a lower frequency of positive interactions between work and family. Quite the contrary, more impacts emerged from positive events than from negative events; the kind of impact just was not specifically tied to the kind of trigger. We think that the difference may lie in the specificity of reactions to positive vs. negative events. Negative emotions tend to narrow people's attention and to provoke more specific reaction tendencies, whereas positive emotions tend to broaden attention and behavioral repertoires (Fredrickson and Branigan, 2005). With reactions being more varied, the chances of finding a specific chain of event must necessarily diminish.

Discussion

Our aim in this chapter was to advocate a stronger focus on events, their characteristics, their triggers, and their consequences and to illustrate ways of doing research in that way. The case-crossover design works "backwards", starting with an outcome and trying to identify triggers for that outcome; using the person as his or her own control, more specifically the person's situation/behavior at another time, it is quite strong in terms of causal interpretations. Our approach, as illustrated by our study, also tries to establish connections between events but starts with a triggering event and follows the development of its consequences, focusing more strongly on *chains* of events. Thus, unlike the case-crossover design, our approach allows for identifying several typical constellations, some of which tend to lead to a specific outcome, while others do not. Both approaches emphasize specific characteristics, rather than general descriptions, of events, implying that this type of research is rather time-consuming and laborious.

We could not find a case-crossover study in the work–family domain, and as far as we know ours is the first study investigating chains of events in that domain; however, the unfolding model of turnover has followed a similar approach by working backwards (i.e. from the decision to quit one's job back to preceding developments; cf. Holtom *et al.*, 2008). We feel that more studies that adapt the event-focus we tried to illustrate with the two approaches discussed here could advance our understanding of the processes involved in work–family spillover. Also, we could imagine enlarging the case-crossover design by trying to identify typical *constellations,* rather than single events, as triggers for a given outcome. Research that follows our approach is likely to be helpful in a first stage, which identifies potential constellations; it could be followed by a case-crossover study that tries to establish a causal link between these constellations and specific outcomes. Such research could complement existing research by going beyond general descriptions of phenomena, such as work–family conflict, and their associations with general outcomes (such as well-being), thus shedding light on the specific mechanisms involved (cf. Maertz and Boyar, 2011). Our model is only a first approximation towards such a goal, and it undoubtedly will have to be refined as a consequence of such research, but we feel it does represent a starting point that is useful.

Acknowledgements

The presented study was supported by a grant from the Swiss National Science Foundation (101411-103593/1).

We would like to thank Cornelia Meier Tschudi and Regula Zimmermann for their support in the presented study.

References

Allen, T.D., Herst, D.E.L., Bruck, C.S. and Sutton, M. (2000). Consequences associated with work-to-family conflict: A review and agenda for future research. *Journal of Occupational Health Psychology* 5, 278–308.

Amstad, F.T. and Semmer, N.K. (2009). Recovery and the work-family interface. In S. Sonnentag, P.L. Perrewé and D.C. Ganster (eds) *Research in occupational stress and well-being* 7. "Current perspectives on job-stress recovery research" (125–166). Oxford: Elsevier Science.

Amstad, F.T., Meier, L.L., Elfering, A., Fasel, U. and Semmer, N.K. (2011). A meta-analysis of work-family conflict and various outcomes with a special emphasis on cross-domain vs. matching domain relations. *Journal of Occupational Health Psychology* 16, 151–169.

Argyle, M. and Henderson, M. (1986). The informal rules of working relationships. *Journal of Occupational Behavior* 7, 259–275.

Baumeister, R.F. and Leary, M.R. (1995). The need to belong: Desire for interpersonal attachments as a fundamental human motivation. *Psychological Bulletin* 117, 497–529.

Bolger, N., Davis, A. and Rafaeli, E. (2003). Diary methods: Capturing life as it is lived. *Annual Review of Psychology* 54, 579–616.

Bolger, N., DeLonis, A., Kessler, R.C. and Schilling, E.A. (1989). Effects of daily stress on negative mood. *Journal of Personality and Social Psychology* 57, 808–818.

Bolger, N., DeLongis, A., Kessler, R.C. and Wethington, E. (1990). The microstructure of daily role-related stress in married couples. In J. Eckenrode and S. Gore, (eds) *Stress between work and family* (95–115). New York: Plenum Press.

Byron, K. (2005). A meta-analytic review of work-family conflict and its antecedents. *Journal of Vocational Behavior* 67, 169–198.

Carver, C.S., Scheier, M.F. and Weintraub, J.K. (1989). Assessing coping strategies: A theoretically based approach. *Journal of Personality and Social Psychology* 56, 267–283.

Cohen, J. (1960). A coefficient of agreement for nominal scales. *Educational and Psychological Measurement* 20, 37–46.

Cohen, S. (2004). Social relationships and health. *American Psychologist* 59, 676–684.

Crouter, A.C., Perry-Jenkins, M., Huston, T.L. and Crawford, D.W. (1989). The influence of work-induced psychological states on behavior at home. *Basic and Applied Social Psychology* 10, 273–292.

DeLongis, A., Folkman, S. and Lazarus, R.S. (1988). The impact of daily stress on health and mood: Psychological and social resources as mediators. *Journal of Personality and Social Psychology* 54, 486–495.

Demerouti, E., Taris, T.W. and Bakker, A.B. (2007). Need for recovery, home-work interference and performance: Is lack of concentration the link? *Journal of Vocational Behavior* 71, 204–220.

Dormann, C. and Zapf, D. (1999). Social support, social stressors at work, and depressive symptoms: Testing for main and moderating effects with structural equations in a three-wave longitudinal study. *Journal of Applied Psychology* 84, 874–884.

—— (2002). Social stressors at work, irritation, and depressive symptoms: Accounting for unmeasured third variables in a multi-wave study. *Journal of Occupational and Organizational Psychology* 75, 33–58.

Eagle, B.W., Miles, E.W. and Icenogle, M.L. (1997). Interrole conflicts and the permeability of work and family domains: Are there gender differences? *Journal of Vocational Behavior* 50, 168–184.

Eby, L.T., Maher, C.P. and Butts, M.M. (2010). The intersection of work and family life: The role of affect. *Annual Review of Psychology* 61, 599–622.

Fassnacht, G. (1982). *Theory and Practice of Observing Behaviour.* London: Academic Press.

Flanagan, J.C. (1954). The critical incident technique. *Psychological Bulletin, 51,* 327–358.

Fleiss, J.L. (1975). Measuring agreement between two judges on the presence or absence of a trait. *Biometrics* 31, 651–659.

Ford, M.T., Heinen, B.A. and Langkamer, K.L. (2007). Work and family satisfaction and conflict: A meta-analysis of cross-domain relations. *Journal of Applied Psychology* 92, 57–80.

Fredrickson, B.L. and Branigan, C. (2005). Positive emotions broaden the scope of attention and thought-action repertoires. *Cognition and Emotion* 19, 313–332.

Frone, M.R. (2003). Work-family balance. In J. Campbell Quick and L.E. Tetrick (eds) *Handbook of Occupational Health Psychology* (143–162). Washington, DC: APA.

Frone, M.R., Russell, M. and Cooper, M.L. (1992). Prevalence of work-family conflict: Are work and family boundaries asymmetrically permeable? *Journal of Organizational Behavior* 13, 723–729.

Geurts, S.A.E. and Demerouti, E. (2003). Work/non-work interface: A review of theories and findings. In M.J. Schabracq, J.A.M. Winnubst and C.L. Cooper (eds) *Handbook of Work and Health Psychology* (279–312). Chichester: John Wiley & Sons.

Grebner, S., Elfering, A. and Semmer, N.K. (2010). The success resource model of job stress. In P.L. Perrewé and D.C. Ganster (eds) *Research in occupational stress and well being* 8. "New developments in theoretical and conceptual approaches to job stress" (61–108). Bingley, UK: Emerald Group Publishing.

Greenhaus J.H and Allen T.D. (2011). Work-family balance: A review and extension of the literature. In J. C Quick and L. E. Tetrick (eds) *Handbook of occupational health psychology* 2nd ed. (165–183). Washington, DC: American Psychological Association;

Gross, S., Semmer, N.K., Meier, L.L., Kälin, W., Jacobshagen, N. and Tschan, F. (2011). The effect of positive events at work on after-work fatigue: They matter most in face of adversity. *Journal of Applied Psychology* 96, 654–664. doi: 10.1037/a0022992.

Grzywacz, J.G. and Marks, N.F. (2000). Reconceptualizing the work-family interface: An ecological perspective on the correlates of positive and negative spillover between work and family. *Journal of Occupational Health Psychology* 5, 111–126.

Grzywacz, J.G., Arcury, T.A., Marin, A., Carrillo, L., Burke, B., Coates, M.L. and Quandt, S.A. (2007). Work-family conflict: Experiences and health implications among immigrant latinos. *Journal of Applied Psychology* 92, 1119–1130.

Heller, D. and Watson, D. (2005). The dynamic spillover of satisfaction between work and marriage: The role of time and mood. *Journal of Applied Psychology* 90, 1273–1279.

Higgins, C., Duxbury, L. and Lee, C. (1994). Impact of life-cycle stage and gender on the ability to balance work and family responsibilities. *Family Relations* 43, 144–150.

Holtom, B.C., Mitchell, T.R., Lee, T.W. and Eberly, M.B. (2008). Turnover and retention research: A glance at the past, a closer review of the present, and aventure into the future. *The Academy of Management Annals* 2, 231–274.

Holtom, B.C., Mitchell, T.R., Lee, T.W. and Inderrieden, E.J. (2005). Shocks as causes of turnover: What they are and how organizations can manage them. *Human Resource Management* 44, 337–352.

Kanner, A.D., Coyne, J.C., Schaefer, C. and Lazarus, R.S. (1981). Comparison of two modes of stress measurement: Daily hassles and uplifts versus major life events. *Journal of Behavioral Medicine* 4, 1–39.

Kossek, E.E. and Ozeki, C. (1998). Work-family conflict, policies, and the job-life satisfaction relationship: A review and directions for organization behavior-human resources research. *Journal of Applied Psychology* 83, 139–149.

Kossek, E.E., Pichler, S., Bodner, T. and Hammer, L.B. (2011). Workplace social support and work-family conflict: ameta-analysis clarifying the influence of general and work-family-specific supervisor and organizational support. *Personnel Psychology* 64, 289–313.

Kreiner, G.E., Hollensbe, E.C. and Sheep, M.L. (2009). Balancing borders and bridges: Netotiating the work-home interface via boundary work tactics. *Academy of Management Journal* 52, 704–730.

Lazarus, R.S. (1999). *Stress and emotion. A new synthesis*. New York: Springer.

Lee, T.W. and Mitchell, T.R. (1994). An alternative approach: The unfolding model of voluntary employee turnover. *Academy of Management Review* 19, 51–89.

Lyubomirsky, S., King, L. and Diener, E. (2005). The benefits of frequent positive affect: Does happiness lead to success? *Psychological Bulletin* 131, 803–855

Maertz, C.P. and Boyar, S.L. (2011). Work-family conflict, enrichment, and balance under "levels" and "episodes" approaches. *Journal of Management* 37, 68–98.

Michel, J.S., Kotrba, L.M., Mitchelson, J.K., Clark, M.A. and Baltes, B.B. (2011). Antecedents of work-family conflict: A meta-analytic review. *Journal of Organizational Behavior* 32, 689–725.

Michel, J.S., Mitchelson, J.K., Kotrba, L.M., LeBreton, J.M. and Baltes, B.B. (2009). A comparative test of work-family conflict models and critical examination of work-family linkages. *Journal of Vocational Behavior* 74, 199–218.

Mittleman, M.A., Maclure, M., Sherwood, J.B., Mulry, R. P., Tofler, G.H. and Jacobs, S.C. (1995). Triggering of acute myocardial infarction onset by episodes of anger. *Circulation* 92, 1720–1725.

Mittleman, M.A., Maclure, M., Tofler, G.H., Sherwood, J.B., Goldberg, R.J. and Muller, J.E. (1993). Triggering of acute myocardial infarction by physical exertion: Protection against triggering by regular exertion. *New England Journal of Medicine* 329, 1677–1683.

Möller, G., Hallqvist, J., Diderichsen, F., Theorell, T., Reuterwall, C. and Ahlbom, A. (1999). Do episodes of anger trigger myocardial infarction? A case-crossover analysis in the Stockholm Heart Epidemiology Program (SHEEP). *Psychosomatic Medicine* 61, 842–849.

Pearlin, L.I. and McCall, M.E. (1990). Occupational stress and marital support: A description of microprocesses. In J. Eckenrode and S. Gore (eds) *Stress between work and family* (39–60). New York: Plenum Press.

Perrez, M., Schoebi, D. and Wilhelm, P. (2000). How to assess social regulation of stress and emotions in daily family life? A computer-assisted family self-monitoring system (FASEM-C). *Clinical Psychology and Psychotherapy* 7, 326–339.

Repetti, R.L. (1992). Social withdrawal as a short-term coping response to daily stressors. In, H.S. Friedman (ed.) *Hostility, Coping & Health* (151–165). Washington: American Psychological Association.

Repetti, R.L. and Wood, J. (1997). Effects of daily stress at work on mothers' interactions with preschoolers. *Journal of Family Psychology* 11, 90–108.

Resch, M. (1999). *Arbeitsanalyse im Haushalt. Erhebung und Bewertung von Tätigkeiten außerhalb der Erwerbsarbeit mit dem AVAH-Verfahren* [Work analysis in the household. The survey and appraisal of tasks outside of paid work with the AVAH-survey]. Zürich: Verlag der Fachvereine.

Romesburg, H.C. (1984). *Cluster analysis for researchers*. Belmont, CA: Lifetime Learning Publications.

Sarason, I.G., Sarason, B.R., Brock, D.M. and Pierce, G.R. (1996). Social support: Current status, current issues. In C.D. Spielberger, I.G. Sarason, J.M.T. Brebner, E. Greenglass, P.Laungani and A.M. O'Roark (eds) *Stress and Emotion: Anxiety, Anger, and Curiosity* 16 (3–27). Philadelphia: Taylor & Francis.

Schönpflug, W. and Battmann, W. (1988). The costs and benefits of coping. In S. Fisher and J. Reason (eds) *Handbook of life stress, cognition and health* (699–713). New York, NY: Wiley.

Schwarz, N. (1990). Assessing frequency reports of mundane behaviours: Contributions of cognitive psychology to questionnaire construction. In C. Hendrick, & M.S. Clark (eds.) *Research methods in personality and social psychology* (Vol. 11, pp. 98-119). Thousand Oaks, CA: Sage.

Semmer, N.K., McGrath, J.E. and Beehr, T.A. (2005). Conceptual issues in research on stress and health. In C.L. Cooper (ed.), *Handbook of stress, medicine and health*, 2nd ed. (1–43). Boca Raton: CRC Press.

Semmer, N.K., Jacobshagen, N., Meier, L.L. and Elfering, A. (2007). Occupational stress research: The Stress-as-Offense-to-Self perspective. In J. Houdmont and S. McIntyre, (eds) *Occupational health psychology: European perspectives on research, education and practice* 2 (43–60). Castelo da Maia, Portugal: ISMAI Publishing.

Semmer, N.K., Elfering, A., Jacobshagen, N., Perrot, T., Beehr, T.A. and Boos, N. (2008). The emotional meaning of instrumental social support. *International Journal of Stress Management* 15, 235–251.

Sonnentag, S. and Bayer, U.V. (2005). Switching off mentally: Predictors and consequences of psychological detachment from work during off-job time. *Journal of Occupational Health Psychology* 10, 393–414.

Sonnentag, S. and Zijlstra, F.R.H. (2006). Job characteristics and off-job activities as predictors of need for recovery, well-being, and fatigue. *Journal of Applied Psychology* 91, 330–350.

Spector, P E. and Jex, S.M. (1998). Development of four self-report measures of job stressors and strain: Interpersonal conflict at work scale, organizational constraints scale, quantitative workload inventory, and physical symptoms inventory. *Journal of Occupational Health Psychology* 3, 356–367.

Spencer, L.M. Jr. and Spencer, S.M. (1993). *Competence at work: Models for superior performance*. New York: Wiley.

Stanley, R.O. and Burrows, G.D. (2001). Varieties and functions of human emotions. In R.L. Payne and C.L. Cooper (eds) *Emotions at work: Theory, research and applications for management* (3–19). Chichester, UK: Wiley.

Weiss, H. and Cropanzano, R. (1996). Affective events theory: A theoretical discussion of the structure, causes and consequences of affective experiences at work. In B.M. Staw and L.L. Cummings (eds) *Research in Organizational Behavior* 18 (1–74). Greenwich, CT: JAI Press.

Williams, K.J. and Alliger, G.M. (1994). Role stressors, mood spillover, and perceptions of work-family conflict in employed parents. *Academy of Management Journal* 37, 837–868.

Zohar, D. (1999). When things go wrong: The effect of daily work hassles on effort, exertion and negative mood. *Journal of Occupational and Organizational Psychology* 72, 265–283.

10 Biomarkers in work and family research

*Orfeu Marcello Buxton, Laura Cousino Klein,
Julia Whinnery, Sharon Williams and
Thomas McDade*

What is a biomarker?

Key features and general utility

Biomarkers are directly measured traits that provide insight into the functioning of biological systems. They often involve the collection and subsequent analysis of biological specimens such as blood, saliva, and urine. Biomarkers also include physical and functional measures such as blood pressure and actigraphy (i.e., assessment of human rest/activity cycles). Biomarkers provide valuable information about biological processes ranging from normal to pathogenic that may contribute clinically identifiable disease.

A detailed picture of the typicality of individuals' biological processes requires a diverse range of biomarkers. While extremely diverse in complexity and source, the inclusion of biomarkers in work and family research offers great potential for advancing the field, particularly with regard to understanding work, family and health. For example, a fundamental premise in the literature is that difficulties at the work–family interface act as stressors that initiate the sympathetic and parasympathetic nervous system, which if repeated over time, undermines physical and mental health. Biomarkers provide a direct opportunity for definitively testing this core premise.

Lessons from other fields

Biomarkers are extremely useful tools across multiple disciplines, including medicine, cell biology, genetics, psychology, sociology, demography, and social epidemiology. Within each discipline, early phase validity and reliability biomarker research was used to uncover both hidden disease risk and provide longitudinal prediction of health outcomes. In these instances, biomarkers that are accurate, durable (i.e., they can survive the lag between sample collection and implementation of the lab assay to extract the biomarker), and versatile (i.e., useful in a variety of models) are required.

Exploration of the relationships between biomarkers, the external environment, and disease has become quite advanced. To use the relatively new field of sleep medicine as one example, the current literature demonstrates how fluctuating levels of hormones linked to sleep and health, particularly melatonin, cortisol, leptin, and ghrelin across the circadian cycle are modified by environmental and social context (Yaggi, Araujo *et al.* 2006; Reiter, Tan *et al.* 2007; Tengattini, Reiter *et al.* 2008). In diabetes research several recent Genome-Wide Association Studies (GWAS) have made both advances in the genetic profile of diabetes, as well as major improvements and refinements of diabetic phenotypes characterized by distinct biomarker profiles that are relatively easier to capture in large and at-risk populations than previous clinical measures (Scott, Mohlke *et al.* 2007; Benyamin, Middelberg *et al.* 2011). However, this research is only the beginning; further examination of the genetic basis of the disease is required in order to gain a thorough understanding of the pathogenesis of diabetes. Other more advanced research areas, such as cardiometabolic risk assessment, have long relied upon biomarkers such as C-reactive protein (CRP), insulin, and glycated hemoglobin (HbA1C) for early detection and prevention efforts, as well as biomarkers of "hard endpoints" for cardiovascular disease (CVD) risk and CVD-associated mortality (Gerszten and Wang 2008). Clinical epidemiology frequently assesses biomarkers to prospectively predict cardiometabolic risk outcomes such as heart disease and Type II diabetes. Perhaps the most widely used of all biomarkers is the Framingham risk score, a composite that includes blood pressure, HDL cholesterol levels and total cholesterols levels that has demonstrated utility in predicting CVD (D'Agostino, Grundy *et al.* 2001). However, the Framingham score has experienced some technical controversies, and has limitations in studies focused on linking social and environmental factors to health, suggesting the need for more accurate and specific biomarkers related to cardiovascular research.

Practical comments for biomarker usage

Bearing in mind that a panel of biomarkers, rather than a lone biomarker, is most useful in the fields of cardiovascular and diabetes research, biomarkers need to be considered along with a variety of contextual factors in order to maximize their utility. Biomarker research can be expensive, however, both financially and in time for data collection. Thus, while it is vital to choose biomarkers that are accurate, durable, and versatile, work and family biomarker research must be rooted in practicality by selecting biomarkers that are inexpensive, appropriate and can be collected quickly with ease. Furthermore, practical considerations often result in having to pick two out of three potential elements: cheap, good, and fast. Herein lays the next steps in health biomarker research within the work and family context. The field of biomarkers research is currently in a period of dramatic growth; however, most of the work is yet to come. It is important to note that there are many laboratories available to assist researchers in developing the methods required for successfully including biomarkers in their research. This chapter serves as a guide to understanding the practical issues involved in biomarker data collection and use in work and family research.

Biomarkers in work–family research

The standard reductionist approach tends to incorporate mechanistic studies over time at increasingly finer biological resolution and within individuals. In contrast, work and family research frequently attempts to use a multi-level approach and, importantly, incorporates multiple contexts simultaneously (see Figure 10.1). The use of biomarkers in work and family research is not new, but increasing because of the information that biomarkers provide on within-individual biological variation that allows rigorous assessment of core questions, like to what extent do challenges combining work and family contribute to a physiological stress response. This basic research framework can be extended to allow development and evaluation of alternative points for intervention (e.g., family, community, workplace). For example, biomarkers can be used to track the consequences and processes by which a workplace intervention may impact health through another context (e.g., family / household). Also, there is an opportunity for more dynamic, bi-directional analyses, such as work to health to family, and back again, with longitudinal data.

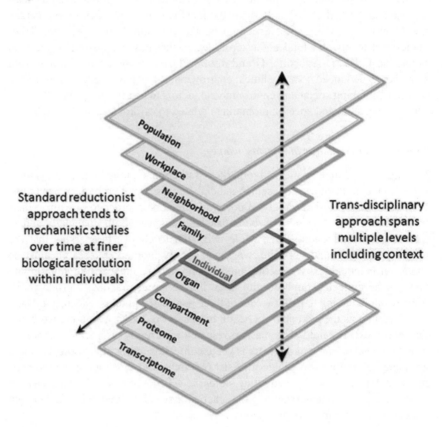

Figure 10.1 A schematic of a transdisciplinary approach to work and family research enhanced by use of biomarkers

Discipline-specific biomarkers

Biomarkers in medicine

Biomarkers are descriptive indicators and effective predictors that vary in important ways between disciplines. As such, the specific definition of a biomarker is contingent on the discipline in which it is being studied. In medicine, biomarkers are widely used to predict the onset of disease, examine the body's responsiveness to specific therapies, or to test for harmful drug interactions. A useful biomarker in the field of medicine may, for example, be a substance whose presence indicates a particular disease state, such as an antibody that may indicate infection. In addition to identifying existing disease states, biomarkers also can be utilized as predictors of risk or susceptibility to disease. These types of biomarkers range anywhere from a substance that indicates the change in expression or state of a protein, such as DNA hypermethylation as a risk factor for cardiovascular disease (Stenvinkel, Karimi *et al.* 2007), or an analyte found in blood that could be used to identify the genetic cause for a disease, such as schizophrenia. Furthermore, biomarkers that can be introduced into an organism and traced successfully have a number of different uses, such as revealing a drug's site of action or allowing researchers to examine the function of specific organs. Lastly, the discovery and validation of a prospective diabetes biomarker panel from hundreds of candidates (Goldfine, Gerwien *et al.* 2011) may provide a detailed look at the pathogenesis of diabetes, and become a technique applicable to the discovery of biomarkers in other diseases.

The concept of personalized medicine is of particular interest for work and family research. A panel of biomarkers gathered from one subject that can collectively be used to predict the onset of disease or identify the subject's susceptibility for a disease is an extremely useful dataset that is both individualized and standardized. Further, comparison of individual biomarkers collected in distinct social environments (e.g., workplace or household) allows for even greater depth when it comes to analyzing the effect of work and family balance on health outcomes.

Biomarkers in cell biology

In cell biology, a biomarker is a particle or substance that is either present or absent in a particular cell type. Biomarkers in this field are readily used to identify certain populations of cells, such as cancer cells, to make a diagnosis, or to measure the progression of treatment for a disease. For example, two biomarkers, serum trefoil factor 2 and growth/differentiation factor 15, were recently found to be associated with the metastatic behavior of lymph nodes in colorectal cancer (Xue, Lu *et al.* 2010). This finding is important, as these serum proteins may be able to serve as potential biomarkers for the diagnosis or possible onset of colorectal cancer. Early identification of cancer or warning signs for the development of the disease may allow for preventative measures that may improve or alleviate the progression of the disease in the affected individual. As the work and family research expands, having these kinds of biomarkers in the research arsenal may allow for a more well-rounded exploration of disease causation and progression, which may further expand the realm of possible treatment outcomes.

Biomarkers in genetics

A genetic marker is a specific sequence of DNA that causes a disease or is linked to an individual's susceptibility for a disease. As genes are not directly modifiable by environmental influences, genes themselves cannot be classified as biomarkers. However, genes may interact with work and family contexts to shape biology. For example, a genetic predisposition for a disease combined with a stressful work or home environment may increase an individual's risk for that disease, compared to the presence of just one of these risk factors. Some common genetic markers include gene sequences that have recently come to indicate an underlying susceptibility for diabetes. One genome-wide association study confirmed several variants near specific genes, including genes TCF7L2 and SLC30A8, to be associated with Type 2 Diabetes (Scott, Mohlke *et al.* 2007). Research consortia that increased samples sizes by pooling samples and phenotypes to n>100,000 have revealed over a hundred genetic variants associated with frank diabetes and diabetic phenotypes, although each variant may only predict a tiny proportion of the overall risk (1 per cent). According to the biological susceptibility model, certain individuals have a larger genetic reactivity to stress, indicating worse outcome in poor environments, but better outcomes in good environments (Mitchell, Notterman *et al.* 2011).

Biomarkers in social science

When they are applied to population and social sciences biomarkers need to be easy to obtain, transport, and analyze, but also need to provide detailed biological information about study participants. The primary goal in this field is credible generalizability of the findings, as is rarely accomplished in laboratory studies, by bringing biomarker collection to the research participant. Gathering biomarker information from a diverse research population is a secondary goal in this field, which also helps to accomplish the primary goal of external validity of study findings. Several different methods can be employed to gather biomarkers in this field, including the collection of height, weight, body mass index (BMI), salivary cortisol, and dried blood spots (DBS). Height, weight, and BMI are preferred biomarkers because they can be accurately assessed with equipment and training. Furthermore, daily salivary cortisol levels are relatively easy to collect, and function as a reliable biological indicator of emotional well-being (Steptoe and Wardle 2005), although most indicators currently used reflect a relatively transient state. Lastly, dried blood spots are becoming an increasingly preferred method for collecting biomarkers in whole blood; in addition to being relatively painless, noninvasive and easy to collect, DBS samples can be analyzed for a variety of different blood analytes, including cholesterol, C-reactive protein, glycated

Table 10.1 Biomarker resources

Exploring the changes in labor force participation and the health transitions that individuals undergo toward the end of their work lives and the years to follow: The Health and Retirement Study (HRS)	http://hrsonline.isr.umich.edu/index.php
How social environment and behaviors in adolescence are linked to health and achievement in young adulthood: The National Longitudinal Study of Adolescent Health (Add Health)	http://www.cpc.unc.edu/projects/addhealth
A National longitudinal study of health and well-being: Midlife in the United States (MIDUS Study)	http://midus.wisc.edu/index.php
How changes in work environment can improve the health of workers and their families while benefitting organizations: The Work, Family, and Health Study	http://www.kpchr.org/workfamilyhealthnetwork/
What is a biomarker, according to the U.S. National Institute of Health (NIH)?	http://riskfactor.cancer.gov/areas/biomarkers/

hemoglobin, and Epstein-Barr virus antibodies. Furthermore, DBS samples require minimal storage requirements compared to other biomarkers (e.g., they do not need to be immediately frozen, and can be stored for a long period of time in a stable freezer environment before analysis).

Such straightforward biomarkers allow for the creation of large databases of information, which then can be used in combination with self-report and field interviews to draw important connections between health and environmental influences. Biomarkers make this possible by highlighting specific physiological pathways that account for the influence of individual, household, and community-level factors on the development and progression of disease. In doing so, biomarkers also allow for the identification of trends that can be used to predict patterns of morbidity and mortality (McDade, Williams *et al.* 2007).

Biomarkers in bodily fluids

Biomarkers in blood

C-reactive protein (CRP) is an acute phase blood protein synthesized by the liver and is used as a biomarker of inflammation (e.g., high levels of CRP suggest high levels of inflammation), indicating a decreased immune response in the body and, thus, a poorer ability to fight infection. CRP levels play an important role in the early identification of disease, as elevated levels may be predictive of certain disease states, such as type 2 diabetes mellitus (T2DM) and CVD. In a recent study, CRP measured in fasting blood samples was found to be associated with insulin sensitivity, glucose tolerance, and insulin secretion, three physiological measures important in the pathogenesis of T2DM (Goldfine, Gerwien *et al.* 2011).

High levels of CRP are a risk factor for cardiovascular disease, independent of cholesterol, which has been the number-one cause of mortality in the United States for decades (Williams, Pham-Kanter *et al.* 2009). With regard to work and family research, CRP is a potentially valuable biomarker. As stress is often at the root of decreased immune response and subsequent inflammation, blood CRP levels provide enormous insight into how environmental stressors affecting an individual in the workplace, household, or community can subsequently affect health.

HbA1c, or glycated hemoglobin, is a form of hemoglobin that is directly proportional to the average glucose level in the blood over an extended period of time (i.e., up to 90 days). Similar to CRP, HbA1c has been identified as a risk factor in the development of diabetes: a recent study found that HbA1c levels are associated with impaired glucose tolerance important in the pathogenesis of T2DM (Goldfine, Gerwien *et al.* 2011). Furthermore, because of its association with diabetes, increased HbA1c is also considered a risk factor for cardiovascular disease. In the field of work and family research, HbA1c may respond to periods of elevated exposure to environmental stressors, particularly in the workplace. In general, it has been found that low levels of supervisor support, combined with other dimensions of job strain related to job control and demands, may increase susceptibility to CVD by influencing bad habits such as tobacco use, physical activity, and diet (Berkman, Buxton *et al.* 2010). As with all other biological samples, it is imperative to verify collection and post-collection conditions that influence the validity of the assay of interest, from subject characteristics and confounders, tubes and processing conditions, transportation conditions, etc. For example, HbA1c levels may vary in samples depending on storage conditions (Buxton, Malarick *et al.* 2009).

Epstein-Barr virus (EBV) antibodies are produced by the immune system when an individual is exposed to the Epstein-Barr virus or infectious mononucleosis (human herpes virus 4). In the United States, it is estimated that about 90 per cent of the adult population has been previously infected with this virus, resulting in a latent infection that exists for the life of the individual (Larson, Ader *et al.* 2001). Reactivation of the virus and the subsequent production of antibodies typically results from biological and psychosocial stressors from the workplace, community, or household (Glaser, Friedman *et al.* 1999). Given that reactivation of the virus has been implicated in a host of diverse disease outcomes (Maeda, Akahane *et al.* 2009), the relationship between environmental stressors and EBV antibody production is widely studied in clinical epidemiology. In one 2010 study, it was found that women who reported a higher degree of perceived stress, or reported experiences of discrimination had significantly higher levels of EBV than women who did not (Borders, Grobman *et al.* 2010). Clearly, this research presents a strong link between stressors that can be confronted in the workplace and health outcomes. Further research in the work and family sphere will go on to examine the effects of managerial support on the overall health and well-being of employees.

Leptin is a circulating hormone important in the regulation of appetite and metabolism. While normal levels of leptin indicate satiation, too-low levels are associated with extreme hunger. Another hormone important in the regulation of appetite and metabolism is **ghrelin**. In contrast to leptin, increased ghrelin levels are associated with extreme hunger, whereas normal levels indicate satiation. Several studies have shown a relationship between sleep duration, leptin, and ghrelin levels. Taheri and colleagues (Taheri, Lin *et al.* 2004) demonstrated that acute partial sleep deprivation increases plasma concentrations of ghrelin while decreasing those of leptin. In the study, healthy participants classified as short sleepers (i.e. sleeping less than or equal six hours per night) had reduced leptin and elevated ghrelin, compared to subjects sleeping 8 hours per night. The study also found that participants sleeping less than 8 hours a night had increased BMI, proportional to their amount of decreased sleep. As reduced leptin and elevated ghrelin are both associated with an increased appetite, it is possible that these hormones explain the increased BMI seen with short sleep duration (Taheri, Lin *et al.* 2004). In another study, subjects who had insufficient sleep duration for two consecutive nights consumed 22 per cent more energy on the day after sleep restriction (compared to subjects with an 8-hour sleep opportunity), and reported higher hunger levels before breakfast and dinner (Brondel, Romer *et al.* 2010).

In addition to having measurable effects on fluctuating plasma levels of leptin and ghrelin, sleep duration also has an influence on **glucose** and **insulin**, two biomarkers commonly measured and studied in obesity and diabetes research. In fact, there is a growing association between decreased sleep and the development of obesity and diabetes. Yaggi and colleagues (Yaggi, Araujo *et al.* 2006) examined the relationship between glucose, insulin and sleep duration and showed that, compared to men who obtained between seven and eight hours of sleep per night, men reporting short sleep duration (less than or equal to six hours per night) were twice as likely to develop diabetes. Furthermore, men reporting extended sleep duration (greater than 8 hours per night) were more than three times as likely to develop diabetes over the 15-year follow-up period (Yaggi, Araujo *et al.* 2006). Additionally, it has been suggested that the relationship between sleep restriction, weight gain, and diabetes risk involved three pathways: alterations in glucose metabolism (which leads to insulin resistance), upregulation of appetite and decrease in energy expenditure, which both lead to weight gain (Knutson, Spiegel *et al.* 2007). These findings have begun to inform work and family research, in that increased stress and decreased managerial support have been shown to lead to decreased sleep duration (Berkman, Buxton *et al.* 2010) and quality (Åkerstedt, Knutsson *et al.* 2002).

Biomarkers in saliva

The use of saliva to determine hormone and drug levels has become a cornerstone of biobehavioral research (Kirschbaum, Read *et al.* 1992; Smyth, Ockenfels *et al.* 1997; Piazza, Almeida *et al.* 2010; Strahler, Berndt *et al.* 2010). Each year, several health biomarkers typically become available for assay through saliva, and testing laboratories are widely available to assist investigators in adding this simple collection method to their field research. For the purpose of this review, we focus on two of the most abundantly examined salivary biomarkers that would apply to work and family research, cortisol and cotinine. However, several excellent reviews are available on additional, exciting biomarkers in the health-stress field that readily can be translated to work and family research such as salivary alpha amylase, dehydroepiandrosterone (DHEA), and dehydroepiandrosterone-sulfate (DHEA-S); (Hucklebridge, Hussain *et al.* 2005; Nater, Rohleder *et al.* 2007; Piazza, Almeida *et al.* 2010). Of particular interest to work and family researchers, saliva collection can be adapted to children without the concerns associated with blood collection (Granger, Blair *et al.* 2007; Halpern, Whitsel *et al.* 2012; McHale, Blocklin *et al.*, in press).

Cortisol (corticosteroid) is a glutocorticoid produced by the adrenal cortex that is released in response to stimulation of the hypothalamic-pituitary-adrenal (HPA) axis by exposure to stressors. Cortisol is a catabolic hormone that helps the body deal with stress by mobilizing energy stores, communicating with the immune system and working as an anti-inflammatory hormone (Klein and Corwin 2007). Under conditions of prolonged stress or disease states that dysregulate the HPA-axis, cortisol's ability to shut off the HPA-axis response through a negative feedback loop is uncoupled. This cortisol uncoupling results in chronically elevated cortisol levels that can be associated with cardiovascular disease, T2DM, reduced immune function, depression, and cognitive impairment (Sapolsky 1996; Lundberg 2005; Duval, Mokrani *et al.* 2006; Klein and Corwin 2007; Whetzel, Corwin *et al.* 2007). Stress in the workplace due to factors such as lack of social support, managerial support, or low flexibility may lead to elevated stress levels which, if prolonged, could result in an increase in cortisol levels and depression. In a recent study, it was shown that cortisol secretion was higher in those reporting high job demands together with a greater anticipation of work (Devereux, Rydstedt *et al.* 2011). Another study reported that saliva cortisol levels were lower in women in low strain jobs (with high control and low demands) than women in high strain jobs (with low control and high demands) (Alderling, Theorell *et al.* 2006).

When developing methods for collecting salivary cortisol in population studies, it is important to understand and highlight the diurnal rhythmicity of cortisol (Ockenfels, Porter *et al.* 1995; Smyth, Ockenfels *et al.* 1997). As a biological indicator of an individual's chronobiology, salivary cortisol tends to peak in the morning and decline for the duration of the day (Dorn, Lucke *et al.* 2007; Dickmeis 2009). However, because physical and psychological stress promotes secretion of cortisol, these daily stressors can confound diurnal cortisol patterns and, thus, need to be accounted for in data analyses (Ockenfels, Porter *et al.* 1995; Smyth, Ockenfels *et al.* 1997; Stone, Schwartz *et al.* 2001; Miller, Chen *et al.* 2007). To control for this within-person stressor reactivity, it is advisable to implement a daily diary method that provides context for each salivary cortisol sample. In the National Study of Daily Experiences (NSDE), subjects were required to complete a daily telephone diary at the end of the day and answer specific questions regarding physical and psychological stressors they may have experienced during the day. The addition of a daily diary protocol in this study increased the feasibility, reliability, and validity of using salivary cortisol as a biomarker of stress by accounting for fluctuations in the hormone previously unexplainable by studies asking only generalized questions about individual stressors (Almeida, McGonagle *et al.* 2009).

Cotinine is the primary metabolite of nicotine, the active addictive ingredient in cigarettes (Office of the Surgeon General, 1988). Cotinine can be measured in blood, urine and saliva at least a day after tobacco use or exposure. Therefore, it can be used as a biomarker to indicate exposure to tobacco smoke (first-, second-, or third-hand) (Benowitz 1996; Roche, Callais *et al.* 2001). In addition to the negative side effects of tobacco smoking, such as increased risk for lung cancer, coronary heart disease, stroke, obstructive lung disease, and other cardiovascular risks (CDC 2011), smoking also is a risk factor for sleep disorders. Relative to nonsmokers without secondhand smoke exposure, smokers were significantly more likely to have been diagnosed with a sleep disorder (Davila, Lee *et al.* 2010). Further, second-hand smoke exposure by a caregiver or parent more than doubles the risk of Sudden Infant Death Syndrome in infants and increases rates of middle ear infections and asthma in children (Britton 2010). In the field of work and family research, cotinine levels may be related to the amount of work stress an individual is experiencing. One study showed that behavioral risk factors, including smoking, made up part of the mechanism underlying the association between work stress and coronary heart disease (Kouvonen, Kivimaki *et al.* 2005). Similarly, results from other studies have shown that increased daily stress, whether in the workplace or at home, leads to increased smoking behavior (Steptoe, Wardle *et al.* 1996; Aronson, Almeida *et al.* 2008), demonstrating an empirical relationship between environmental stressors and serious disease risk. Cotinine is an invaluable biomarker to determine individual exposure to tobacco smoke, such that the relationship between work stress, cardiovascular disease, and poor health outcomes can be fully examined. Nicotine exposure, even second-hand smoke, also stimulates the HPA axis and results in elevated cortisol levels (Granger, Blair *et al.* 2007). Therefore, the addition of cotinine to salivary stress-health research is useful to help understand salivary cortisol responses to daily stressors across participants.

Biomarkers in urine

Melatonin is a hormone secreted by the pineal gland responsible for maintaining the body's circadian rhythm and regulating levels of other fluctuating hormones. When melatonin levels become abnormal, such as through prolonged shift work, nighttime exposure to light, or extreme sleep deprivation, serious health consequences may result. While most well-known for its role in sleep regulation, melatonin is a diverse hormone that can be used as a biomarker in a number of different settings. Some studies have shown that normal levels of melatonin are associated with cholesterol levels in the body: because melatonin converts cholesterol to bile in the liver and regulates the amount of cholesterol that passes through the intestinal walls, it is able to decrease the total amount of cholesterol made in the gall bladder (Koppisetti, Jenigiri *et al.* 2008). Furthermore, normal melatonin levels may help prevent obesity by regulating brown adipose tissue metabolism (Tan, Manchester *et al.* 2011). In terms of work and family research, collecting data on melatonin levels may be useful in order to gain a better understanding of an individual's sleep patterns, which could further be associated with levels of stress both in the workplace and at home.

Collection methods

Blood

In population research it is important to include biomarkers that not only are relatively straightforward to take, but which can be stored easily, such that the integrity of the sample is maintained if immediate analysis is not an option (which it often is not). Blood samples obtained through venipuncture have long been the gold standard for the collection of biomarkers in blood. However, obtaining, storing, and shipping blood samples requires adherence to a number of protocols and health codes, which may not be feasible for certain work and family researchers. For example, serum blood collection requires sterile blood drawing equipment (i.e., needles, tubes, tourniquets, and a proper outlet for disposing of sharps), a trained phlebotomist, and a volunteer willing to have their blood drawn. Furthermore, blood samples must be processed (i.e., serum or plasma extracted from the blood sample via centrifugation or standing at room temperature for a given period of time), and frozen between −20 and −70 degrees Celsius (the latter being preferential), in order to prevent the degradation of analytes. Finally, in adherence to guidelines set forth by the CDC, shipment of samples requires that the shipper be certified in the transportation of dangerous goods (http://www.cdc. gov/od/eaipp/). The institution hosting the research study can frequently provide the needed certification courses; nevertheless, it is an issue that requires attention.

While venipuncture allows for the analysis of almost all analytes measureable in blood, it is not always the most practical method for obtaining these biomarkers. As an alternative, taking dried blood spots is becoming increasingly preferred over venipuncture: DBS is not only easier to collect, ship, and store, but properly-obtained samples can also be assayed for a variety of different biomarkers, including HbA1c, CRP, and EBV antibodies. In the realm of work and family research, interviewers and staff who obtain dried blood spots can be trained according to specific guidelines. Unlike phlebotomy; however, DBS sampling procedures are fairly straight-forward, and do not require official certification. To obtain a DBS sample, the participant's finger is first cleaned with an alcohol swab, allowed to air-dry, and then pricked with a sterile, disposable micro-lancet. The first drop of blood is wiped clean with gauze, and subsequent blood drops are applied to the filter paper, without the finger actually touching the paper. The drop should be thick enough to fully soak through the filter paper. If the blood flow is not sufficient to fill all spots, the skin puncture can be repeated as necessary. Once the filter paper has been allowed to air-dry, it is placed in an air-tight container with a desiccant and stored in a freezer at a minimum of –30 degrees Celsius (closer to –70 degrees is preferred). Although it is preferable to freeze samples soon after they are obtained, doing so is not necessary: the filter paper matrix in each DBS card stabilizes most analytes in the dried blood spot (McDade, Williams *et al.* 2007). This stability provides flexibility in the collection of samples in field studies, and is thus preferred over serum blood collection in work and family research.

Saliva

In population-based field studies, saliva samples can be obtained through the use of self-administered saliva collection kits. Although the collection protocol differs between studies, it is usually as simple as having subjects spit into a tube until a predetermined volume is achieved (about 2–3 ml), cap it, and place it on ice or in the refrigerator. Another common salivary collection method asks subjects to gently roll a cotton swab (e.g., Salivette) over their tongue for a few minutes, and then place the saturated cotton in a capped tube. The tubes are later centrifuged to obtain the saliva (Whetzel and Klein 2010). Collected saliva samples can be returned to the researcher via mail, where they can then be analyzed. Unlike the blood shipping protocol, it is not typically necessary for saliva samples to remain frozen during shipment. Rather, samples can be shipped overnight without dry ice to preserve the integrity of the analytes. The shipping/packaging instructions are determined by the salivary analytes.

Biomarker determination in saliva samples can be affected by several factors including how the sample is collected (e.g., passive drool, cotton swab), time of sample collection, and factors related to the participant such as health status, menstrual cycle/hormone use, age, tobacco use, alcohol consumption and medication use (Smyth, Ockenfels *et al.* 1997; Kirschbaum, Kudielka *et al.* 1999; Stone, Schwartz *et al.* 2001; Granger, Blair *et al.* 2007; Granger, Hibel *et al.* 2009; Beltzer, Fortunato *et al.* 2010; Piazza, Almeida *et al.* 2010; Strahler, Berndt *et al.* 2010). With regard to sample collection, subjects should refrain from eating, drinking, brushing their teeth or using toothpaste at least 20 minutes prior to producing a saliva sample. These activities should be avoided due to potential blood contamination from the oral mucosa that may result from these activities that can affect the assay results (Kivlighan, Granger *et al.* 2004). Furthermore, many salivary hormone levels fluctuate with the circadian cycle (Smyth, Ockenfels *et al.* 1997; Hucklebridge, Hussain *et al.* 2005; Nater, Rohleder *et al.* 2007). Therefore, it is imperative that subjects provide samples at the appropriate data collection times and that these times are recorded by the participant (in the field) and the investigator (in the research setting). The addition of saliva collection devices that automatically time stamp the saliva collection time through photo-activated caps greatly improves the accuracy of time recordings (Halpern, Whitsel *et al.* 2012). Finally, with regard to individual difference variables that can alter salivary biomarker levels (e.g., health status, menstrual cycle/hormone use, age, tobacco use, alcohol consumption and medication use), it is imperative that researchers include a comprehensive assessment of these variables that later can be used as covariates in the appropriate data analyses.

Unfortunately, data obtained from saliva samples can be confounded by between-person differences in the ability to comply with the data collection protocol. A common saliva sampling protocol requires the collection of one sample immediately upon waking, another sample 30 minutes after waking, then additional samples at lunch, dinner and bedtime. In trying to understand the "challenges of daily work and family life": individuals who are able to fit this protocol into their daily routine are likely to be systematically different from individuals who are unable to accommodate this protocol. Indeed, one study examining subject compliance with saliva sampling protocols found that approximately 25 per cent of subjects failed at least once to obtain a saliva sample at the correct time (Kudielka, Broderick *et al.* 2003; Halpern, Whitsel *et al.* 2012). Despite these restrictions, saliva continues to be a reliable medium for the accurate measurement of salivary biomarkers, and is preferable if blood samples cannot be taken. Fewer restrictions exist for the measurement of salivary cotinine; instructions are usually as simple as having the subject rinse their mouth with water before producing the sample (Abrams, Follick *et al.* 1987; Foulds, Bryant *et al.* 1994). It is important to note that, if a saliva sample is to be assayed for multiple biomarkers, work and family researchers should work closely with the laboratory that will conduct salivary assays to determine the appropriate saliva collection and shipping procedures required for accurate biomarker assessment.

Urine

The collection of urine in population studies is fairly straightforward, regardless of whether it requires a first morning void, a spot void, or a 24-hour collection. Subjects are instructed to urinate in a labeled collection cup, which is then refrigerated. Trained staff members aliquot (i.e., transfer) a specific amount of urine from the cup into an alternate vessel that is frozen and later assayed. This type of urine collection can be completed either at home or in the field.

When collecting urinary samples of metabolites of melatonin (and cortisol), it is important to remember that melatonin fluctuates based on circadian phase. Thus, subjects must adhere to the timing protocol of the study in order to produce an appropriate sample. Melatonin is also reliably measured in blood and saliva (Nowak, McMillen *et al.*, 1987), although several regulations must be followed when taking these samples. In addition to the strict timing protocol, subjects must also maintain a specific posture when producing salivary or plasma melatonin samples, as posture has a significant influence on the concentrations of these biomarkers in humans (Deacon and Arendt, 1994).

Physical biomarkers

Actigraphy

An **actigraphy recorder** is a wrist-worn, non-invasive device that measures physical activity during wake and sleep over extended periods of time. In the sleep community, actigraphy is recognized as a reliable, valid measure of sleep that, while unable to diagnose sleep disorders, is useful in large-scale studies (Berkman, Buxton *et al.*, 2010). Many population-based research studies compare actigraphy information with other biomarkers, such as CRP and HbA1c, as well as with objective and subjective measures of environmental stress, in order to examine the relationship between such stressors and overall health. Berkman and colleagues (Berkman, Buxton *et al.*, 2010) examined the effect of manager practices related to work–family balance on sleep duration and cardiovascular risk. In the study, managers were given a score based on their overall openness and creativity in regards to work–family balance: low scores corresponded to the least amount of job flexibility, and vice versa for high scores. Results of this study found an association between sleep duration and manager scores: on average, employees whose manager scored low slept 29 minutes less than employees whose managers scored high. Furthermore, the study found that employees whose managers scored low were likely to have an elevated risk for cardiovascular disease, based on both biomarker assessment and doctor diagnoses (Berkman, Buxton *et al.*, 2010). These results display a clear relationship between environmental workplace factors and health outcomes in individuals, some of which are potentially life threatening. These outcomes emphasize both the need for and usefulness of actigraphy as a biomarker in large-scale studies.

While many researchers deem actigraphy used alone to be a valid and reliable measure of sleep, actigraphy has limitations in that it may accurately measure the sleep state but less accurately determine the wake state in standard 30-second epochs versus the gold standard of polysomnography. A recent validation describes the accuracy, sensitivity, specificity, and systematic bias associated with actigraphy (Marino *et al.*, 2012) As is the historical standard for the sleep field and especially clinical trials, some researchers choose to supplement actigraphy data with sleep diaries, daily calls, and/or event markers to obtain additional data useful for determining sleep latency, sleep efficiency, and environmental context, to name a few. However, these supplemental measures are not always useful or feasible for use in population studies. Event markers, for example, are only present on some, not all, actigraphy devices, and the feature may incur an additional cost, and are not always a reliable indicator, as subjects may only use them sporadically and inconsistently. Similarly, daily phone calls, in which subjects call in at bedtime and upon waking, are not always feasible, and may increase participant burden for those with limited or no access to a computer or phone. Furthermore, even when subjects are not limited by their socioeconomic status, problems of systematic compliance differences may exist where a subject either does not call in at all, or does not accurately report his or her sleep and wake times. Similar problems exist for the usage of sleep diaries. In one study, it was found that only about two third of subjects provided an accurate and complete account of their sleep habits in the sleep diary or event markers (Lauderdale, Knutson *et al.*, 2006). It may be logical, then, to simply use actigraphy when objectively measuring sleep in some population studies.

Besides the limitations of actigraphy related to self-reports, actigraphy is measuring wrist activity movements, not sleep via the gold standard of polysomnography, which is a rich stream of physiological measures. Emerging evidence further suggests that wrist actigraphy validated for sleep may be a rough surrogate of physical activity energy expenditure, or that hip placement of the actigraphic device may be useful for sleep as well as validated energy expenditure, these advances in technology are only just emerging and not widely validated or accepted for physical placement on the body, exact analysis methods, and generalizability.

Blood pressure

Blood pressure is defined as the pressure that blood exerts on the walls of blood vessels while circulating the body. It is measured in millimeters of mercury (mmHg) as a reading of systolic pressure (SBP; when cardiac muscles contract) over diastolic pressure (DBP; when cardiac muscles relax). Normal blood pressure levels are below 120 systolic and 80 diastolic mmHg, while levels of at least 140 systolic or 90 diastolic mmHg indicate the presence of hypertension. Hypertension is a disease that may result from a variety of risk factors, including genetic, physiological, lifestyle, and sociogeographic factors. Genetic and physiological risk factors, while dangerous on their own, can become further aggravated by lifestyle factors such as smoking, high-sodium or high-fat diets, low exercise levels, and alcohol or drug abuse (Holmes and Marcelli 2012). Combinations of these factors can result in cardiovascular disease, kidney disease, and even death.

As such, blood pressure is important to measure and analyze in the field of work and family research, especially as it relates to stress in the workplace and at home. A seminal work and family study found that elevated work–family conflict predicted new incidence of hypertension (Frone, Russell *et al.* 1997). A more recent study found that immigrants in the United States had a higher risk of developing hypertension than their native-born counterparts. The research indicated that this increased risk was primarily the result of sociogeographic factors, such as having a low socioeconomic status and living in a more residentially segregated neighborhood, which can together or separately increase stress and anxiety, leading to hypertension (Holmes and Marcelli 2012). This study emphasizes the importance of measuring blood pressure and analyzing it alongside a host of other environmental factors and biomarkers, in order to develop a comprehensive profile of health and disease on both an individual and community level.

Limitations of blood pressure include the need to take carefully controlled measurements with respect to posture and context, and recent smoking, exercise, and other behaviors. "Resting" blood pressure provides useful physiological information but ambulatory blood pressure responses across the day, at work and at home, may even be more informative (Schnall, Dobson *et al.* 2008).

Future directions

This chapter outlines several biomarkers, directly measured traits that can provide insight into the functioning of multiple biological systems and overall health, in the context of work and family research. Biomarkers provide important information about within-individual biological variation that allows rigorous assessment of core research questions and interventions. We have provided an overview of several currently available, widely used biomarkers that range across multiple media (blood, urine, saliva), including issues to consider when collecting these types of measures. It is important to note that interdisciplinary collaboration can be a key to success when integrating lab-based biomarker assessments into work and family field research. Work–family and biobehavioral health scientists who bridge their expertise can develop exciting and innovative research projects that address public health concerns, such as the potentially modifiable impact of work–family conflict on cardiovascular disease risk markers.

Transdisciplinary collaborations also can lead to the development of new biomarker assessment techniques such as new collection devices (e.g., real time biomarker collection via the skin) and new techniques. Indeed, biomarker research moves forward in responses to the needs of field researchers and vice versa. For example, a growing technique to measure long-term stress or tobacco exposure in the field is hair sampling (Stalder *et al.*, 2012), and this technique is being used in workplace research. Manenschijn and colleagues (2011) used scalp hair samples to measure long-term cortisol levels in shift workers that were significantly higher than day workers. Each new biomarker technique brings with it a set of collection and measurement techniques that need special consideration (e.g., see Stalder and Kirschbaum, 2012, for new hair cortisol technique considerations) but that can move the field of work and family research forward in exciting new directions. The opportunities for understanding how the intersection of work and family interact to get under the skin to alter health are limitless.

References

Abrams, D. B., Follick, M. J., Biener, L., Carey, K. B., & Hitti, J. (1987). Saliva cotinine as a measure of smoking status in field settings. *American Journal of Public Health, 77*(7), 846-848.

Åkerstedt, T., Knutsson, A., Westerholm, P., Theorell, T., Alfredsson, L., & Kecklund, G. (2002). Sleep disturbances, work stress and work hours: A cross-sectional study. *Journal of Psychosomatic Research, 53*(3), 741-748.

Alderling, M., Theorell, T., de la Torre, B., & Lundberg, I. (2006). The demand control model and circadian saliva cortisol variations in a Swedish population based sample (The PART study). *BMC Public Health, 6*, 288. doi: 10.1186/1471-2458-6-288

Almeida, D. M., McGonagle, K., & King, H. (2009). Assessing daily stress processes in social surveys by combining stressor exposure and salivary cortisol. *Biodemography and Social Biology, 55*(2), 219-237. doi: 10.1080/19485560903382338

Aronson, K. R., Almeida, D. M., Stawski, R. S., Klein, L. C., & Kozlowski, L. T. (2008). Smoking is associated with worse mood on stressful days: results from a national diary study. *Annals of Behavioral Medicine, 36*(3), 259-269. doi: 10.1007/s12160-008-9068-1

Beltzer, E. K., Fortunato, C. K., Guaderrama, M. M., Peckins, M. K., Garramone, B. M., & Granger, D. A. (2010). Salivary flow and alpha-amylase: collection technique, duration, and oral fluid type. *Physiology & Behavior, 101*(2), 289-296. doi: 10.1016/j.physbeh.2010.05.016

Benowitz, N. L. (1996). Cotinine as a biomarker of environmental tobacco smoke exposure. *Epidemiologic Reviews, 18*(2), 188-204.

Benyamin, B., Middelberg, R. P., Lind, P. A., Valle, A. M., Gordon, S., Nyholt, D. R., Whitfield, J. B. (2011). GWAS of butyrylcholinesterase activity identifies four novel loci, independent effects within BCHE and secondary associations with metabolic risk factors. *Human Molecular Genetics.* doi: 10.1093/hmg/ddr375

Berkman, L. F., Buxton, O. M., Ertel, K., & Okechukwu, C. (2010). Manager's practices related to work-family balance predict employee cardiovascular risk and sleep duration in extended care settings. *Journal of Occupational Health Psychology, 115*(3), 316-329.

Borders, A. E., Grobman, W. A., Amsden, L. B., McDade, T. W., Sharp, L. K., & Holl, J. L. (2010). The relationship between self-report and biomarkers of stress in low-income reproductive-age women. *American Journal of Obstetrics and Gynecology, 203*(6), 577 e571-578. doi: 10.1016/j.ajog.2010.08.002

Britton, J. (2010). Passive smoking damages children's health. *The Practitioner, 254*(1729), 27-30, 23.

Brondel, L., Romer, M. A., Nougues, P. M., Touyarou, P., & Davenne, D. (2010). Acute partial sleep deprivation increases food intake in healthy men. *The American Journal of Clinical Nutrition, 91*(6), 1550-1559. doi: 10.3945/ajcn.2009.28523

Buxton, O. M., Malarick, K., Wang, W., & Seeman, T. (2009). Changes in dried blood spot Hb A1c with varied postcollection conditions. *Clinical Chemistry, 55*(5), 1034-1036.

Centers for Disease Control. (2012) Fact Sheet: Health Effects of Cigarette Smoking. *Centers for Disease Control and Prevention.* Retrieved 11/30/2012 from http://www.cdc.gov/tobacco/data_statistics/fact_sheets/health_effects/effects_cig_smoking/index.htm

D'Agostino, R. B., Sr., Grundy, S., Sullivan, L. M., & Wilson, P. (2001). Validation of the Framingham coronary heart disease prediction scores: results of a multiple ethnic groups investigation. *JAMA, 286*(2), 180-187.

Davila, E. P., Lee, D. J., Fleming, L. E., LeBlanc, W. G., Arheart, K., Dietz, N., Bandiera, F. (2010). Sleep disorders and secondhand smoke exposure in the U.S. population. *Nicotine & Tobacco Research, 12*(3), 294-299. doi: 10.1093/ntr/ntp193

Deacon, S., & Arendt, J. (1994). Posture influences melatonin concentrations in plasma and saliva in humans. *Neuroscience Letters, 167*, 191-194.

Devereux, J., Rydstedt, L. W., & Cropley, M. (2011). An exploratory study to assess the impact of work demands and the anticipation of work on awakening saliva cortisol. *Psychological Reports, 108*(1), 274-280.

Dickmeis, T. (2009). Glucocorticoids and the circadian clock. *The Journal of Endocrinology, 200*(1), 3-22. doi: 10.1677/JOE-08-0415

Dorn, L. D., Lucke, J. F., Loucks, T. L., & Berga, S. L. (2007). Salivary cortisol reflects serum cortisol: analysis of circadian profiles. *Annals of Clinical Biochemistry, 44*(Pt 3), 281-284.

Duval, F., Mokrani, M. C., Monreal-Ortiz, J. A., Fattah, S., Champeval, C., Schulz, P., & Macher, J. P. (2006). Cortisol hypersecretion in unipolar major depression with melancholic and psychotic features: dopaminergic, noradrenergic and thyroid correlates. *Psychoneuroendocrinology, 31*(7), 876-888. doi: 10.1016/j.psyneuen.2006.04.003

Foulds, J., Bryant, A., Stapleton, J., Jarvis, M. J., & Russell, M. A. (1994). The stability of cotinine in unfrozen saliva mailed to the laboratory. *American Journal of Public Health, 84*(7), 1182-1183.

Frone, M., Russell, M., & Cooper, M. (1997). Relation of work-family conflict to health outcomes: a four-year longitudinal study of employed parents. *Journal of Occupational and Organizational Psychology, 70*, 325-336.

Gerszten, R. E., & Wang, T. J. (2008). The search for new cardiovascular biomarkers. *Nature, 451*(7181), 949-952. doi: 10.1038/nature06802

Glaser, R., Friedman, S. B., Smyth, J., Ader, R., Bijur, P., Brunell, P., Toffler, P. (1999). The differential impact of training stress and final examination stress on herpesvirus latency at the United States Military Academy at West Point. *Brain, Behavior, and Immunity, 13*(3), 240-251. doi: 10.1006/brbi.1999.0566

Goldfine, A. B., Gerwien, R. W., Kolberg, J. A., O'Shea, S., Hamren, S., Hein, G. P. & Patti, M. E. (2011). Biomarkers in fasting serum to estimate glucose tolerance, insulin sensitivity, and insulin secretion. *Clinical Chemistry, 57*(2), 326-337. doi: 10.1373/clinchem.2010.156133

Grandner, MA, Buxton O.M., Jackson, N.J., Pandey, A., Pak, V.M., Jean-Louis, G. (Under Review) Extreme Sleep Durations and Increased C-Reactive Protein: Effects of Sex and Ethnoracial Group. *Sleep, 35*: A294.

Granger, D. A., Blair, C., Willoughby, M., Kivlighan, K. T., Hibel, L. C., Fortunato, C. K., & Wiegand, L. E. (2007). Individual differences in salivary cortisol and alpha-amylase in mothers and their infants: relation to tobacco smoke exposure. *Developmental Psychobiology, 49*(7), 692-701. doi: 10.1002/dev.20247

Granger, D. A., Hibel, L. C., Fortunato, C. K., & Kapelewski, C. H. (2009). Medication effects on salivary cortisol: tactics and strategy to minimize impact in behavioral and developmental science. *Psychoneuroendocrinology, 34*(10), 1437-1448. doi: 10.1016/j.psyneuen.2009.06.017

Halpern, C. T., Whitsel, E. A., Wagner, B., & Harris, K. M. (2012). Challenges of measuring diurnal cortisol concentrations in a large population-based field study. *Psychoneuroendocrinology, 37*(4), 499-508. doi: 10.1016/j.psyneuen.2011.07.019

Holmes, L. M., & Marcelli, E. A. (2012). Neighborhoods and systemic inflammation: high CRP among legal and unauthorized Brazilian migrants. *Health & Place, 18*(3), 683-693. doi: 10.1016/j.healthplace.2011.11.006

Hucklebridge, F., Hussain, T., Evans, P., & Clow, A. (2005). The diurnal patterns of the adrenal steroids cortisol and dehydroepiandrosterone (DHEA) in relation to awakening. *Psychoneuroendocrinology, 30*(1), 51-57. doi: 10.1016/j.psyneuen.2004.04.007

Kirschbaum, C., Kudielka, B. M., Gaab, J., Schommer, N. C., & Hellhammer, D. H. (1999). Impact of gender, menstrual cycle phase, and oral contraceptives on the activity of the hypothalamus-pituitary-adrenal axis. *Psychosomatic Medicine, 61*(2), 154-162.

Kirschbaum, C., Read, G. F., & Hellhammer, D. H. (1992). *Assessment of hormone and drugs in saliva in biobehavioral research*. Seattle, WA: Hogrefe & Huber Publishers.

Kivlighan, K. T., Granger, D. A., Schwartz, E. B., Nelson, V., Curran, M., & Shirtcliff, E. A. (2004). Quantifying blood leakage into the oral mucosa and its effects on the measurement of cortisol, dehydroepiandrosterone, and testosterone in saliva. *Hormones and Behavior, 46*(1), 39-46. doi: 10.1016/j.yhbeh.2004.01.006

Klein, L. C., & Corwin, E. J. (2007). Homestasis and the stress response. In E. J. Corwin (Ed.), *Handbook of Pathophysiology* (3rd ed., pp. 159-172). Philadelphia, PA: Lippincott Williams and Wilkins.

Knutson, K. L., Spiegel, K., Penev, P., & Van Cauter, E. (2007). The metabolic consequences of sleep deprivation. *Sleep Medicine Reviews, 11*(3), 163-178.

Koppisetti, S., Jenigiri, B., Terron, M. P., Tengattini, S., Tamura, H., Flores, L. J. & Reiter, R. J. (2008). Reactive oxygen species and the hypomotility of the gall bladder as targets for the treatment of gallstones with melatonin: a review. *Digestive Diseases and Sciences, 53*(10), 2592-2603. doi: 10.1007/s10620-007-0195-5

Kouvonen, A., Kivimaki, M., Virtanen, M., Pentti, J., & Vahtera, J. (2005). Work stress, smoking status, and smoking intensity: an observational study of 46,190 employees. *Journal of Epidemiology and Community Health, 59*(1), 63-69. doi: 10.1136/jech.2004.019752

Kudielka, B. M., Broderick, J. E., & Kirschbaum, C. (2003). Compliance with saliva sampling protocols: electronic monitoring reveals invalid cortisol daytime profiles in noncompliant subjects. *Psychosomatic Medicine, 65*(2), 313-319.

Larson, M. R., Ader, R., & Moynihan, J. A. (2001). Heart rate, neuroendocrine, and immunological reactivity in response to an acute laboratory stressor. *Psychosomatic Medicine, 63*(3), 493-501.

Lauderdale, D. S., Knutson, K. L., Yan, L. L., Rathouz, P. J., Hulley, S. B., Sidney, S., & Liu, K. (2006). Objectively measured sleep characteristics among early-middle-aged adults: the CARDIA study. *American Journal of Epidemiology, 164*(1), 5-16.

Lundberg, U. (2005). Stress hormones in health and illness: the roles of work and gender. *Psychoneuroendocrinology, 30*(10), 1017-1021. doi: 10.1016/j.psyneuen.2005.03.014

Maeda, E., Akahane, M., Kiryu, S., Kato, N., Yoshikawa, T., Hayashi, N., Ohtomo, K. (2009). Spectrum of Epstein-Barr virus-related diseases: a pictorial review. *Japanese Journal of Radiology, 27*(1), 4-19. doi: 10.1007/s11604-008-0291-2

Manenschijn, L., van Kruysbergen, R.G., de Jong, F.H., Koper, J.W. & van Rossum, E.F. (2011). Shift work at young age is associated with elevated long-term cortisol levels and body mass index. *Journal of Clinical Endocrinology and Metabolism, 96*(11):E1862-5.

Marino, M., Li, Y., Rueschman, M., Winkelman, J.W., Ellenbogen, J., Solet, J.M., Dulin, H., Berkman, L. & Buxton, O.M. (2012). Accuracy, sensitivity, and specificity of a wrist actigraphy algorithm for sleep/wake and WASO versus polysomnography. *Sleep, 35*: S-440-441.

McDade, T. W., Williams, S., & Snodgrass, J. J. (2007). What a drop can do: dried blood spots as a minimally invasivemethod for integrating biomarkers into population-based research. *Demography, 44*(4), 899-925.

McHale, S. M., Blocklin, M. K., Walker, K. N., Davis, K. D., Almeida, D. M., & Klein, L. C. (In Press). The role of daily activities in youths' stress physiology. *Journal of Adolescent Health.*

Miller, G. E., Chen, E., & Zhou, E. S. (2007). If it goes up, must it come down? Chronic stress and the hypothalamic-pituitary-adrenocortical axis in humans. *Psychological Bulletin, 133*(1), 25-45. doi: 10.1037/0033-2909.133.1.25

Mitchell, C., Notterman, D., Brooks-Gunn, J., Hobcraft, J., Garfinkel, I., Jaeger, K. & McLanahan, S. (2011). Role of mother's genes and environment in postpartum depression. *Proceedings of the National Academy of Sciences of the United States of America, 108*(20), 8189-8193. doi: 10.1073/pnas.1014129108

Nater, U. M., Rohleder, N., Schlotz, W., Ehlert, U., & Kirschbaum, C. (2007). Determinants of the diurnal course of salivary alpha-amylase. *Psychoneuroendocrinology, 32*(4), 392-401. doi: 10.1016/j.psyneuen.2007.02.007

Nowak, R., McMillen, I. C., Redman, J., & Short, R. V. (1987). The correlation between serum and salivary melatonin concentrations and urinary 6-hydroxymelatonin sulphate excretion rates: Two non-invasive techniques for monitoring human circadian rhythmicity. *Clinical Endocrinology, 27*, 445-452.

Ockenfels, M. C., Porter, L., Smyth, J., Kirschbaum, C., Hellhammer, D. H., & Stone, A. A. (1995). Effect of chronic stress associated with unemployment on salivary cortisol: overall cortisol levels, diurnal rhythm, and acute stress reactivity. *Psychosomatic Medicine, 57*(5), 460-467.

Office of the Surgeon General. (1988). The Health Consequences of Smoking: Nicotine Addiction. Rockville, MD: U.S. Department of Health and Human Services, Public Health Service, Centers for Disease Contro, Center for Health Promotion and Education, Office on Smoking and Health.

Piazza, J. R., Almeida, D. M., Dmitrieva, N. O., & Klein, L. C. (2010). Frontiers in the use of biomarkers of health in research on stress and aging. *The Journal of Gerontology. Series B, PsychologicalSsciences and Social Sciences, 65*(5), 513-525. doi: 10.1093/geronb/gbq049

Reiter, R. J., Tan, D. X., Korkmaz, A., Erren, T. C., Piekarski, C., Tamura, H., & Manchester, L. C. (2007). Light at night, chronodisruption, melatonin suppression, and cancer risk: a review. *Critical Reviews in Oncogenesis, 13*(4), 303-328.

Roche, D., Callais, F., Reungoat, P., & Momas, I. (2001). Adaptation of an enzyme immunoassay to assess urinary cotinine in nonsmokers exposed to tobacco smoke. *Clinical Chemistry, 47*(5), 950-952.

Sapolsky, R. M. (1996). Why stress is bad for your brain. *Science, 273*(5276), 749-750.

Schnall, P. L., Dobson, M., Rosskam, E., Baker, D., & Lansbergid, P. (2008). *Unhealthy Work: Causes, Consequences and Cures*. Amityville, NY: Baywood Press.

Scott, L. J., Mohlke, K. L., Bonnycastle, L. L., Willer, C. J., Li, Y., Duren, W. L. & Boehnke, M. (2007). A genome-wide association study of type 2 diabetes in Finns detects multiple susceptibility variants. *Science, 316*(5829), 1341-1345. doi: 10.1126/science.1142382

Smyth, J. M., Ockenfels, M. C., Gorin, A. A., Catley, D., Porter, L. S., Kirschbaum, C. & Stone, A. A. (1997). Individual differences in the diurnal cycle of cortisol. *Psychoneuroendocrinology, 22*(2), 89-105.

Stalder, T., Steudte, S., Alexander, N., Miller, R., Gao, W., Dettenborn, L. & Kirschbaum, C. (2012). Cortisol in hair, body mass index and stress-related measures. *Biol Psychol, 90*(3):218-23.

Stalder, T., Kirschbaum, C. (2012) Analysis of cortisol in hair--state of the art and future directions. *Brain, Behavior, and Immunity, 26*(7):1019-29. doi: 10.1016/j.bbi.2012.02.002.

Stenvinkel, P., Karimi, M., Johansson, S., Axelsson, J., Suliman, M., Lindholm, B. & Schalling, M. (2007). Impact of inflammation on epigenetic DNA methylation - a novel risk factor for cardiovascular disease? *Journal of Internal Medicine, 261*(5), 488-499. doi: 10.1111/j.1365-2796.2007.01777.x

Steptoe, A., & Wardle, J. (2005). Positive affect and biological function in everyday life. *Neurobiology of Aging, 26 Suppl 1*, 108-112. doi: 10.1016/j.neurobiolaging.2005.08.016

Steptoe, A., Wardle, J., Pollard, T. M., Canaan, L., & Davies, G. J. (1996). Stress, social support and health-related behavior: a study of smoking, alcohol consumption and physical exercise. *Journal of Psychosomatic Research, 41*(2), 171-180.

Stone, A. A., Schwartz, J. E., Smyth, J., Kirschbaum, C., Cohen, S., Hellhammer, D., & Grossman, S. (2001). Individual differences in the diurnal cycle of salivary free cortisol: a replication of flattened cycles for some individuals. *Psychoneuroendocrinology, 26*(3), 295-306.

Strahler, J., Berndt, C., Kirschbaum, C., & Rohleder, N. (2010). Aging diurnal rhythms and chronic stress: Distinct alteration of diurnal rhythmicity of salivary alpha-amylase and cortisol. *Biological Psychology, 84*(2), 248-256. doi: 10.1016/j.biopsycho.2010.01.019

Taheri, S., Lin, L., Austin, D., Young, T., & Mignot, E. (2004). Short sleep duration is associated with reduced leptin, elevated ghrelin, and increased body mass index. *PLoS Medicine, 1*(3), e62.

Tan, D. X., Manchester, L. C., Fuentes-Broto, L., Paredes, S. D., & Reiter, R. J. (2011). Significance and application of melatonin in the regulation of brown adipose tissue metabolism: relation to human obesity. *Obesity Reviews, 12*(3), 167-188. doi: 10.1111/j.1467-789X.2010.00756.x

Tengattini, S., Reiter, R. J., Tan, D. X., Terron, M. P., Rodella, L. F., & Rezzani, R. (2008). Cardiovascular diseases: protective effects of melatonin. *Journal of Pineal Research, 44*(1), 16-25.

Whetzel, C. A., Corwin, E. J., & Klein, L. C. (2007). Disruption in Th1/Th2 immune response in young adult smokers. *Addictive Behaviors, 32*(1), 1-8. doi: 10.1016/j.addbeh.2006.03.007

Whetzel, C. A., & Klein, L. C. (2010). Measuring DHEA-S in saliva: time of day differences and positive correlations between two different types of collection methods. *BMC Research Notes, 3*, 204. doi: 10.1186/1756-0500-3-204

Williams, S. R., Pham-Kanter, G., & Leitsch, S. A. (2009). Measures of chronic conditions and iseases associated with aging in the National Social Life, Health, and Aging Project. *Journal of Gerontology: Social Sciences, 64B*(S1), i65-i75.

Xue, H., Lu, B., Zhang, J., Wu, M., Huang, Q., Wu, Q. & Lai, M. (2010). Identification of serum biomarkers for colorectal cancer metastasis using a differential secretome approach. *Journal of Proteome Research, 9*(1), 545-555. doi: 10.1021/pr9008817

Yaggi, H. K., Araujo, A. B., & McKinlay, J. B. (2006). Sleep duration as a risk factor for the development of type 2 diabetes. *Diabetes Care, 29*(3), 657-661.

11 Using direct observational methods to study the real lives of families

Advantages, complexities, and conceptual and practical considerations

Rena L. Repetti, Shu-wen Wang and Meredith S. Sears

Whether describing jobs, families, or work–family processes, research on the interface between work experiences and family life has relied almost exclusively on participant-report measures in which the respondent describes the self or another target, such as a spouse. These methods offer an obvious advantage to researchers in that they are relatively inexpensive and easy to use. But there are shortcomings, and direct observational methods offer an alternative. This chapter focuses on the use of direct observational methods to address research questions in the work–family field, particularly their use in the assessment of families. We begin by discussing sources of error in participant reports and then move to a discussion of key issues involved in designing a direct observational study and in making sense of the data. Throughout, we distinguish between naturalistic designs and approaches that incorporate greater researcher control over what is observed.

Measuring work and family constructs through indirect and direct observations

Psychological constructs are explanatory variables that are not directly measurable but make sense of the complexity of human behavior. Constructs such as interpersonal conflict, positive and negative emotion, social support, spillover, and cross-over are common and meaningful in the work–family research literature. Instead of directly observing these phenomena, indicators or manifestations of them are observed and recorded, either by researchers or the participants themselves. The approaches used to assess manifestations of a construct rely on some form of either indirect or direct observation. With indirect methods, such as questionnaires, the research participant describes his or her observations of a target (e.g., experiences on the job, a family characteristic, a spouse's behavior). With direct observational techniques, the work or family variable is observed in the here-and-now by a third party. Direct observations have been used to assess both family interaction (Costigan, Cox and Cauce, 2003; Grossman, Pollack and Golding, 1988; Repetti and Wood, 1997; Wang, Repetti and Campos, 2011) and work conditions (Repetti, 1989) in studies addressing work–family questions. As we move from indirect to direct observations, the work of observing the target and of processing and recording those observations shifts from the participants to the researcher.

Researchers use constructs to organize observations, which can be represented by anything from numbered ratings on questionnaires to images on video. Although all measurement techniques – whether based on participant reports or direct observations made by third parties – involve processes of choosing, defining, and interpreting constructs, the approaches vary with respect to the point at which the construct is defined and the process by which it is interpreted. Because constructs themselves are not directly observable, decisions must be made about the indicators that constitute the construct (e.g., what comprises family conflict) and whether the manifestations of the construct have been observed. The direct and indirect measurement approaches discussed in this chapter vary according to how those decisions are made, and how participants and researchers contribute to the decision-making process.

The phenomena of interest to psychologists (i.e., the manifestations of a psychological construct) can be thought of as roughly falling into two categories. Conscious "internal" psychological processes – such as beliefs, thoughts, and feelings – can only be described by the individual. A larger class of externally measurable, observable phenomena – such as behaviors that constitute marital conflict or emotion expression, job characteristics, or indicators of mental and physical health – can be described by a range of observers. These might include the individual him or herself, a family member or co-worker, or an independent observer, such as a researcher. When the indicators of a construct are subjective experiences and thought patterns, such as participants' *perceptions* of their experiences or the environment, self-report instruments are ideal. For example, marital satisfaction is a consequence of an individual's subjective cognitive and emotional experience of a marriage, and can only be addressed by self-report. Though most constructs in the field of work and family research refer to observable phenomena, they are almost always assessed at the level of individual impressions only. We argue that, when constructs are manifested by phenomena other than purely subjective experiences and perceptions, there is an advantage to supplementing self-reports with observations made by others. The field's understanding of familiar constructs, such as work–family balance, would benefit from integrated methods that assess both internal as well as external phenomena. That's because we do not yet know the extent to which work–family balance is a psychological concept that exists in the minds of individuals, and the extent to which it is enacted in social space shared with family members, co-workers, and supervisors.

Sources of error in participant reports

The limitations of participant-report methods most commonly mentioned in the work–family research literature are the predispositions, attitudes, and beliefs that participants bring to the task of responding to items on questionnaires and surveys. Respondent biases – whether due to social desirability, mood, or another individual characteristic – introduce systematic error and, as a result, correlations between variables assessed with scales completed by the same person are inflated. For example, cross-sectional correlations between self-report scales assessing job satisfaction and marital satisfaction are sometimes attributed to "positive spillover" between experiences in the two settings. However, it is impossible to distinguish any actual spillover effects (work influencing married life, or vice versa) from individual characteristics that contribute to responses on both scales. When responding to items like "I feel good about my job," or "how happy are you in your marriage," an individual's tendency to look at the glass as "half empty" would lead to a focus on deficits, or what could be better in *both domains*. On the other hand, a wish to view one's life in the best possible light would direct attention to positive experiences *both at work and at home*, or perhaps to comparisons with people who are in worse situations. In either case, the participant's responses would be biased in the same direction on the two scales, and the correlation between them would at least partially reflect that response bias. The consequence of this common method variance is an increase in Type I error, or false-positives in the research literature. In short, a reliance on cross-sectional correlations between self-report measures in the work–family field has undoubtedly led to an overestimation of the robustness of concepts like spillover. To address that problem, rather than rely on self-report data alone, work–family researchers sometimes include observations made by other participants, such as spouses or coworkers (Repetti, 1994; Story and Repetti, 2006; Schulz, Cowan, Cowan and Brennan, 2004).

There are also a number of sources of random error in measures that rely on the reports of participants including differences among respondents in the way that questions and response scales are interpreted. The reliability of a scale provides information about the degree to which individual users respond similarly to items designed to assess the same construct or to the same items on different occasions; it does not provide information about the extent to which respondents differ in their interpretation of key terms or in their use of a response scale. Although the researcher may have one meaning in mind for a term on a scale, participants may introduce nuances in their interpretation of the term. For instance, when responding to a typical item on a family conflict scale, such as "we fight a lot in our family," participants may conceive of the terms "fight" and "a lot" in different ways. "Fight" can be interpreted to mean overt physical aggression, or a heated verbal argument, or more subtle forms of aggression without any overt hostility at all. Because the language used on a scale is open to interpretation, each respondent plays some role in shaping the way that the construct is defined in his or her data. Thus, for example, the strategy of testing correlations between a self-report family conflict scale and a measure of job stress to assess negative spillover is undermined if the interpretations of family conflict and job stress items vary randomly across participants, thereby introducing noise that obscures the identification of true underlying associations. The consequence of non-systematic measurement error is an increase in Type II error, or false-negatives in the research literature. The failure to detect true associations, which is especially likely when effect sizes are small, is just as consequential for advancements in the work–family field as are false-positive associations due to systematic biases. Aggregating ratings of a single target made by multiple participants is one way to reduce both types of measurement error. For instance Repetti (1987) averaged coworkers' ratings to assess the social climates of bank branches.

Another source of random error is the simple inability to accurately provide the information that is being requested. The description of behavioral and interactional patterns places a substantial cognitive burden on participants with respect to basic recall as well as the aggregation of memories across many contexts and occasions, some of which may be more or less salient depending on the participant's mood or recent events (Stone and Shiffman, 2002). To even attempt to respond with accuracy to the sort of scale items used in work–family studies involves complex processing of information. The example used above ("we fight a lot in our family") requires the respondent to first operationalize terms like "fighting" and "a lot" and then apply those definitions in a consistent manner to daily memories that extend back over a long period of time and countless situations. Corrections must be made to the estimating process. For instance, respondents for whom there is little family conflict to recall must overcome a tendency to overestimate the frequency of fighting from recall of a single (but rare) or recent fight in the family. Of course, measurement error is compounded as the phenomena that participants are asked to describe become more complex. Participants in work–family studies are often asked to describe psychological processes, such as positive and negative spillover and coping responses to work stress. For example, they might be asked whether "stress at work makes you irritable at home." Responding to that item requires – in addition to a shared understanding of what the researcher means by "stress" and "irritability" and a keen awareness and accurate reporting of both – an ability to correctly infer whether irritable behavior, mood, and attitudes expressed at home are *caused by* stress at work. Making the causal inference involves a comparison of periods when work is more and less stressful, and decisions about when behavior at home is a response to job conditions and not some other factor. A complex cognitive calculus is needed to compute changes in behavior and affect and accurately link those changes to specific conditions in the environment. Items like this are just as likely to assess a respondent's *beliefs* as they are to reflect actual associations between experiences and behavior in the work and family domains. However, self-report measures of complex constructs like work–family conflict and spillover are rarely interpreted as measures of impressions, attitudes, or beliefs.

Daily report studies reduce the information processing demands placed on the participant by inquiring about specific behavior or events during a recent limited period of time, such as that day, or the last few hours (Stone and Shiffman, 2002). Clearly less information needs to be recalled and processed, resulting in less error, when responding to a family conflict item on a daily report scale such as, "my husband and I argued tonight," compared to the item, "we fight a lot in our family." The influence of social desirability is likely to be more limited in reports about behavior on a single day compared to asking participants what they or their families are "usually" like. More important, the processing demands shift from the participant and onto the researcher. For example, in order to determine what participants or their families are "usually" like, person-level or family-level variables can be computed from daily-level data. Moreover, the respondent is relieved of the task of calculating a connection between experiences and behavior at work and at home. That calculus is now performed through statistical analysis of the repeated measures.

Direct observation of families

Direct observation provides a drastically different approach to the definition and examination of constructs than that offered by participant reports. With direct observation, constructs are assessed through phenomena that are directly surveyed by the researcher, bypassing participants as reporters. By gaining a fly-on-the-wall view that directly taps into the behavior or events of interest, these methods allow researchers to more objectively assess what is occurring in real-time rather than rely on subsequent accounts delivered by participants. We believe greater use of direct observational data would benefit the work–family field. Because they remove much of the subjectivity and noise inherent in participant reports, direct observations reduce the amount of Type I and Type II error contained in correlations based purely on self-report scales. This section begins with a discussion of the design and data collection stages of direct observational research, focusing on factors that underlie decisions about whether to observe families in the laboratory or in the field and the issues that arise in choosing specific design features and methodologies for naturalistic studies. Next, we discuss characteristics of observational data, and the steps involved in organizing and coding observations. Throughout, we emphasize naturalistic observational data and the ways in which they differ from observations made in the laboratory.

Designing a direct observational study of families

Methods used by researchers to directly observe families vary with respect to the researcher's role in deciding what about a family or its life is observed, as well as where, when and how the family is observed. The circumstances under which families are observed range from the artificial setting of the research laboratory – in which families might be instructed about what to discuss, for how long, and with whom – to field settings in which families can be recorded as they go about their daily lives. An overriding issue that differentiates among the various approaches to direct observation methods is the degree of control exerted by the researcher.

Choosing the observational situation

Characteristics of the settings in which families are observed include physical location as well as situational factors, such as who is present and the specific instructions given to family members. Most direct observational assessments of couple or family behavior take place in the structured setting of the laboratory where, typically, a situation is designed to elicit the behavior that constitutes the construct of interest. Researcher demands that shape what occurs in the laboratory constrain participants' behavior such that a restricted but relatively uniform view of a specific process is observed. For example, there is a rich tradition in the marital observation literature of eliciting conflict by asking couples to discuss a highly problematic issue in their relationship for a designated period of time (for a review, see Heyman, 2001). A relatively newer area of marital investigation involves the observation of marital support processes; in these laboratory studies, the researcher structures opportunities for the solicitation and provision of support by having each member of a couple discuss something personal that they would like to change about him or herself (e.g., Pasch and Bradbury, 1998). Behavior in the laboratory may be influenced not only by instructions (e.g., topics for a dyad to discuss, or a particular game for the family to play), but also by space and movement limitations (e.g., having an individual connected to a blood pressure monitor throughout a task), the people present (e.g., a parent–child interaction task that does not include siblings or the other parent), and other controls imposed by the researcher on the observational setting. Attempts to study family behavior in 'seminatural' settings designed to approximate an actual home (e.g., 'apartment laboratory') have revealed that conflict observed in a more typical laboratory setting differed from conflict observed during dinnertime in the 'apartment laboratory' (Gottman and Driver, 2005). Overall, the evidence suggests that behaviors and processes observed in the laboratory do not necessarily map onto the behaviors and processes that unfold in everyday life (Gottman and Krokoff, 1989).

Observations are also made outside of researcher-controlled environments, in locations where family members can be tracked as they go about their normal routines with minimal interference from the researcher, a procedure we refer to here as "naturalistic observation." In comparison to data collected in the artificial setting of most research labs, the ecological validity of observations made in the field is assumed to improve the external validity, and therefore the generalizability, of a study's results. Family interactions have been systematically observed in a variety of natural settings, ranging from the privacy of the family home, to semi-private settings such as daycare centers, to public places like playgrounds or museums. Of course behavior (whether observed by a researcher or not) is also constrained by situational demands in natural settings. For example, emotions and behavior in private settings (e.g., the home) have been found to differ from those displayed in public settings (e.g., the workplace; Larson, Richards and Perry-Jenkins, 1994).

Of course, just because an observation is conducted in the field doesn't necessarily mean that the targets of the observation are behaving in a completely natural manner as they are being observed. First, the level of intrusiveness on the part of the researchers (e.g., how cameras are placed, who is present) may influence how free participants are to act in a "normal" way. Observations made outside of the laboratory are also sometimes directed in some manner by the researcher. For instance, to study parent–child interaction at home, parents might be asked to play with their infant for 15 minutes as they normally would (e.g., Costigan, Cox and Cauce, 2003), or they might be asked to arrange a family dinner to be filmed (e.g., Hayden *et al.*, 1998). There are several reasons why prompted behavior in response to a researcher's instructions, regardless of the setting, would not necessarily map on to everyday behaviors and experiences. Missing are the normal sequencing of events, behaviors, and feelings that usually precede, and give rise to, a particular type of interaction. The presence (or absence) of certain family members can also reduce the observations' external validity. For instance, the researcher might ask that all family members be present for a dinner or that siblings not be present during parent–child play in the home, conditions that may not reflect the social environments in which these events typically occur. Consider, for example, the Costigan *et al.* (2003) study, in which mothers' descriptions of their social climate at work were linked to the observed quality of both parents' interactions with their infant at home; a less supportive job climate was associated with more negative and intrusive, and less positive behavior. The external validity of the 15-minute "play session" was reduced to the degree that the investigators' arrangement of the observational setting did not match the circumstances of everyday life at home.

In addition, just as with participant reports, there are individual differences in social desirability biases that lead to varying degrees of self-correction or editing of behavior. Of course, a research participant has much more control over self-presentation when deciding which number to circle in response to a question about how she argues with her spouse than when asked to discuss a conflict-laden topic with her husband. Not only is her own emotion aroused in the latter situation, her spouse's emotion is also aroused and his behavior is not under her control. Family members in naturalistic observational studies have the least awareness of and control over what they reveal. In addition to having only limited control over the events that occur and the behavior and activities of others as their everyday lives are recorded, they cannot know all of the potential foci of interest in the observations that are collected. Indeed, as discussed below, even a researcher may not be aware of all of the constructs that ultimately will be identified and studied once the data are collected.

Although naturalistic family observations maximize external validity, there are pragmatic considerations for researchers to consider. Extra resources are needed to collect direct observational data in natural settings. Study recruitment can be especially challenging when asking families to allow one or more researchers into their lives. Home observations can be uncomfortable for participants and one uninterested family member can prevent the rest of the family's entry into the study. In addition, a large and well-trained staff is required to collect and process the data. And, if the construct of interest has a relatively low base rate occurrence (e.g., overt family conflict), researchers may have to collect data for quite some time before capturing even a minimal amount of relevant behavior. Low base rates are one of the primary reasons psychologists observe families in controlled settings in which a desired behavioral situation can be elicited. All of these factors, as well as providing sufficient monetary compensation to participating families, can become quite expensive compared to the typical laboratory-based study. The next two sections focus on occasions when a researcher decides that the advantages of naturalistic observation outweigh the costs and challenges. Two critical design issues are discussed: decisions about the timing of data collection and the choice of recording methods.

Naturalistic methods: Deciding when families are observed

Naturalistic studies can focus on a particular time of day in which an identified interaction or behavior routinely occurs. In a sense, control over the timing of naturalistic observations is comparable to the intentional elicitation of particular social situations in laboratory studies. Naturalistic participant reports such as daily diaries and other momentary techniques (e.g., Ecological Momentary Assessment; Shiffman, Stone and Hufford, 2008; Experience Sampling Method; Larson and Csikszentmihalyi, 1983) describe events as they play out in the natural environment by tracking perceptions and behaviors on repeated occasions. Our understanding of complex phenomena like work–family spillover has been advanced by studies relating daily conditions at work to same-day mood and behavior as assessed by self- and spouse-reports (Story and Repetti, 2006; Schulz, *et al.*, 2004). For example, in a sample of air traffic controllers, Repetti (1989, 1994) studied work–family spillover by examining associations between daily reports of job stress and daily descriptions of marital and parent–child interactions later that evening. The data showed same-day linkages between reports of job stress and the level of social involvement and anger in subsequent family interactions later that evening. Daily behavior was also linked to direct observational measures of workload: visibility at the airport during the air traffic controller's shift each day (based on hourly weather observations from the National Climatic Data Center) and FAA records of daily air traffic volume. These studies show how repeated measures can be used to assess psychological and behavioral processes as they unfold in real time.

Well-timed direct observations of families in their natural settings can be incorporated into daily research designs. Although the isolation of naturally-occurring events that families or individuals have in common is often a knotty process, "universal" events have been studied through naturalistic designs, particularly when the participants share some common characteristics. For instance, Repetti and Wood (1997) assessed mother–child interactions in a direct observational study of employed mothers as they were reuniting each evening with their preschool-aged children at a worksite daycare center. Behavioral coding of the videotaped reunions indicated that the mothers spoke less and appeared less emotionally involved with their children (e.g., fewer verbal and nonverbal expressions of affection) during reunions that followed more difficult days at work. Thus, an analysis of mothers' daily reports of job conditions in combination with direct observations of their behavior at the moment of reunion with their children at the end of each workday suggested that daily job stress was often linked to a short-term increase in parental withdrawal. This study allowed researchers to observe a purely naturalistic (i.e., not prescribed) event while maintaining some control over the parameters of the situation.

The best example of the use of naturalistic video data to study work–family processes is found in the work of the UCLA Center on Everyday Lives of Families (CELF). With funding from the Alfred P. Sloan Foundation, our interdisciplinary group studied 32 middle-class dual-earner families with school-age children over the course of a week. Multiple methods, including questionnaires, daily self-reports, interviews, home tours, and salivary cortisol samples were used, but the hallmark of this project is the ethnographic videotaping of everyday family routines and interactions. Family members were filmed as they went about their daily lives inside and outside of the home over two weekdays and two weekend days, permitting direct observation of family behavior and process (Ochs, Graesch, Mittmann, Bradbury and Repetti, 2006). Using the CELF data, Wang, Repetti, and Campos (2011) coded rates of talking, social engagement (i.e., intensity of response to another's initiation of interaction), and negative emotion expression (e.g., frowns) in employed adults with their spouse and children in the first hour after they returned home from work. When those direct observations were linked with self-reported levels of job stress and trait neuroticism (i.e., emotional instability), two pictures emerged. On the one hand, a pattern of negative emotion spillover was observed among husbands and fathers who scored high on neuroticism: more job stress was associated with more involved and negatively valenced interactions. On the other hand, a pattern of social withdrawal was found among the men who scored low on neuroticism: more job stress was associated with less social interaction and less negative emotion expression. There were no associations between job stress and the after-work social behavior of the women in this sample. The contrast with typical questionnaire methods to assess work–family processes is striking. It would be unreasonable to expect research participants to recognize or describe the kind of subtle behavioral changes that were observed in conjunction with job stressors. This approach provides a more detailed and accurate picture of the links between experiences at work and behavior at home. While the larger observation effort recorded hundreds of hours of footage inside the home, this particular investigation "zoomed in" on the first hour window of after-work behavior in order to study work–family process. Thus, timing at the level of coding and analysis – in addition to timing in the initial filming effort – is critical to research that uses naturalistic observations of continuous and non-specific streams of behavior.

Naturalistic methods: Deciding how families are observed

There are a variety of methods that researchers use to document family behavior in natural settings. In addition to video and audio recordings, trained observers can directly register their observations immediately as they occur through notes made on paper or into electronic devices. For example, the CELF study supplemented video with a scan-sampling method in which live observers used hand-held computers to note the locations and describe the activities in which family members were involved at 10-minute intervals, such as watching TV, preparing dinner, doing homework, talking on the telephone, playing with a video game, or brushing teeth; the activities were later sorted into larger categories such as leisure, housework, communication, and personal care (Ochs, *et al.*, 2006; Saxbe, Repetti and Graesch, 2011). The scan-sampling observational data were used to address questions about how activities at home influence physiological recovery after a day at work. Findings indicated that an individual's recovery from the work day – as assessed by cortisol, a stress hormone – was associated with his or her spouse's observed activities at home. Physiological unwinding was enhanced among women whose husbands spent more time involved in housework activities, whereas men's physiological unwinding was more effective if their wives apportioned less of their time to leisure (Saxbe, Repetti and Graesch, 2011). Another recording approach has live observers describe families during set periods of time according to a predetermined reporting scheme. In one study, an observer with a hand-held computer followed family members at home and noted the occurrence of specific behaviors. The variables of interest had already been operationalized; for instance, during the 20-minutes each hour that the target child was observed, behaviors such as hitting, yelling, and destructiveness were noted (Patterson and Forgatch, 1995).

Technological advancements have permitted the recording of behavior and interaction such that continuous streams of raw data are captured prior to any coding or data reduction. Audio-recordings can be taken in the field by the use of devices worn on the person as he or she goes about his or her daily life. One such audio-recording apparatus is the Electronically Activated Recorder (EAR, Mehl, Pennebaker, Crow, Dabbs and Price, 2001), an event sampling device that has been used to sample brief clips of participants' acoustic social environments, capturing everything from self-talk, to laughter, to conversation. For example, Slatcher and Robles (2012) assessed children's social conflicts at home with this methodology. Direct observations can also be collected using video-recordings that capture both auditory and visual information that build archives of rich multisensory data. Videotaping captures non-specific streams of behavior and interactions that occur in a given context. The CELF study is one example of continuous videotaping of family interactions inside families' homes and community settings (e.g., Campos, Graesch, Repetti, Ochs and Bradbury, 2009; Ochs *et al.*, 2006; Wang, *et al.*, 2011).

Making sense of family observations

Whether in the laboratory or in the field, direct observation affords windows onto behavior and interactional processes for researchers to study in real-time. In order to gain an understanding of families from direct observations, constructs must be operationalized through coding and analysis of the data. The variety of behaviors and situations captured by the observations, the degree of detail contained in the recordings, the level of order and organization inherent in the raw data, and the uniformity of information across participants have important implications for behavioral coding.

Detail and variability in observational data

The specific features of a direct observational study of families determine the depth and breadth of the data that are collected. A much broader span of behavior is observed in naturalistic studies than when participant behavior is to some degree scripted and controlled by researchers. Naturalistic observations are subject to the idiosyncrasies of the phenomena as they naturally occur. For example, an investigation of dinnertime interactions in the CELF study found that the family composition sitting down to dinner (e.g., in unison with Dad missing, in partial unison with all members present at some point of the dinner), lengths of mealtime (range of 16–40 minutes), types of concurrent activities (e.g., watching TV, doing homework), and how the food was prepared (e.g., cooked from scratch, take-out) all varied considerably (Ochs, Shohet, Campos and Beck, 2010). Conversely, a laboratory investigation of family dinners might invite family members into a structured setting (e.g., an "apartment laboratory"; Driver and Gottman, 2004) in which these factors vary to a lesser extent. In a controlled setting there is more clarity and uniformity in what is captured on film. In fact, the point of researcher control over settings and instructions is precisely that – to reduce variability and limit the scope of what is observed. The goal of live observers' notes is the same; they are designed to limit and organize what is recorded. Both approaches seek to impose order and organization on observations during the data collection stage. The strategy is analogous to indirect observational methods in which items are selected in advance to direct the attention of participants to the particular phenomena (e.g., perceptions, behaviors, experiences) that the researcher wants to assess.

The breadth and level of detail in the raw data that are collected is also determined by the recording methods that are used. For example, video recordings include information about both verbal and nonverbal behavior whereas audio recordings gather verbal behavior only. Setting characteristics influence the level of detail that can be captured in the video or audio recordings. The investigator can collect more detail about certain variables by including the ability to "zoom in" or "zoom out" on the phenomena of interest. For instance, an observational study using videotapes in the laboratory can deliver close-up views of discrete facial movements that reveal miniscule details about facial expressions, a prerequisite for such widely used emotion coding systems as the Specific Affect Coding System (SPAFF; Coan and Gottman, 2007) and Facial Action Coding System (FACS; Ekman, Friesen and Hager, 2002) which require direct unobstructed footage at close proximity. This level of clarity and detail in vantage point is conceded with video observations taken in the field, which contend with shifting angles and movement, ambient noise, changing actors, and spontaneous activity in pursuit of the advantages of ecologically valid data. Similarly, the amount of detail derived from the work of live observers in naturalistic settings will fluctuate depending on the method by which observations are recorded. For instance, observers who use technologies that facilitate note-keeping (e.g., voice recorders, handheld computers) have the potential to quickly record more detailed observations than if they relied on hand-written notes alone. Additionally, the structure of observers' note-keeping – for example, registering the occurrence of specific pre-determined behaviors or activities versus open-ended descriptions – will also determine the amount of detail and the scope of the data.

Ultimately, researchers who use direct observation are faced with the monumental task of imposing order on the data in order to measure the constructs of interest. Across methods, there are inherent differences in the extent to which the data are collected in an organized manner from the start versus imposing organization *after* the raw data are collected. With participant reports and live observer notes, there is an effort to define key constructs before the data are collected. Similarly, when researchers control family observations through instructions to participants, the constructs are largely defined and decisions made about how to organize observations prior to data collection. For work–family scholars who are considering the use of direct observational methods and are clear about the particular family circumstances and behaviors of interest, it may be optimal to use settings and data recording methods that limit the breadth of behavior and variety of situations that are observed. For instance, in the study mentioned above, reunion behavior after work was assessed by observing employed mothers at a worksite daycare center just as they were reuniting with their preschool-aged children at the end of each work day (Repetti and Wood, 1997). Statistical analyses are more efficient when the design of a study and the collection of data were organized with specific settings and constructs in mind. In the case of naturalistic observations, the process of defining and operationalizing constructs often involves a series of steps *after* the data have been collected in which the raw data are divided into meaningful units, coded in some manner, and analyzed. However, the more that the organization was imposed prior to data collection, the less breadth is present in the data that are collected.

Parsing family observations

With continuous streams of raw observational data, the process of imposing order and meaning begins with the *parsing* of the data prior to the implementation of a coding scheme. In laboratory observation, the constructs under study are largely defined by how they are elicited by the researcher, limiting the degree to which any breaking down of the data is required. For example, there will be fewer components to an interaction that lasts a predetermined and manageable 10 minutes for all families, involves the same actors (e.g., a parent–child dyad), and results from the same scripted prompts delivered by the researcher. Direct naturalistic observations, however, yield uninterrupted streams of behavior because little organization was imposed prior to data collection. For statistical analysis, the raw naturalistic data must be divided into units for analysis; consider the challenge of coding hundreds of hours of continuous video footage that varies across and within participants in terms of situations, actors, settings, filming angles, and length of time on-screen. The researcher can choose to parse the data in any number of ways. For example, one approach is to organize the observations according to set intervals in which clips of a specific duration are identified. Other parsing approaches may be more content- or process–specific, and thus anchored to *who* appears on-screen (e.g., a specific family member or dyad), and/or *what* is occurring (e.g., routine events, the occurrence of particular types of behavior or activity).

The extra effort involved in parsing data can be illustrated by comparing the observations of parent–child reunions in the worksite daycare study and in the CELF study. In the first case, the observational data were contained in 10-minute videotaped reunion episodes all of which took place in the same room with a table, two chairs, and some toys (Repetti and Wood, 1997). In the CELF study, a parent–child reunion had to first be defined; we examined the two minutes of video recording that began after the parent's initial arrival home and coded the returning parent's first encounter with children who were at home at the time of arrival. Even with this specific definition of a reunion, the CELF data contained many sources of variance that were not represented in the worksite daycare study: the particular family members who were at home each day; even if a child was at home, whether or not the reunion took place within the 2-minute time span; the length of time a child had been at home when the parent arrived; and interruptions, distractions, and activities that took place during the two-minute period, such as phone calls, opening mail, folding laundry, playing on the computer and homework. The added variables in the CELF video, which complicated the identification and coding of reunions, proved to be critical. We learned, for example, that fathers tended to arrive home later than mothers and were therefore more likely to be immediately involved in ongoing household logistics and routines. Fathers were also more likely to be greeted by children who were distracted by an activity, such as homework (Campos *et al.*, 2009).

Investigations from the CELF study have used a variety of approaches in the analysis of its large archive of naturalistic observations of everyday family life. For example, the Wang *et al.* (2011) analysis of the first hour of interactions with family members after work adopted a "thin-slicing" approach that organized the video into 10-minute intervals and designated the first 30 second clip at the start of each interval for coding. Other investigations have honed in on specific family routines. For example, in the CELF dinner study described earlier, Ochs and colleagues (2010) identified family dinners – defined as the main household meal of the evening – in order to examine the level of participation of each family member in the meal and the length of the meal. As mentioned above, Campos and colleagues (2009) examined another family routine, daily reunions; in that case, greetings that a parent received from children and spouse were coded when the parent arrived home after work.

In several current projects, CELF researchers are targeting the occurrences of particular types of behaviors or activities, such as supportive interactions in couples, parent–child conversations about peers and academic topics, expressions of anger in school-age children and parent responses to child negative emotions. When a particular type of situation is the target, the parsing process takes place in multiple steps that progressively impose greater order and organization onto the data. First, clips are identified in which the individual (e.g., school-age child) or dyad (e.g., the couple) of interest appear on screen. Second, occasions are selected when the specific behavior or activity occurs (e.g.s., a child expresses an emotion, an opportunity for a supportive couple interaction occurs, a certain topic is mentioned in conversation). Only then is a detailed coding system applied to rate the phenomena of interest. Note how the first two steps, both part of what we call the parsing process, serve the function that is represented in a laboratory study by researcher control over the social situation in which the family is observed.

The efficiency of the process of searching and parsing video is largely determined by the manner in which the data are organized. A critical early accomplishment at CELF was the organization of the video in ways that would allow the data to be maximally useful to a wide variety of research programs addressing diverse questions. For example, existing software was modified so that researchers could easily sort video according to (a) the family members appearing on-screen, and (b) their locations inside or outside the home (e.g., kitchen, bathroom, car, restaurant). The investment of resources in software development and the employment of large numbers of research assistants who coded every second of the 1600 hours of footage has paid off thanks to the universal utility of this system and the data it generates. The effort greatly facilitated the first steps of numerous research projects by expediting the identification of relevant video segments for further coding.

Defining constructs through behavioral coding

Whether direct observation of behavior takes place in a laboratory or in the field, the constructs of interest are ultimately operationalized through the coding and analysis of behavior. One of the main advantages of direct observation is the increase in reliability that results when only one person (i.e., the researcher) is "making sense" of raw observations, rather than many participants. For example, to study work–family conflict in a direct observational study, a specific indicator of family conflict – such as hostile questioning or blaming, or pressure for change – would be explicit and applied across families without the involvement of the family members in the coding or counting process. The uniform application of a behavioral code to different families, which significantly reduces random measurement error, is assessed through measures of inter-rater reliability. There are trade-offs in behavioral coding systems between the reliability and the meaningfulness of the codes that are developed. Failure to achieve high reliability on a complex behavior that may be manifested in a variety of ways (e.g., frustration) may call for the use of a variable that can be more reliably coded (e.g., negative emotion expression).

Behavioral coding variables can represent notably different units of analysis. For example, the units analyzed by a micro-analytic video coding system like the

Social Support Interaction Coding System (SSICS; Bradbury and Pasch, 1994), which assesses turn-by-turn couple support behavior, differs from the units of analysis in a global rating system like the Couple Interaction Rating System (CIRS; Heavey, Gill and Christensen, 1998), which assesses the overall intensity of demand–withdraw behaviors in a couple interaction. With audio-recordings, a parallel issue exists regarding the scope with which transcripts of speech are coded. Some tackle this at the level of the text itself, using defined categories for grouping and quantifying words (e.g., prepositions, negative emotion; Language Inquiry and Word Count; Pennebaker, Booth and Francis, 2007). This method was applied to the CELF parents' narrations of self-guided tours of their homes in order to address questions about how home life can facilitate or impede physiological and emotional recovery after work. Wives who used words like "cluttered" or "unfinished" to describe their homes showed flatter (i.e., less healthy) diurnal cortisol slopes and increases in depressed mood over the course of an average day. The use of restful words, such as "comfortable" and "peaceful," or references to nature, were associated with steeper (i.e., healthier) cortisol slopes and decreased depressed mood over the day. Other approaches used in coding speech focus on the content or interactional process in conversations (e.g., problem-solving and monitoring in conversations about peer and academic problems). We have focused on methods that are used by psychological and quantitative researchers. Scholars outside of our field studying the same phenomena (e.g., applied linguists, conversation analysts, linguistic anthropologists) often adopt very different analytic techniques. For example, Ochs and Izquierdo (2009) examined the socialization of responsibility in childhood in the CELF data using an anthropological framework and qualitative methods that differ considerably from the methods we describe here.

The coding of naturalistic observational data differs from the coding of observations made in the laboratory, where *what* is being observed (e.g., type of interaction, actors present) and the *way* in which it is observed (e.g., camera angle, sound quality, close-ups) are tightly controlled and uniform across participants. Imagine trying to apply a system developed to code turn-by-turn interaction in couples instructed to discuss a specific topic to a stream of naturalistic observations. It is analogous to the expectation that a response scale developed for couples to respond to specific questions about their relationship (e.g., "how many times each week do you and your spouse argue?") be used to code responses to an open-ended question (e.g., "tell us a bit about your relationship"). It just isn't possible. In the real world, interactions occur alongside other activities, conversations on topics of interest to the researcher (when they do spontaneously occur) may be interrupted by another family member and fail to resume, or participants may walk in and out of a room mid-conversation, limiting the ability of the researcher to capture the full content of a conversation. Recording devices that have to move with participants may not be sensitive enough to pick up quiet or poorly articulated phrases. In addition, a particular topic, or a particular family member, may weave in and out of an interaction. As a result, rather than a continuous (and uniform) "conversation" on a single subject of interest, the relevant "talk" between two family members may start and stop at multiple points over an extended period. Similar difficulties occur with visual recordings, such as participants' faces being in shadow, turned away from the camera, or behind an object that obscures full view. More subtle behaviors like facial expressions may be very difficult for coders to notice or agree upon, and phenomena of interest may occur at extremely low base rates, all resulting in lower reliability coefficients than are typically obtained in more controlled laboratory settings.

Naturalistic observational data call for new coding systems, often developed through an iterative process in which concepts are defined, shaped, and re-defined through repeat engagement with the raw data. A manualized coding system develops through a primarily bottom-up, data-driven process in which the researcher may be discovering – rather than imposing – a definition for a behavior or process. Coded behaviors may reflect lower order constructs that are descriptively preserved throughout analysis (e.g., ratings of the amount of touches exchanged by a couple); higher order constructs can also emerge from these lower order constructs during data analysis (e.g., touches as one indicator of expressions of emotional support).

Reconceptualizing and reinterpreting observational data

Participant reports are in many ways locked in time. Constructs, having been defined in advance of data collection, are resistant to later revision. A work–family researcher's preconceived notions about what constitutes balance, conflict, facilitation, or spillover between the job and home domains are embedded within the selection of items and the choice of wording on participant-report scales. Direct observational data, on the other hand, can be revisited by different scholars, even decades later, with new coding systems and entirely rewritten constructs. The opportunity to reconceptualize and reinterpret the raw data with fresh ideas and the promise of "future" research are probably the most overlooked benefits of direct observational research. When a study's raw data consist of ratings made by an observer – whether that observer is a family member responding to items on a questionnaire or a researcher making notes about a family behavior – it is certainly possible to return to the data and redefine concepts of interest, but the options are limited. With participants' responses to items on a questionnaire and researchers' real-time coding of live interaction, conceptual constraints are reflected in the questions that were posed to the participants or in the guidelines followed by live observers.

There is more flexibility when the raw data consist of video and audio recordings of families. For example, even though the behavior observed in a typical laboratory study is constrained and controlled to some degree, the researcher can return to the recordings with a new set of concepts or to examine different aspects of the raw data. Video, in particular, offers a storehouse of information – images, language, movement – comprising a dense encyclopedia of information that can be deciphered for multiple purposes. In the CELF study, video taken during weekday afternoons were included in the study of daily family reunions described earlier;

greetings that parents received when they arrived home were coded for constructs such as positive behaviors, distraction, and reports of information (Campos, *et al.*, 2009). The same recordings were also included as part of the analysis mentioned earlier of working couples' after-work family interactions for which levels of behavioral involvement (talking, social engagement) and negative emotion expression were coded (Wang, *et al.*, 2011). And a current project uses the same video data in an investigation of marital social support that includes constructs such as solicitations and offers of support, support quality, and type of support (instrumental, emotional). Direct detailed raw observations of families – such as video and audio recordings – provide an ideal medium for researchers to engage and re-engage with different questions and constructs.

Conclusion

We have argued that work–family researchers have much to gain from direct observational methods. The advantages over participant report methods include improvements in external validity, protection against correlations inflated by respondent biases (the most common source of Type I error in our field), and reduction of random measurement error (i.e., reductions in Type II error). In addition, direct observation can be used with a wider population; for example, pre-literate children can be included as participants in a family study. Perhaps most important, direct observational data can contribute to the development of key constructs and the generation of new hypotheses. One pattern of findings from the CELF investigation of links between job stress and family social behavior after work highlighted the intensity of an employed family member's reactions to others' initiations of interaction. Response intensity was coded only in response to openings for a social interaction that were presented by others, regardless of the affective quality or valence of the response; amount of talking and expression of emotion were coded as separate variables. For instance, a response to a question could range from simply ignoring it to an effusive and articulate answer (with either a positive or a negative tone) (Wang *et al.*, 2011). Although our interest in social withdrawal as a response to job stress provided the impetus for examining this variable, response intensity itself is not a familiar concept in the work–family literature. It is probably too subtle and complex a variable for family members to observe and accurately describe in a participant report measure. Nonetheless, CELF's naturalistic data provided novel information about response intensity for work–family researchers by suggesting how the quality of social behavior at home is influenced by stress at work.

Unquestionably, the benefits of direct observational studies are balanced by challenges. The intensity and complexity of data collection procedures, especially when conducted in the context of a naturalistic design, translate into extra expenses and smaller sample sizes. One result is a reduction in statistical power that all but rules out the testing of small effects. That problem can be minimized to some extent by increasing the homogeneity of the sample (based on individual and family characteristics, such as SES, occupation, age of children, etc.), which reduces variance in the data attributable to group differences. However, that solution reduces the generalizability of the study's findings to more narrow populations. Naturalistic observational studies also add analytic complexities associated with parsing and coding of the data. Fortunately, the challenges are not insurmountable. The elasticity of naturalistic observational data, particularly when collected with minimal processing by an observer (i.e., video and audio recordings) is its greatest selling point. As demonstrated by the CELF study, resources can be pooled and scholars from different disciplines and sub-disciplines can coordinate methodologies to produce a multi-layered archive of naturalistic data. (See Ochs *et al.*, 2006 for a more detailed description of the video and scan sampling methods used by CELF.) Although initial investments in time and funding may seem burdensome, the picture changes drastically when the archive's many purposes and applications across different fields are considered.

Ultimately, a mixture of methods provides the most valuable and valid information about a construct and the most complete answer to a research question. Findings based on both direct and indirect observations, each flawed in its own way, will offer unique insights that contribute to a rich mosaic of knowledge in our field.

References

Bradbury, T.N. and Pasch, L. (1994) *The Social Support Interaction Coding System (SSICS)*. Unpublished coding manual, University of California, Los Angeles.

Campos, B., Graesch, A., Repetti, R.L., Ochs, E. and Bradbury, T. (2009). Naturalistic observation of opportunities for social interaction in contemporary family life. *Journal of Family Psychology*, 23(6), 798–807.

Coan, J.A. and Gottman, J.M. (2007). The specific affect (SPAFF) coding system. In J.A. Coan and J.J.B. Allen (Eds.) *Handbook of Emotion Elicitation and Assessment* (pp. 106–123). New York, NY: Oxford University Press.

Costigan, C.L., Cox, M.J. and Cauce, A.M. (2003). Work-parenting linkages among dual-earner couples at the transition to parenthood. *Journal of Family Psychology, 17*, 397–408.

Driver, J.L. and Gottman, J. M. (2004). Daily marital interactions and positive affect during marital conflict among newlywed couples. *Family Process, 43*, 301–314.

Ekman, P., Friesen, W.V. and Hager, J.C. (2002). *Facial Action Coding System* [E-book]. Salt Lake City, UT: Research Nexus.

Gottman, J. M. and Krokoff, L.J. (1989). Marital interaction and satisfaction: A longitudinal view. *Journal of Consulting and Clinical Psychology, 57*(1), 47–52.

Gottman, J.M. and Driver, J.L. (2005). Dysfunctional marital conflict and everyday marital interaction. *Journal of Divorce and Remarriage, 43*(3/4), 63–77.

Grossman, F.K., Pollack, W.S. and Golding, E. (1988). Fathers and children: Predicting the quality and quantity of fathering. *Development Psychology, 24,* 82–91.

Hayden, L.C., Schiller, M., Dickstein, S., Seifer, R., Sameroff, S., Miller, I., Keitner, G. and Rasmussen, S. (1998). Levels of family assessment I: Family, marital, and parent–child interaction. *Journal of Family Psychology, 12*(1), 7–22.

Heavey, G., Gill, D.S. and Christensen, A. (1998). *The Couple Interaction Rating System.* Unpublished document. University of California, Los Angeles.

Heyman, R.E. (2001). Observation of couple conflicts: Clinical assessment applications, stubborn truths, and shaky foundations. *Psychological Assessment, 13*(1), 5–35.

Larson, R. and Csikszentmihalyi, M. (1983). The experience sampling method. *New Directions for Methodology of Social and Behavioral Science*, 15, 41–56.

Larson, R.W., Richards, M.H. and Perry-Jenkins, M. (1994). Divergent worlds: The daily emotional experiences of mothers and fathers in the domestic and public spheres. *Journal of Personality and Social Psychology, 67*, 1034–1046.

Mehl, M.R., Pennebaker, J.W., Crow, D.M., Dabbs. J. and Price, J.H. (2001). The Electronically Activated Recorder (EAR): A device for sampling naturalistic daily activities and conversations. *Behavior Research Methods, Instruments and Computers, 33*(4), 517–523.

Ochs, E., Graesch, A.P., Mittmann, A., Bradbury, T. and Repetti, R. (2006). Video ethnography and ethnoarchaeological tracking. In M. Pitt-Catsouphes, E.E. Kossek and S. Sweet (Eds.), *The work and family handbook: Multi-disciplinary perspectives, methods and approaches* (pp. 387–409). Mahwah, NJ: Lawrence Erlbaum Associates.

Ochs, E. and Izquierdo, C. (2009). Responsibility in childhood: Three developmental trajectories. *Ethos, 37*(4), 391–413.

Ochs, E., Shohet, M., Campos, B. and Beck, M. (2010). Coming together for dinner: A study of working families. In K. Christensen and B. Schneider (Eds.), *Workplace Flexibility: Realigning 20th Century Jobs to 21st Century Workforce* (pg. 57–70). Ithaca, NY: Cornell University Press.

Pasch, L.A. and Bradbury, T.N. (1998). Social support, conflict, and the development of marital dysfunction. *Journal of Consulting and Clinical Psychology, 66*(2), 219–230.

Patterson, G.R. and Forgatch, M.S. (1995). Predicting future clinical adjustment from treatment outcome and process variables. *Psychological Assessment, 7*(3), 275–285.

Pennebaker, J.W., Booth, R.J. and Francis, M.E. (2007). *Linguistic Inquiry and Word Count: LIWC 2007*. Austin, TX: LIWC (www.liwc.net).

Repetti, R.L. (1987). Individual and common components of the social environment at work and psychological well being. *Journal of Personality and Social Psychology, 52* (4), 710–720.

Repetti, R.L. (1989). Effects of daily workload on subsequent behavior during marital interaction: The roles of social withdrawal and spouse support. *Journal of Personality and Social Psychology, 57* (4), 651–659.

Repetti, R.L. (1994). Short-term and long-term processes linking job stressors to father-child interaction. *Social Development, 3* (1), 1–15.

Repetti, R.L. and Wood, J. (1997). Effects of daily stress at work on mothers' interactions with preschoolers. *Journal of Family Psychology, 11,* 90–108.

Saxbe, D.E. and Repetti, R.L. (2010). No place like home: Home tours correlate with daily patterns of mood and cortisol. *Personality and Social Psychology Bulletin, 36*, 71–81.

Saxbe, D.E., Repetti, R.L. and Graesch, A.P. (2011). Time spent in housework and leisure: Links with parent's physiological recovery from work. *Journal of Family Psychology, 25*(2), 271–281.

Schulz, M.S., Cowan, P.A., Cowan, C.P. and Brennan, R.T. (2004). Coming home upset: Gender, marital satisfaction and the daily spillover of workday experience into couple interactions. *Journal of Family Psychology*, 18, 250–263.

Shiffman, S., Stone, A.A. and Hufford, M.R. (2008). Ecological momentary assessment. *Annual Review of Clinical Psychology, 4,* 1–32.

Slatcher, R.B. and Robles, T.F. (2012). Preschoolers' everyday conflict at home and diurnal cortisol patterns. *Health Psychology, 31*, 834–838

Stone, AA. and Shiffman, S. (2002). Capturing momentary, self-report data: A proposal for reporting guidelines. *Annals of Behavioral Medicine, 24*(3), 236–243.

Story, L.B. and Repetti, R.L. (2006). Daily occupational stressors and marital behavior. *Journal of Family Psychology, 20(4),* 690–700.

Wang, S., Repetti, R.L. and Campos, B. (2011). Job stress and family social behavior: The moderating role of distress. *Journal of Occupational Health Psychology, 16(4),* 441–456.

Index